JCMS Annual Review of the European Union in 2020

Edited by

Theofanis Exadaktylos,
Roberta Guerrina
and
Emanuele Massetti

General Editors: Toni Haastrup and Richard Whitman

WILEY

CONTENTS

JCMS 2021 Volume 59. Annual Review. pp. 5–10   DOI: 10.1111/jcms.13296

A Year like no Other: Hope out of Despair?

THEOFANIS EXADAKTYLOS,[1] ROBERTA GUERRINA[2] and EMANUELE MASSETTI[3]
[1]University of Surrey, Guildford [2]University of Bristol, Bristol [3]University of Trento, Trento

When we took over the editorship of the *Annual Review* in 2018, we reflected on the institutional and political challenges facing the EU (Exadaktylos *et al.*, 2018). Over the last three years we have explored the way the EU and its member states adapted to manage the unfolding of multiple and overlapping crises (Exadaktylos *et al.*, 2019, 2020). However, we did not anticipate that the EU – likewise all the other political systems – would have to face such a dramatic crisis as the one triggered by the Covid-19 global pandemic. This is exactly where the story of 2020 starts: with a public health emergency that entails an economic fall and the risk of a fatal political crisis.

As the EU and its Member States were preparing for a next phase of the Brexit process, after the formal withdrawal of the UK from the EU, a new and unexpected crisis was looming on the horizon. The end of 2019 was marked by a growing concern with reports of a novel virus spreading across China. It was clear from this outset that this novel virus had the potential to disrupt the global political economy, and it could be a challenge like no other for the institutions of the EU (Christiansen, 2020). As Northern Italy became the epicentre of the Covid-19 crisis in the month of February, the European Commission and the Member States' governments struggled to get to grips with the complexity of the challenge facing them. A degree of panic, coupled with competing interests and ambiguity over competencies led to a delay in establishing a coordinated response. Rather, the 'political instinct' of managing security issues at national level appeared to prevail on European co-operation, as physical borders were re-established and significant restrictions on people's movement within member states and across the EU were imposed.

However, eventually the EU was able to agree on and implement a co-ordinated response. Undoubtedly, dealing with the public health emergency took up a lot of the EU's political and economic capital. Coordinating national efforts to contain the spread of the virus, providing support for cross national research aimed at developing a vaccine, and managing the impact of national quarantines and 'lockdowns' on the European economy, superseded all other policy interests. It is easy to see how managing the pandemic could have become the one and only driver of public policy in 2020. In many ways, just like the virus it sought to contain, public policy responses deprived oxygen form other policy domains. It is therefore worth noting that despite this shock, European institutions continued to pursue the agenda presented in late 2019. The Green Deal remained a linchpin of the Commission's agenda (von der Leyen, 2019), and the budget was more ambitious than ever. Undoubtedly, the innovation included by von der Leyen in 2019 was delayed, but it was not completely disrupted by Covid-19.

In fact, what 2020 demonstrated is that the Commission has put forward a very resilient agenda. All the key drivers of von der Leyen's agenda were included in the State of the Union (von der Leyen, 2020). Perhaps what is most significant is that by the end of

2020 the pandemic was absorbed within the programme of action, rather than replacing it. Even the national plans for resilience and recovery were to align with the pre-pandemic aspiration espoused by Green Deal and the Digital Innovation Policy. Federica Mogherini's (2021) Annual Lecture captures this sentiment, seeing 2020 as the year in which the EU – and the project of European integration more broadly – went from near collapse to a new hope. Specifically, Mogherini's lecture points to the way the European project has emerged out of crises. There is creativity and a strengthened political aspiration to be found amidst political and economic crises. After all, these are moments that disrupt the status quo, thus offering alternative ways of approaching established problems.

From this perspective, the post-Covid-19 recovery deal[1] marks the relaunch of the European project with a range of ambitious new policies and instruments. Particularly worth noting is the recovery budget and the common EU bonds. These were not envisaged before the pandemic. Covid-19 changed perceptions in relation to coordination in key policy areas such as public health, thus generating the political will required to carry out such an ambitious programme.

Two articles in this year's *Annual Review* pick up on the themes introduced by Mogherini's Annual Lecture. Eckert's (2021) analysis of the European Green Deal (EGD) sees this as a potential turning point. It is not just the moment that European institutions acknowledge the climate crisis looming on the horizon, it also commits the EU and all its constituent parts to lead on the conversation about a green post-Covid recovery. Specifically, Eckert's analysis finds that, despite attempts to curtail the impact of the EGD by some member-states' governments, the last year has proved its resilience in the face of crisis. This analysis is echoed by Ladi and Wolff's (2021) discussion of the emergence of a form of coordinative Europeanisation as a result of the Covid-19 emergency. Ladi and Wolff specifically argue that the EU's response to Covid can be best understood as a continuation of its almost permanent state of emergency condition. This state has helped to develop new modes of governance that either neither supranational nor intergovernmental, but that allows direct engagement with key stakeholders in the process of European integration. The question that arises from this analysis is whether this form of coordinative Europeanisation is to become a feature of European governance or is it only a response to crisis or emergency situations.

Not all the contributors to this year's *Annual Review* see such possibility in the developments of 2020. These pieces point to a learning process from the Eurocrisis, but not a settlement that can see the EU through future crises. Schelkle (2021) in particular does not find 2020 to have generated a breakthrough moment in Hamiltonian terms. Certainly, 2020 was a critical juncture in terms of decision making and competencies, however it did not commit to some kind of European federalism. In other words, the political economy of the block has not changed substantially. What we have is a breakthrough response, rather than a ground-breaking response. This analysis is supported by Auer and Scicluna (2021) who question the legitimacy of decision making at the EU level, especially in the context of crisis and emergency. Echoing Schelkle's analysis, they also do not find this to be the kind of Hamiltonian moment that would see the EU rising through adversity. European institutions did find a path through the

[1]See NextGenerationEU information page: https://europa.eu/next-generation-eu/index_en

crisis, however, the shift into "emergency mode" also highlighted long standing problems of legitimacy in EU decision-making. Covid-19 has only been the latest in a long series of crises that have marked the last decade. It is in this context that Auer and Scicluna urge us to think about the difficulties (or impossibility) of constitutionalizing emergency powers at the EU level, and to reflect on the underlying dysfunctionality of the EU polity and project more broadly. In their view, the only level of the EU system of governance that has the democratic legitimacy to adopt emergency measures is the national (member-state) one.

Forman and Mossialos's (2021) contribution provides a useful illustration of the difficult transition from emergency decision making to strategic decision making. This contribution focuses specifically on the evolution of EU health care and public health policy and the impact of Covid-19 on EU-level decision making. The challenge, they argue, is whether the EU can learn from the last eighteen months and move towards more strategic decision making, at least in the context of managing future public health emergencies and pandemics. This assessment dovetails with the previous analysis about governance, legitimacy and decision-making processes. Covid-19 has exposed both rising nationalism within Member States, as well as the EU's capacity to play a key strategic role in the context of crisis. The challenge now will be to move EU level governance from emergency management to horizon scoping and planning.

Zooming in on the social dimension Hantrais (2021) points out that the tension between national sovereignty and international solidarity has been a long-standing tension within EU governance structures. The tensions emerged during the pandemic, as outlined also by Forman and Mossialos, simply exacerbated existing inequalities within and between Member States. In this regard, Hantrais argues, 2020 did not create a space to advance social integration. The impact of social inequalities on Covid outcomes is further evidence of the inextricably linked nature of economic and social policies. This link is something that European institutions and Member States governments are starting to acknowledge, even though there is evidence that social cohesion policies are the only viable way to deal with future emergencies.

Despite the fact that the social dimension is often relegated to the lower end of the political spectrum, a number of the contributions to this year's *Annual Review* point to this area in order to understand the challenges facing European institutions and the Member States. Two contributions provide particularly important insights into the impact of historical hierarchies on the politics of social inclusion in 2020. Freedman (2021) examines the issue of social cohesion through the prism of the New Pact on Migration and Asylum presented by the European Commission as a way forward for the development of a migration management system. Here, the issue at stake dovetails well with issues previous contributors to the *Annual Review* also identified – that is, the limits of intra-European solidarity, this time in relation to 'burden sharing'. What is, however, highly visible is the bounded nature of solidarity, which struggles to accommodate migrants and refugees. As Freedman outlines in her contribution, whereas Covid-19 was used to justify the strengthening of physical borders to safeguard the 'security' of European populations, little or no consideration was given to the growing level of insecurity faced by people on the move in the context of a global pandemic.

In a similar way, Beaman (2021) reflects on the manifestation of the Black Lives Matter movement in Europe. She focuses on the impact of racialized social and economic cleavages that support the process of European integration. Understanding the connections between Europe's history, its position in the world today and the endurance of social cleavages should be part of any future conversation about social inclusion and cohesion in the EU. Specifically, Beaman challenges Europe's idea of exceptionalism when it comes to race. Rather, this powerful piece points to the way European social and political actors have sanitized the history of race and racism. In so doing, Beaman's argument goes, they have contributed to the construction of an idea of Europe, and Europeanness, that centres on whiteness. In this vision, individuals and groups racialized as non-white remain Europe's permanent Other. This contribution thus reflects on the interconnections between Europe's past, present and future, especially in relation to the position of minoritized groups living within the boundaries of the EU, as well as the plight of refugees coming to Europe.

Turning to the ongoing reconfiguration of Britain's new relationship with Europe, Usherwood (2021) explores the latest developments in the Brexit process focusing on the hinge between the internal and external dimension of the EU. This contribution starts at the end of 2019 with the UK General Election that gave Boris Johnson and his government a significant majority in Westminster, allowing to take forward the Brexit process. As a result, during 2020 the focus of the negotiations was on finding a way forward through a Trade and Cooperation Agreement that would apply at the end of the transition period. The key to understanding the way this process evolved is the status of the UK, which now negotiates as a third country rather than as a Member State. The Covid-19 emergency placed additional pressures and strains on both parties and further deepened differences between them in an already difficult relationship.

Covid-19 came to be the backdrop to most of the EU's external actions in 2020 shaping the direction of the relationship with its neighbours. Schumacher and Günay (2021) remind us that the public health emergency, was not the only event that had an impact on international affairs. The South Caucasus region experienced an outbreak of an armed conflict between Armenia and Azerbaijan as well as major internal political crises. The reason this development matters is that both countries are part of the European Neighbourhood and thus have a direct connection with (and impact on) the EU and its external affairs. Schumacher and Günay point to important differences in the EU's response to these crises in the region on the back of the pandemic. Whereas the political crises were marked by passivity, the EU's response to the Covid-19 crisis in the region was prompt and focused. This highlights the centrality of Covid-19 to the EU's internal and external work during 2020.

Also focused on the neighbourhood, Korosteleva and Petrova (2021) look at the EU's response to the emergence of organized social movements in Belarus. This crisis in the neighbourhood raises important questions about the EU's commitment to its own core values and its relationship with fragile environments. Korosteleva and Petrova's analysis looks specifically at the emergence of flexible mechanisms of interaction that would allow the building of resilience and responses to local dynamics and challenges. Looking at another region of salience for the EU, Grigoriadis (2021) also points to a shift of focus to EU's external action that can further explain the EU's response to the South Caucasus region examined by Schumacher and Günay. For Grigoriadis, the Eastern Mediterranean is now in the direct the focus of the EU's foreign and security policy, possibly because it provides an occasion for the EU's long-standing ambition to develop its own strategic autonomy. In this regard the crisis in the Eastern Mediterranean, in the race to exploit hydrocarbon reserves, provides an important test case for the EU, especially in its relations with Turkey. These two contributions point to a tension in the EU's approach to external affairs, especially in relation to the question of what kind of role the EU is looking to play as a regional/global actor post-Brexit.

Part of an answer to this question arises from examining the EU's relationship with the United States and China. Hofmann's (2021) and Telò's (2021) contributions examine in depth developments across this dimension for 2020. Hofmann's article starts from the simple observation that EU–US relationship was under significant strain in 2020, especially in the run-up to the US Presidential Election. However, the transatlantic relationship seems to be able to withstand such tensions, demonstrating its elasticity and resilience. Hofmann sees Covid-19 as posing as significant challenge to the development of European strategic autonomy, in so far as despite significant steps taken to augment a cohesive, pan-European approach, the block continues to rely on the transatlantic relationship in areas of security and defence.

The EU–China relationship is equally complicated, albeit for different reasons. Telò (2021) points in his contribution to the attempt of creating of a new international regime through the ratification of the Comprehensive Agreement on Investment (CAI) between the EU and China after seven years of negotiations. It is difficult to know at the time of writing the full implications of this comprehensive agreement or regime, which is likely to be determined by a range of domestic and international drivers. Interestingly, this contribution also points to the EU's quest for enhanced strategic autonomy as a key variable in determining the evolution of this complex relationship.

The contributions in the *JCMS Annual Review of 2020* highlight the degrees of complexity of the challenges facing the EU, its institutions and Member States. These challenges have a direct impact in national politics, inter- and intra-institutional relations, EU-level politics and external affairs. In its history, the EU has been called to manage a series of crises in which the Covid-19 pandemic and the subsequent public health crisis are simply the latest ones. Indeed, despite the dominance of Covid-19 in policy responses, it was not the only crisis facing the EU and challenging the process of European integration as a whole. The key question that is raised by the contributions in this *Annual Review*, both at an individual level and as a collective volume, is whether these multiple and overlapping crises provide the platform and motivation for deeper integration or pose an existential challenge to the legitimacy of the integration process and the institutions of the EU. The answer to this overarching question starts to unfold in 2021 and there is no doubt that it will form the subject of many of the future contributions at the *Annual Review* in 2022 and the years to come.

References

Auer, S. and Scicluna, N. (2021) 'The Impossibility of Constitutionalizing Emergency Europe'. *JCMS*, Vol. 59, No. S1. https://doi.org/10.1111/jcms.13240

Beaman, J. (2021) 'Towards a Reading of Black Lives Matter in Europe'. *JCMS*, Vol. 59, No. S1. https://doi.org/10.1111/jcms.13275

Christiansen, T. (2020) 'The EU's New Normal: Consolidating European Integration in an Era of Populism and Geo-Economics'. *JCMS*, Vol. 58, No. S1, pp. 13–27.

Eckert, S. (2021) 'The European Green Deal and the EU's Regulatory Power in Times of Crisis'. *JCMS*, Vol. 59, No. S1. https://doi.org/10.1111/jcms.13241

Exadaktylos, T., Guerrina, R. and Massetti, E. (2018) 'Editorial: 2017 – A Year in Review'. *JCMS*, Vol. 56, No. S1, pp. 5–10.

Exadaktylos, T., Guerrina, R. and Massetti, E. (2019) 'Sailing through Troubled Waters and towards "Someplace ..."'. *JCMS*, Vol. 57, No. S1, pp. 5–12.

Exadaktylos, T., Guerrina, R. and Massetti, E. (2020) 'Calm before the Storm? 2019 in Perspective'. *JCMS*, Vol. 58, No. S1, pp. 5–12.

Forman, R. and Mossialos, E. (2021) 'The EU Response to COVID-19: From Reactive Policies to Strategic Decision-Making'. *JCMS*, Vol. 59, No. S1. https://doi.org/10.1111/jcms.13259

Freedman, J. (2021) 'Immigration, Refugees and Responses'. *JCMS*, Vol. 59, No. S1. https://doi.org/10.1111/jcms.13258

Grigoriadis, I.N. (2021) 'The European Union in the Eastern Mediterranean in 2020: Whither Strategic Autonomy'. *JCMS*, Vol. 59, No. S1. https://doi.org/10.1111/jcms.13247

Hantrais, L. (2021) 'Social Perspectives on Brexit, COVID-19 and European (Dis)Integration'. *JCMS*, Vol. 59, No. S1. https://doi.org/10.1111/jcms.13218

Hofmann, S.C. (2021) 'Elastic Relations: Looking to both Sides of the Atlantic in the 2020 US Presidential Election Year'. *JCMS*, Vol. 59, No. S1. https://doi.org/10.1111/jcms.13245

Korosteleva, E. and Petrova, I. (2021) 'Societal Resilience in Belarus and the EU Response'. *JCMS*, Vol. 59, No. S1. https://doi.org/10.1111/jcms.13248

Ladi, S. and Wolff, S. (2021) 'The EU Institutional Architecture in the Covid-19 Response: Coordinative Europeanization in Times of Permanent Emergency'. *JCMS*, Vol. 59, No. S1. https://doi.org/10.1111/jcms.13254

Mogherini, F. (2021) 'How 2020 has Shaped the Future of the European Union: When a Crisis Turns into an Opportunity'. *JCMS*, Vol. 59, No. S1.

Schelkle, W. (2021) 'Fiscal Integration in an Experimental Union: How Path-Breaking Was the EU's Response to the COVID-19 Pandemic?' *JCMS*, Vol. 59, No. S1. https://doi.org/10.1111/jcms.13246

Schumacher, T. and Günay, C. (2021) 'Territorial Conflict, Domestic Crisis, and the Covid-19 Pandemic in the South Caucasus. Explaining Variegated EU Response'. *JCMS*, Vol. 59, No. S1. https://doi.org/10.1111/jcms.13255

Telò, M. (2021) 'Controversial Developments of EU–China Relations: Main Drivers and Geopolitical Implications of the Comprehensive Agreement on Investments'. *JCMS*, Vol. 59, No. S1. https://doi.org/10.1111/jcms.13226

Usherwood, S. (2021) 'Our European Friends and Partners'? Negotiating the Trade and Cooperation'. *JCMS*, Vol. 59, No. S1. https://doi.org/10.1111/jcms.13238

von der Leyen, U. (2019) 'Presentation of the European Green Deal', 11 December 2019. https://ec.europa.eu/info/strategy/priorities-2019-2024/european-green-deal_en

von der Leyen, U. (2020) 'State of the Union Address' at the European Parliament Plenary Brussels, 16 September 2020. https://ec.europa.eu/commission/presscorner/api/files/document/print/en/speech_20_1655/SPEECH_20_1655_EN.pdf

JCMS 2021 Volume 59. Annual Review. pp. 11–19   DOI: 10.1111/jcms.13278

How 2020 Has Shaped the Future of the European Union: When a Crisis Turns into an Opportunity

FEDERICA MOGHERINI[1,2]
[1]Rector, College of Europe, Bruges, Belgium [2]Rector, College of Europe, Natolin (Warsaw), Poland

The first two decades of the new millennium have been a solid reminder of how wise and correct Jean Monnet was by predicting that '[l]'Europe se fera dans les crises et elle sera la somme des solutions apportées à ces crises'.[1] In order to understand how the year 2020 has impacted the future of the European Union, we need to take a step back and read carefully how Europe got to the end of the second decade of the century, and how the multiple crises that have shaken our continent before that year have contributed to shaping the Union's reaction to the pandemic, and its connected and related effects.

The 21st century started with a major economic and financial crisis, which has, in turn, had heavy social repercussions; terrorist attacks on European soil; conflicts in the East of our continent, and all across the Mediterranean; large flows of refugees and migrants, desperately searching for a place to live safely; a shrinking space for democracy, human rights and the rule of law, that has affected also our continent, as part of a more global trend; the loss, for the first time ever, of one Member State, with the UK decision to leave the Union; devastating climate disruption; and an unprecedented global pandemic.

This quite dramatic picture allows us to fully capture, at a glance, the magnitude of the challenges that our continent has faced in recent years. The sequence and combination of these challenges had the potential to create an existential threat to the very pursuit of the European integration project. In fact, only five years ago, during the summer of 2016, many commentators and analysts were arguing that the Brexit Referendum would mark the beginning of the end for the European Union. Many were predicting that our Union would soon collapse, as more Member States would follow the UK's path towards disintegration. As we discuss today the future of Europe, just five years ago, we were discussing how to avoid the EU not having a future at all.

Instead, what actually happened as the Brexit negotiations started to develop, notwithstanding countless difficulties, is that all those political movements and leaders that were founding their political discourse, and their very identity, on the anti-European and anti-system narrative, realized at once that criticizing the European Union was probably much less complicated and much more convenient (both politically and economically) if done while keeping their respective countries solidly within the block, rather than facing the unexplored, risky and bumpy road of exit negotiations. The actual start of the Brexit process acted as an extremely effective wake-up call to reality: staying in the European Union is very convenient, even when you do not like every aspect of the organization.

---

[1]Jean Monnet, Mémoires, Paris: Librairie Arthème Fayard, p. 488.

So, the prediction of a long list of countries deciding to exit the Union proved to be based on a number of wrong assumptions. What actually happened was rather the opposite, with a strong determination from the remaining 27 Member States to relaunch and strengthen the symbols, the narrative, the politics and the policies of the European integration process. The boldest message of unity, and the clearest sign that the 27 had understood the risk, and were determined to react together, came in March 2017, during the celebrations for the anniversary of the Treaty of Rome. I perfectly remember the sense of belonging, pride and hope that those days brought to the European landscape, not only across institutions but also in public opinions all over the continent. Not only was it not going to be the beginning of the end: it was set to become the beginning of a relaunched European unity. A unity that, in fact, the 27 managed to keep all along during the difficult negotiations that have then led to the effective exit of the UK from the EU. It is worth noting that this is something not many were ready to bet on, in those early months.

The turning point of the EU's collective, unified reaction to the Brexit referendum has constituted a solid element of hope, self-confidence, trust and even a sense of relief. Still, the multiplicity of crises was exposing our societies and institutions to a perfect storm, in which the point of no return seemed to be inevitably getting closer by the day. The EU was perceived, and most importantly perceived itself, as on the edge of collapse. The European integration, which had so far been the most successful political integration experiment in history, seemed destined to turn soon and irremediably into a disintegration process.

I personally remember very vividly this sense of frustration within the European institutions during those years. Every single day seemed to bring a new crisis – or a new ramification and development of a pre-existing one. Many good things were done – and yet, every step taken in the direction of solutions seemed to be shadowed and partially even deactivated by the challenge of the day. And while the rest of the world often looked at the European Union as a beacon of hope in an increasingly conflictual and fragmented global order, the political discourse, media narrative and public opinions inside Europe were reflecting the image of a continent in an existential identity crisis. The Union was probably performing better than perceived, and this was much more evident from the perspective of our external partners across the world than from that of our citizens and even of our own leaders.

But all those that were predicting the collapse of the European Union were clearly wrong. Whereas, Jean Monnet was clearly right. All those crises, including the one of self-confidence and self-perception, have provided to our Union the opportunity to test its limits, identify shortcomings and gaps, open a critical public reflection on changes that might be needed, shape new instruments and new policies, relaunch some elements internal understanding and solidarity (within and among institutions, and across societies), and most importantly prove its relevance on issues of literally vital importance for communities and individuals across the entire continent, and far beyond.

Years ago, one of the main arguments used to attack and try to dismantle the European integration process was the irrelevance of the institutions and of their actions for ordinary citizens' lives. Over time, as crises accumulated and multiplied dramatically, the narrative of the anti-European political discourse has shifted from the irrelevance of the EU institutions to their shortcomings. There is now a focus on the institutions' failure to deliver on competences that are not theirs. There are more and more expectations projected to the European level as the national governments find it increasingly difficult – if not im-possible – to deliver themselves on the needs of their own citizens. Today, at almost any stage of any crisis, at any turn of the bumpy roads of our times, the instinctive temp-tation of public opinions and national institutions across the continent is to turn towards Brussels and ask for solutions – even when the Treaties do not give any institutional com-petence or responsibility to the EU institutions on those specific policies, that are instead exclusive domain for national authorities to exercise their sovereign decision-making re-sponsibilities. This unexpected and extraordinary rise of expectations was simply unimag-inable a few years ago, before the tornado of crises that has hit Europe – and not only Europe, in some cases the entire globe – had put an extra burden over the shoulders of any institution that is expected to deliver for its citizens.

Is this new perceived, or rather projected, level of ambition, this demand for European policies and solutions, a stepping stone on which further elements of the integration pro-cess can be built? Or, is it a political trap, a self-fulfilling prophecy that over time will only fuel frustrations and serve the anti-European discourse? Expecting solutions and ac-tions that do not align with powers and competences can be an extraordinarily powerful push for change, increasing and deepening instruments, resources and tools. However, it can also lead to inevitable short-term failures, providing an easy scapegoat for all those who do not manage to identify effective responses to difficult challenges at the national or local level, and turn to Europe to discharge responsibilities they cannot carry or deliver upon.

I believe 2020 has marked a turning point in this process. Shaping the future of our Union much more than it could have been expected or predicted. The year started with high expectations on the new institutional cycle. After a short delay in the appointment and confirmation of Commissioners by the European Parliament in the late months of 2019, and in the midst of complex and controversial Brexit arrangements and negotia-tions, a brand new Commission was finally in place, led for the very first time by a woman. The new Comission had a clear and very ambitious political agenda centred on the digital transformation of our societies and economies and a green deal set to serve both the European and the global interests in the key domain of climate change and sus-tainability. The European Council, the Parliament and the Commission seemed to a large extent aligned and ready to back solid, consistent and coordinated actions to give sub-stance to these priorities, indicated by the institutions but also largely shared by the European public opinions.

And then, the pandemic came. At first, Covid hit some countries disproportionally more than others, reaffirming the gap in perceptions about the gravity and urgency of dif-ferent issues. We often point at divisions in policies and politics across Europe, well be-yond political families and affiliations, without realising that – in most cases – priorities and decisions are defined not so much by ideological or theoretical approaches but rather by a divergence in perceived gravity across societies and public opinions.

The European Union has experienced this gap of perceived urgency several times dur-ing its most recent history. Geography, economy, culture and history itself constantly con-tribute to fueling this diversity of perception. It is a challenge but also an incredible opportunity to listen and understand concerns, analysis and proposals well beyond one's local or national background and environment. The fundamental value-added of having all EU nationalities represented in all institutions is precisely the fact that this helps to shape approaches, proposals and responses that factor in, from the very first stages, a plurality of viewpoints and perceptions. This should help, in turn, to deliver outputs that correspond and match better with the expectations of citizens across the continent. Commissioners themselves, while not representing their country,[2] serve the vital purpose of bringing to the consideration, debate and deliberations of the College of Commissioners the unique insight of local and national dynamics and perceptions, that would otherwise not always be fully and instinctively understood and retained at European level.

In recent years, profound divergences of perception on the relevance, urgency and magnitude of the challenges posed to the Union clearly emerged during the financial crisis, for instance, and then while facing the flows of migrants and refugees across the Middle East and the Mediterranean. The closest a Member State was to the problem, financially or geographically, the most acute was its sense of urgency, and consequently its readiness to adopt drastic and unprecedented measures to address it. Such action was multi-faceted, whether at the level of national institutions, governments and parliaments, or of public opinion, as one needs the other to advance and move from narrative to decisions and actions.

It has been argued that the same divergence of perception had emerged also during the crisis in Ukraine in 2014, first with the Russian aggression in the East of the country, and then with the illegal annexation of Crimea. In fact, on the contrary, those actions were clearly and immediately identified by the entire European Union – no Member State excluded – as blatant violations of international law. As such, they represented a threat to the entire international legal order and multilateral architecture, and most specifically to security and cooperation in the European continent, that had to be addressed with a united and consistent reaction. The discussion among Member States and across the international community on the appropriateness of measures to be taken in order to respond to the Russian actions in Ukraine was not centred on whether it was necessary or appropriate to react, nor on the urgency and gravity of the matter and consequently on the extraordinary need for exceptional measures, but rather on what would have been – in practical terms – the most effective response the EU and the entire global community could have adopted. So, in that case, unity of purpose was not under any doubt or discussion, and the sense of urgency and gravity was equally spread across the continent – even if in some countries, due to history and geography, the narrative was presented more forcefully than in others. But the substance was commonly shared, and this has in fact allowed the EU to take decisions unanimously and then keep a consistent course of action over time, once decisions were taken on the measures to be adopted – namely, sanctions matched with a set of diplomatic efforts that led to some achievements, but unfortunately not to the solution of the crisis.

During the first months of 2020, instead, facing the initial spread of the Covid-19 pandemic, the dynamic in the continent seemed to duplicate the one that the European Union had experienced in relation to the migration flows: a completely different perception of the sense of gravity of the phenomenon across countries, leading to dramatically diverging analyses and proposals on measures and policies at institutional level. I personally remember very well following the news in different Member States in late February 2020:

---

[2]See the explicit reference in the swearing-in formula to the impossibility to receive or follow instructions from national governments, and the commitment to serve uniquely the European common interest.

you could easily believe that they were reporting two completely different realities, far away in time and space. And yet, over a few weeks, the entire European continent – and the entire world – realized that the pandemic was set to change the way lives were lived, economies and societies were organized, health systems were responding, and even global interactions were reshaped and reoriented. In the course of March 2020, everything, every single aspect of life, changed everywhere. Our societies were suddenly and unexpectedly exposed to dramatic losses of lives and a sense of profound vulnerability. The mourning, combined with the devastating psychological, social and economic impact of the pandemic itself and of the measures imposed by the need to contain it, brought the entire continent (and far beyond) into a collective state of mind it had never experienced before: fear, loss, isolation, uncertainty on even the most basic aspects of daily life. The other is perceived as a literally vital threat, and – at the same time – there is the need to come together as a community to try to survive and recover in solidarity. During those months in the Spring of 2020, Europe faced probably the most dramatic and acute collective crisis it had ever experienced since the end of World War II.

The EU institutions had just started their cycle. Plans and priorities were discussed, approved, set. Working methods evaluated and defined, teams built, contacts established, interlocutors identified, inside and outside the EU. All processes that require an immense amount of work, time, energy, focus, consensus, but most of all constant and deep personal connections. The newly established European leadership started to exercise its functions in the most challenging environment ever experienced by any generation of European leaders. Not only they had to face and handle the complexity of challenges and crises we already mentioned above (from the pandemic itself to the Brexit negotiations, just to mention two), but they had to do it as a newly composed team, without the time nor the possibility to elaborate and consolidate practices, formats, policies and even channels of communication that would have been vital for effectiveness and efficiency of actions at all levels and in all fields, both internally and externally.

The risk of disruption between March and April 2020 was concrete and high. Had the European Union failed to react properly, immediately, boldly and in a united manner, it would have probably resulted in the end of the integration process once and for all. The challenge was immense, the tools to respond to the crisis were not in place, and the magnitude of the potential for disruption so dramatic that it was even difficult to describe at the time.

It took some time – precious time – if you consider the speed of the contagion and the impressive number of deaths in those initial weeks. But the European Union reacted – and it reacted incredibly well. In unity and solidarity, mobilizing resources that were not predictably available, and even taking decisions and action on issues that were completely out of its institutional competences. It could have been much easier for the EU institutions to simply ignore or decline the call for action that was dramatically rising from our communities, and remain in the comfort zone clearly designed by the intersection of their well-defined institutional competences and the lack of instruments and tools at their disposal for an appropriate reaction.

Instead, the EU leadership was wise and brave enough to accept the risk and navigate in the uncharted waters of building and shaping a common, coordinated, shared European response to the pandemic. Far from perfect, and with some delay, yet the decisions and actions that the European Union chose to take in spring 2020 not only provided literally life-saving instruments at the disposal of Member States and local communities – both in the health sector and in the one related to the economic recovery –, but they also showed that the institutions had full awareness of the relevance of the challenge. After two decades of multiple and multi-faceted crises, in the midst of the most dramatic existential threat Europe ever faced in almost a century, accepting the challenge of entering the unknown and unexplored territory of shaping policies and tools (and finding the relevant necessary resources) needed to save Europe from the pandemic and its consequences was not only a moral duty vis-à-vis its citizens, but also a matter of survival for the Union itself. It was a declaration of self-confidence against all odds, and the collective capacity to explore the institutional, political and even financial potential of the Union outside of the beaten track. The EU decided to do something that had never been done before, and that had never been foreseen. Something completely exceptional and unique for any institution, let alone the most complex of all.

The European Union launched major and unexpected initiatives in two different domains, both extremely sensitive and potentially controversial: health, on which the treaties assign extremely limited competences to the European institutions; and the economic recovery, on which political controversies had proliferated during the previous years, making it impossible to imagine that the measures that were actually adopted in 2020 would have been even conceived.

On the health sector, the European Union responded to the pandemic by stretching and expanding its role and functions. It worked to ensure the availability of medical equipment and supplies, uniting efforts to overcome the limits of long supply chains that exposed Europe to a major risk of shortages. Under the Union civil protection mechanism, the Union established a 'rescEU' strategic medical stockpile of equipment and supplies; it used the joint procurement of medical equipment to sign more than 50 contracts following calls for tenders; it has strengthened the role of the European Center for Disease Prevention and Control and of the European Medicines Agency; it has encouraged and supported concrete and immediate acts of solidarity among Member States with cross-border delivery of medical equipment and reciprocal offers to take in patients in intensive care structures. The EU action has also been crucial to support Member States to develop effective Coronavirus vaccines and ensure access to them, and to treatments and tests, with an unprecedented investment in support of a truly European pharmaceutical strategy.

This extraordinary combination of new additions to the European policy portfolio makes it possible today to open a reflection on how to strengthen the European Union role in the health sector, using the Conference on the Future of Europe to launch a broad public debate on the perspectives and priorities of the European Health Union. Just a few years ago, before 2020, it would have been highly improbable to develop not only actions (and to mobilize the respective necessary budgetary resources) but even to start and sustain a political debate about competences on issues like those that are today the absolute priority of the European institution: speed and safety of regulatory processes; research investments in the development of therapeutics; large scale EU clinical trials; financing and procurement capacities; securing supply chains and delivery of equipment and therapeutics; facilitating international cooperation and distribution – to mention just a few.

The first and clear impact of 2020 on the future of our Union is the unprecedented focus and investment on the European dimension of Health policies and respective instruments – including research. The second field of action in which extraordinary innovation has been introduced is that of the European support to the economic recovery in Member States.

After the harsh debates and fights around which measures would have been appropriate or needed to contain and overcome the eurozone crisis of the previous years, this was clearly a very dangerous political minefield – even more so for a European leadership that had just started its mandate. And yet, a recovery instrument of around 800 billion euros was established, with the purpose of not only supporting the economies of the continent, but also to incentivize the Green Deal and the Digital agenda, blending in a very smart way the new urgency dictated by the pandemic, with the political priorities set by the institutions at the very beginning of their mandate.

But what was extraordinary in this decision, was not just the magnitude of the instrument, the speed of the decision-making timeline, and the mix of immediate and long-term priorities; it was first and foremost the fact that for the very first time in the history of the European Union, the Commission would have borrowed significant amounts on behalf of the EU on the capital markets, using its high credit rating to negotiate advantageous financial terms for loans and grants and transferring those benefits to Member States, using the EU budget to back the borrowing. No one would have ever imagined, even a few months before 2020, that this decision would have been taken. The pandemic buried a taboo.

This unprecedented step is undoubtedly the most evident sign that the European Union managed to react to the Covid crisis in a way that not only responds to the immediate urgencies of the crisis itself, but also shapes the future of the integration process in a more structural manner. Jean Monnet words must have turned into the European leaders' heads constantly during those crucial negotiations in spring 2020: 'l'Europe se fera dans les crises et elle sera la somme des solutions apportées à ces crises'. One giant step was taken. A taboo was broken.

Overcoming taboos is not only relevant in immediate, practical terms. It does not only impact the field of action to which it is applied. It also shows, in itself, the capacity, will and determination of an institution – in this case, a complex set of complex institutions – to go beyond the natural instinct of conservative practices, processes and policies. The most recurrent attitude in any institution and organization is the tendency to repeat practices and policies of the past. Any innovation is naturally and instinctively confronted with the basic, fundamental question: 'it has always been done this way, it has always worked, so why should we change?'. I believe this is one of the main sources of problems our institutions face, at all levels – from local municipalities to the European and international ones. There is an almost unconscious resistance to transformation and adaptation, the tendency to homologate and absorb people and ideas into a flow of action that in substance represents a reassuring repetition of the past. Shades can change, but the colours remain the same. 'It cannot be done because it has never been done' represents a mantra that is probably also a survival tool, a guarantee of continuity that is vital in institutions and organizations that experience a constant turnover of staff and leadership figures. But it often impedes capturing demands, needs and trends that move fast in society, and long term, it contributes to that sense of disconnection between institutions and 'ordinary people' that fuels so powerfully anti-system feelings in public opinions and in the political discourse. Resistance to change in the institutions can be a very dangerous element in the equation of what we currently refer to as populism.

Breaking taboos, in this framework, represents a major contribution to re-establishing a connection, and eventually a certain decent level of confidence, between public opinions and institutions. Because together with the taboo, what is challenged and overcome is the assumption that change is fundamentally impossible, that messages coming from society are not heard, not understood, and in any case not taken into serious consideration as a valid basis for political decision making.

With the historic decision taken in spring 2020 to create the largest stimulus package ever, with unprecedented use of EU instruments, in the hardest moment for citizens and communities so dramatically hit by the pandemic and its economic and social consequences, has shown that the European institutions have a much higher level of awareness, courage, creativity, and understanding of reality than expected.

This boost in credibility is probably the most relevant element of the way in which 2020 has shaped the future of Europe. Breaking such a heavy taboo signals that the increasing demands and expectations expressed by public opinions and political leaderships towards the EU could turn from being a trap, the easy and comfortable search for a scapegoat, to actually becoming a self-fulfilling prophecy: if in times of existential threats Member States turn towards the European institutions to find and build, together, solutions, they could manage to get them.

This introduces, potentially, two long-term innovative dynamics. On one hand, the distance between capitals and Brussels could diminish. As solutions are actually found, mechanisms are established with a shared responsibility for proper implementation, and the political discourse that used to fuel the anti-European feelings loses ground and arguments. Capitals asked Brussels, Brussels replied, and it is now for capitals to make it work. Whether the recovery plan fails or succeeds, the responsibility will be a shared one. This reduces to zero the interest that some political leaders could be tempted to have, of celebrating the failure of the EU as a national success. National and European interest, and responsibility, finally totally coincide. This happens regularly on basically all policy choices, but the mainstream narrative does not often reflect this reality. In 2020, the shift from a confrontational discourse to a cooperative one based on shared responsibility and solidarity started to be the norm rather than the exception. Not a minor achievement, after the trends of the previous two decades.

On the other hand, the breach of the taboo that the adoption of the Recovery Plan represented sets the already planned Conference on the Future of Europe on a completely different stage. If taboos can be broken, if the urgency of citizens' needs can be heard, then there is a chance that this exercise manages to go beyond a light and vague consultation mechanism on a broad scale, and actually gets to focus on some real innovations in terms of processes or policies. Everything is possible. And the open-ended nature of the Conference turns from being a limition to representing a potential asset. Not to be taken for granted, rather the opposite. But the possibility has opened up, and it is at least not to be excluded. It will be in the hands of the European, national and local institutions, but also of civil society and intermediate bodies, to capture this opportunity and make the best out of it.

2020 also introduced an important potential element of acceleration when it comes to the global role of the European Union. First of all, it became evident more than ever that in times of crisis, what is really needed is a well functioning, cooperative, multilateral institutional framework through which transparent information sharing and constructive solution building can be possible at global or regional scale. The pandemic showed, in fact, beyond the politicisation of narratives and communications around the origins and the effectiveness of responses to Covid, that there is no possible effective solution to a global pandemic in the absence of a truly cooperative and coordinated response at international level. 2020 made it undeniable that national interests coincided with global interests, and vice versa: as long as we are not all free from the pandemic, we will all be hostage of it. No one can live the illusion of being safe if others are not safe. Solidarity, for all those looking at the crisis with some degree of detachment, became the new name for self-interest. The EU being one of the key pillars and sponsors of a cooperative multilateral international order, its role as a catalyst became even more crucial than before when this need was already quite self-evident.

The way in which the European Union supported both the production and supply of medical treatments and vaccines at continental level (not to mention the regulatory role it played and continues to play), and the economic recovery of Member States with the stimulus package, increased the perception of its relevance worldwide and inspired others to follow similar patterns of action. Many, around the world, turned towards the EU for guidance, advice, and support. And many received it. Global power struggles went hand in hand with the search for international cooperation, needless to say. But the EU voice as a strong promoter of a multilateral approach to the crisis has been clear and relevant, in the world dynamics.

The second aspect on which 2020 influenced the global role of the European Union has to do with its external competences. It is well known that consular activities remain in Member States' hands, with extremely limited opportunities for the EU to play a role in this field. When the pandemic started, the massive work required to contact, inform, assist and repatriate all EU nationals from every corner of the globe was largely supported and even directly done by the Union, using the impressive network of EU Delegations in the world, and the economy of scale of a target population with continent size numbers. Another taboo was broken. Building on it will not be self-evident, but a precedent is set (not the first one for sure, but the most relevant one for numbers and impact), and it could contribute to shaping the future of Europe in a very practical manner, pushing towards a systematic common European action in consular activities.

If Europe will be built in times of crisis, and through the responses that will be given to crises, then we can undoubtedly say that 2020 represented a crucial year for shaping the future of our Union. In the key sectors of health and economy, and also in relation to the global role of the EU, the crisis opened the way to potentially impressive opportunities. Doors were opened, paths designed, taboos broken.

Whether these changes will turn into a consolidated trend or will represent a parenthesis, will depend on the political will and capacity of the European leaderships, institutions and societies. As always, the future of Europe will be shaped by Europeans, as the Union is and becomes what its citizens decide to make of it. But there is no doubt that, after 2020, the potential for change is there, if the will for it will also be there. The crisis was turned into an opportunity; now, it is for Europeans to build on it and design what the Union will be.

JCMS 2021 Volume 59. Annual Review. pp. 20–31   DOI: 10.1111/jcms.13240

The Impossibility of Constitutionalizing Emergency Europe[1]

STEFAN AUER[1] (iD) and NICOLE SCICLUNA[2]
[1]The University of Hong Kong, Hong Kong [2]Hong Kong Baptist University, Hong Kong

Introduction

The pandemic year of 2020 started with both the European Commission and national health ministers reassuring European citizens (and each other) that there was not much cause for concern. Pandemics happened elsewhere. While EU leaders were cognizant of the outbreak of a novel respiratory disease in Wuhan, China, and its rapid spread through South East Asia, they believed that Europe was well-prepared. As late as February 26, that is more than a month after the lockdown of Wuhan, the president of the European Commission, Ursula von der Leyen, confidently proclaimed that the infection risk in Europe was 'low to moderate'. She echoed the assessment of the European Centre for Disease Prevention and Control (ECDC), which argued a month earlier that 'EU countries were well-prepared' (Herszenhorn and Wheaton, 2020). They were not. Instead, Europe faced an emergency from which it is yet to recover. Following on a decade-long economic crisis, which has been managed but never resolved, the pandemic further exposed the weaknesses of the EU's constitutional order, diminishing its legitimacy and appeal at a time when citizens looked to Europe in search of support and solutions.

February 26, 2020 can also be seen as the moment at which the EU's Covid-19 crisis began in earnest. As northern Italy was becoming Europe's Wuhan, the 'Italian government issued an emergency request for protective personal equipment to the European Commission', which in turn passed it on to the fellow member states (Genschel and Jachtenfuchs, 2021). For weeks, Italy's call for help remained unheeded. While Italian hospitals and health workers were overwhelmed, member states resorted to unilateral emergency measures – including placing export bans on vital medical equipment – which betrayed the ideal of European solidarity.

As the pandemic worsened and spread across the continent, Europeans rediscovered their commitment to transnational solidarity. By mid-2020, the EU had redeemed itself by reaching agreement on a bold proposal – the Next Generation EU fund – that promised to revolutionize EU financing by enabling the Commission to raise commonly-backed debt. It was hailed as a Hamiltonian moment by commentators and political figures alike – including Olaf Scholz, the German finance minister, signalling the end of Germany's opposition to an EU transfer union. If Covid-19 represented the culmination of the long crisis decade (2010–20), the EU's response to it revived the idea of

[1]We would like to thank Christian Kreuder-Sonnen and Jonathan White for initiating this conversation via their workshop 'The transnational politics of emergency', organized by the Hertie School of Governance in June 2020. We are immensely grateful for their exchange of ideas, support and helpful feedback on earlier drafts of this paper. We would also like to thank Erik Jones for his insightful comments on the paper at the online ISA conference in April 2021. Finally, we are grateful to Emanuele Massetti for his astute feedback and support during the editing process.

Europe growing stronger by defying adversity. Jean Monnet's vision of Europe being 'built through crisis' to become 'the sum of the solutions adopted for those crises' (Monnet, 1978, p. 417) became credible again. Following on from the eurozone crisis, the migration crisis, the crisis of the EU's relationship with its eastern neighbours, and Brexit, the pandemic intensified Europe's ongoing transformation. For some, it was Europe's 'coming of age story' (Laffan, 2020; van Middelaar 2021; Schmidt, 2021), while for others it further exposed Europe's legitimacy problems (Kreuder-Sonnen and White, 2021). It is this latter line of argument that we pick up, analysing the EU's euro crisis and pandemic responses through the lens of 'emergency politics' and with a focus on the impact of crises on the Union's constitutional order.

We suggest that the responses of national and supranational executive bodies to the crises of the past decade have undermined legal coherence insofar as they have precipitated a *dealignment* between law and practice. We raise two, interconnected, questions: (1) Can the exceptional measures taken over the past decade be brought within the EU's constitutional framework (that is, can law and practice be *realigned*)? (2) Can (and should) emergency powers be constitutionalized at the European level?[2]

In pursuing the first question, we signal our scepticism towards celebratory accounts of 'crisis as opportunity'; that is, of Europe being made through crisis management. We suggest, instead, that 'emergency Europe' (White, 2015) is eroding channels of democratic accountability in ways that cannot easily be undone.[3] We will explicate the legal and democratic legitimacy costs of exceptionalism via a focus on supranational and multilateral emergency politics in the euro crisis.

Yet, in raising the second question, we also sound a cautionary note against the idea that recourse to emergency politics is never justified; that is, that there is never an emergency that requires a norm-breaking or law-breaking response (Kreuder-Sonnen, 2019, p. 200; cf. White, 2019). As we argue in the final part of the paper, the rapid spread of the novel coronavirus from early 2020 constituted a challenge that would have been far better addressed had authority holders been able and willing to deviate from established norms and laws earlier (for example those regarding free movement and other civil liberties). For us, the key question is at which level decisions on the invocation and substance of emergency measures ought to be made. While we do not deny that *all* forms of exceptionalism (from domestic to supranational) entail costs, we argue that emergency responses emanating from the national level will usually be more legitimate.

I. Searching for a Sovereign in 'Emergency Europe'

Emergency politics may be defined as comprising (a) practices that deviate from established laws and norms and (b) a rhetoric that rationalizes those practices on the basis of their alleged necessity (Kreuder-Sonnen and White, 2021). Borrowing from Kreuder-Sonnen and White (2021), we may discern different types of emergency politics

---

[2]See Kreuder-Sonnen (2021) for a much more comprehensive treatment of this question, which sets out a blueprint for an EU-level emergency constitution.

[3]Arguably, the erosion of democratic accountability in the EU is a more general trend; for example,owing to the single market's 'over-constitutionalization' and the resulting constriction of the space for political contestation at both national and European levels (Grimm, 2015; Scharpf, 2017). Nevertheless, the prevailing atmosphere of urgency of recent years gives us an opportunity to analyse this trend in a particular form.

in the EU, according to the type of actor that is exercising emergency authority and the type and level of laws and norms that are being suspended. This article focuses particularly on *supranational emergency politics* and *multilateral emergency politics*. The former occurs when EU institutions that hold either delegated authority (for example, the ECB, the European Commission) or pooled authority (for example, the Council), '[expand] their executive discretion by undermining or circumventing the constraints that bind their authority in normal times'. The latter occurs when member state governments collectively expand their executive discretion, *vis-à-vis* democratically legitimated institutions such as national and European parliaments, 'by creating new authority structures outside the EU legal framework' (Kreuder-Sonnen and White, 2021, pp. 5–6).

How does the concept of emergency politics relate to the notion of sovereignty and the question of its location in the EU's hybrid polity? According to Carl Schmitt's famous dictum, the sovereign is the one who decides on the exception. That is, emergencies reveal the sovereign as that actor which is capable of taking the lead and imposing a solution in line with its own interests.[4] In polities in which rules governing the invocation of a state of emergency and the exercise of emergency powers are formally constitutionalized, the constitution itself points to the sovereign (generally, emergency powers will be vested in the executive government). However, the EU does not have a formal constitution, much less a formal emergency constitution. What, then, have the crises of the last decade revealed?

By and large, they reveal the absence of sovereign power at the European level. As Fritz Scharpf (2017, pp. 315–16) has argued, there is no government either at the European or at the national level with sufficient 'capacity to provide effective solutions for manifest common problems and common aspirations'. Instead, we see action without agency and/or technocratic institutions taking up political roles. Thus, in the midst of the Eurozone crisis, Mario Draghi acted as a sovereign by recognizing the urgency of the situation and promising that the ECB would 'do whatever it takes' to safeguard the currency union, downplaying legal constraints. At the start of the pandemic, by contrast, a multitude of actors at all levels of the EU's system of governance largely failed to live up to the challenge of recognizing and acting on the emergency. Both scenarios present a serious challenge to the EU's *de facto* constitution. Bold actions in the name of emergency, which are not underpinned by an enabling legal framework, undermine the EU's self-understanding as a community of law, destabilizing the existing constitutional settlement. Inaction exposes the EU to the charge of being a dysfunctional polity, unable to protect its citizens.

II. How Does Emergency Politics Challenge the EU's Legal Order?

The invocation of a state of emergency is a profoundly political act. The invocation of emergency may be used to simplify complex realities; to frame decision-making as a series of stark choices – ultimately the choice between 'success' and 'failure' (to overcome the crisis). Applied to the euro crisis, recourse to emergency politics – both by supranational actors and member state governments – has served not only to defer

---

[4]As Kreuder-Sonnen and White (2021, p. 3) note, '[b]y invoking irregular, informal, and sometimes extra-legal procedures to enact emergency measures, the role of power (ideational and material) is exponentiated, along with the democratic-legitimacy concerns that accompany it'.

debate about the means of achieving the objectives of European integration, but also to defer debate about the objectives themselves.

Given its emphasis on *urgency*, it is unsurprising that emergency politics has particular implications for law, which is made and interpreted through processes that are slow and deliberate. It is for this reason that many national constitutions provide for the suspension of normal legal and deliberative procedures during designated states of emergency. However, the EU has no formal legal framework governing either the declaration/revocation of states of emergency or the exercise of emergency powers (Kreuder-Sonnen, 2019, pp. 119–23). As a result, there is no clear divide between the state of exception and 'normality'. Measures adopted in circumvention of established EU procedures (that is, outside of the community method) linger semi-permanently; they are neither brought within the EU's constitutional framework via treaty reform, nor wound back in favour of the *status quo ante*.

One way to grasp the supranational and multilateral forms of emergency politics is with the concept of 'evasion' (Dawson, 2020).[5] Evasion of EU law occurs when member states wish to escape the EU's legal strictures without exiting the Union itself. They turn, therefore, to alternative legal and regulatory toolkits, such as the European Financial Stability Facility (EFSF) and European Stability Mechanism (ESM), both of which were established outside of the EU treaty framework, in order to avoid the potential veto points of parliamentary ratification and, potentially, referenda. Evasion also consists in circumventing limits on the EU's supranational competences via soft law regulation. This was the *modus operandi* of the European Semester, through which the Commission gained significant oversight over areas of exclusive national competence (for example, labour and pensions law) via formally non-binding recommendations (Costamagna, 2018).

Finally, evasion has manifested in the *de facto* empowerment of the ECB as lender of last resort and enforcer of austerity. Drawing on the legitimacy conferred by its expertise, the ECB was able to establish its sole competence to define monetary policy and, thereby, the limits of its own mandate. In a move that confirmed the hollowing out of the substance of judicial review of emergency politics, the Court of Justice of the European Union (CJEU) gave the ECB's self-empowerment *de jure* approval in the OMT case (Scicluna, 2018; Grimm, 2020). Thus, evasion of EU law is a key feature of what may be described as 'integration-through-crisis' (Scicluna and Auer, 2019). That is, it is an emergency-driven mode of integration that does not abandon law, but misconstrues it in the service of crisis solutions that are seemingly pre-ordained and *alternativlos*.[6]

To be sure, in seeking to address the interlocking crises of the Eurozone, European leaders faced a series of dilemmas which were not amenable to straightforward solution. Both completion of the half-built house of monetary union (via the construction of a true economic union, including regularized fiscal transfers) and partial disintegration (via the exit of some members of the Eurozone, such as Greece) were deemed politically

---

[5]Adapting Albert Hirschman's tripartite classification of exit, voice and loyalty, Mark Dawson (2020, p. 51) has posited the threat to EU constitutionalism as a series of three, interlinked challenges: exit, evasion and subversion. 'Exit' refers to formal withdrawal from the EU. 'Subversion' describes non-compliance with EU law.
[6]German Chancellor Angela Merkel arguably perfected this approach as her governing style; alternating between the rhetoric of necessity and the politics of the exception (Auer, 2021).

unfeasible and undesirable. Yet, these were (and are) possible choices, which were elided by the 'no alternative' rhetoric of emergency Europe.[7]

The fallout over the German Federal Constitutional Court's (BVerfG) decision on the ECB's Public Sector Purchase Programme (PSPP), handed down on May 5, 2020 was also revealing of the extent to which most commentators have accepted the *ad hoc* legalization of emergency Europe. Rather sensationally, the BVerfG, having referred the question to the CJEU, rejected its endorsement of the PSPP as *ultra vires* and 'simply not comprehensible' ('*schlechterdings nicht mehr nachvollziehbar*') (Grimm, 2020, p. 948). The reaction from scholars and observers of EU politics was swift and hostile. The German court was accused of having 'launched a legal missile into the heart of the EU' (Wolf, 2020), and of 'plunging Europe into a constitutional crisis' (Fabbrini and Kelemen, 2020). On June 9, 2021, the Commission started infringement proceedings against Germany, taking the conflict to the next level, in an attempt to reassert the supremacy of the CJEU's interpretations of European law (Grunert and Gutschker, 2021).

The conflict between the CJEU and the BVerfG exposed two different understandings of the EU and its legitimacy sources. Critics of the BVerfG's judgement continue to view the EU as a quasi-federation that should not be destabilized by its subordinate units. For the BVerfG, on the other hand, 'it is key that the European Union is a union of sovereign states ... and that it must respect their identities, which are reflected primarily in their national constitutions' (Grimm, 2020, p. 945). Taking on more powers in the name of emergency – as the ECB has done with the *ex post facto* blessing of the CJEU – may be justifiable so long as it produces crisis-alleviating *outputs*. However, this cannot make up for the illegitimacy of its *procedures*; an illegitimacy that flows from the EU's nature as a non-sovereign polity, in which it falls to national institutions (e.g. courts and parliaments) to safeguard national constitutional orders. The Schmittian question of 'who is the guardian of the constitution?' thus becomes, in the context of the EU, 'who is the guardian of whose constitution?'

In other words, the hybrid nature of the EU, as an experimental polity located somewhere between a fully-fledged federation (*Bundesstaat*) and a community of sovereign nation states (*Staatenverbund*), creates an irresoluble dilemma about who has the 'final say', which no number of legal proceedings is likely to settle. If one takes the view that a functioning EU requires the prioritization of the European constitution over national constitutions, then the European Court must be the guardian of the European constitution, in which case the judgment of the German Federal Constitutional Court itself was an *ultra vires* act (Mayer, 2020, p. 736). If, by contrast, the authority of EU law is ultimately derived from well-functioning national democracies, as the BVerfG understands it, then the 'final' authority of national constitutional courts over national constitutions is at times impossible to disentangle from their authority over European constitutional issues. Thus, as Everson and Joerges (2014) argued, the Union 'has both national and European masters: masters who may be in disagreement with one another', with disagreements becoming particularly heated in times of crisis.

Emergency politics has undermined the legal legitimacy on which the EU has traditionally relied and replaced it not with expanded channels for democratic inputs, but with

[7]See for example Patberg (2021) for a theoretical discussion of the possibilities for democratically legitimate disintegration in the EU.

a heightened emergency rhetoric, deployed mainly by executive actors (e.g. the ECB and Commission, as well as national governments acting through the European Council), who are (self-)empowered to take 'necessary' decisions in extraordinary circumstances. Consistently with the EU's longstanding preference for output over input legitimacy, emergency Europe claims to operate *for* the people, even if its decisions are not necessarily *of* or *by* them (Schmidt, 2020, p. 31) – as reflected in the decidedly non-majoritarian ECB's new slogan adopted in February 2016, 'we serve the people of Europe' (Lokdam, 2020, p. 985).[8] Whether Greeks, Germans and other Europeans actually feel well-served by the ECB, and what they can do if they do not, is another question. At any rate, the invocation of 'the people' as the ultimate source of the ECB's authority recalls a longstanding, and enduringly relevant, debate – that over the so-called 'no *demos*' problem and its implications for the Union's constitutional potential.

III. Seizing the 'Constitutional Moment'

At the beginning of the millennium, there was a concerted effort to explicitly constitutionalize the EU (Christiansen and Reh, 2009, p. 14). To be sure, the Treaty Establishing a Constitution for Europe (CT) was still an international treaty, which would not have changed the EU's formal legal status as an international organization (IO) governed by a mixture of supranational and intergovernmental organs. Nevertheless, the CT would have consolidated the EU's pre-existing *implicit constitution*; that is, its constitutionalized legal order, which decades of jurisprudence had established as self-contained and autonomous from both the member states' legal orders and international law. Just as importantly, it would have vindicated the possibility of adjusting the EU's constitutional settlement through democratically legitimate means. It is the apparent impossibility of doing this – indeed, of making *any* significant reform of the Treaties – that has driven European leaders' 'evasive' reliance on extra-constitutional emergency politics since 2010.

Indeed, unlike both the judicially-driven process of integration-through-law, through which the EU's implicit constitution was forged, and the executive-driven episodes of treaty-making, through which the EU expanded its policymaking reach, the CT aimed overtly at the politicization of European integration at a mass level. That project was abandoned following the CT's rejection in referenda in France and the Netherlands in 2005. Shorn of its overtly constitutional features, most of the substance of the text was repackaged in the Lisbon Treaty, which entered into force in 2009, following its own bumpy path to ratification (Scicluna, 2015).

This historic episode remains relevant for two reasons. Firstly, as noted above, the entire decade-long process of attempted constitutional reform was an object lesson in the difficulty of securing the support needed to revise the EU treaties. Secondly, and relatedly, it begs the question of when, if ever, the EU will be in a position to seize the 'constitutional moment'. In the lead up to the CT's signature and, then, following its rejection by voters, scholars offered various predictions of, and explanations for, its failure. One line of thought focused on the impossibility of formally constitutionalizing

---

[8]To be sure, the question of whether emergency Europe has delivered positive outputs is very much contested, especially when it comes to the impact of austerity on the countries of the Eurozone's periphery (see for example Matthijs, 2017).

a polity without a *pouvoir constituant* (Craig, 2001; Grimm, 1995; cf. Kumm, 2006) while a more optimistic take saw in the CT's demise a vindication of the durability of the EU's existing constitutional settlement. Moravcsik, in fact, described attempts to politicize European integration as a 'self-inflicted wound', advocating instead further *depoliticization* in order to exploit the 'EU's greatest tactical advantage', which was, as he put it, that it was 'so boring' (Moravcsik, 2008, p. 180–1).[9]

Another dimension of Europe's constitutional debate focused on the presence or absence of a 'constitutional moment'. Well before the negative referenda results in France and the Netherlands, Schmitter (2000, p. 45) noted that a major weakness of the constitutional project was its timing – coming a decade after the EU's foundation and in the absence of any emergency akin to that which energized America's founding fathers in the 1780s. On this view, the CT was a solution in search of a crisis. In marked contrast, the European integration project has faced no shortage of crises since 2010. Yet, as already discussed, the EU response has been to 'muddle through' with a series of *ad hoc* measures. Not only have these not entailed constitutional reform – for example, to bring the ECB's formal mandate into line with its *de facto* expanded role; or to remove Article 125 TFEU (the 'no bailout' clause) and replace it with the legal framework of a transfer union – they have actively evaded it. Instead, EU exceptionalism has unfolded with a certain technocratic automatism, as the authors of major policy initiatives (from bond buying programmes to enforced austerity) have downplayed the *political* nature of their decisions by pointing to an alleged lack of alternative options.

If, then, 2000–05 afforded ample opportunity for debate but no urgency, and 2010–20 has offered lots of urgency, but no time for debate, one must ask whether the conditions will ever be right to embark on major constitutional reform, either to constitutionalize measures taken outside of the treaty framework or to provide the EU itself with constitutionalized emergency powers. The frequent recourse to both supranational and multilateral exceptionalism that marked the euro crisis leads us to doubt whether the EU will ever seize its constitutional moment.

Indeed, it is revealing in this respect that there is no explicit reference to treaty reform in the Joint Declaration on the Conference on the Future of Europe. The rationale for the Conference was very much born out of the crisis decade. Initiated by French President Macron in the immediate aftermath of the Brexit referendum, the Conference was meant to have been launched on 9 May 2020. The pandemic outbreak contributed to a one-year delay (the Conference was formally launched on 9 May 2021), but it also added a sense of purpose. As the Joint Declaration notes, 'the European Union's unique model was challenged like never before' by Covid-19, and 'Europe can and must ... learn the lessons from these crises'. According to the Conference's design, this learning is to take place via a year-long listening exercise 'closely involving [Europe's] citizens and communities'. While there is much to be said about the value of an open-ended and inclusive discussion of Europe's future, one may doubt whether this format will lead to the kind of concrete constitutional renewal that would be necessary to address the EU's manifold challenges.

---

[9]Cf. those scholars, such as Majone (2005) who argued that 'integration by stealth' could not be sustained.

IV. Emergency Politics as Unrestrained Managerialism

In declaring the Draft Treaty Establishing a Constitution for Europe a failure (well before its formal abandonment), Klabbers and Leino (2003, p. 1293) noted its fatal ambivalence on two questions: 'What to do with the Union? And what to do with Europe's citizens?'. A decade of EU emergency politics has not answered these questions. On the contrary, the past ten years of depoliticized crisis management has exacerbated the pathologies inherent in the already dominant managerial (or functional) conception of international organizations. The managerial concept frames IOs as sites of action; bodies constituted and empowered to 'get things done'. This is in contrast to what Klabbers terms the '*agora* concept', which frames IOs as forums for debate, but not necessarily problem-resolution (Klabbers, 2005).

Even outside contexts of exceptionalism, the managerial concept lends itself to the view that transnational cooperation is the domain of executive action guided by techno-cratic expertise. Accordingly, managerialism goes hand-in-glove with depoliticization, understood as the recasting of *political* questions as *technical* questions (Klabbers, 2005, pp. 280–1). More disturbingly, the managerial concept contains within itself the justification needed for bypassing formal legal and procedural constraints when those constraints inhibit action. As Klabbers (2005, p. 283) puts it, 'if formal rules do not allow certain forms of cooperation and stand in the way of solving problems, then things will just be done informally'.

This sentiment describes well the evasive modalities of supranational and multilateral emergency politics during the euro crisis. In contrast to the highly judicialized modes of integration-through-law, integration-through-crisis has relied heavily on extra-constitutional means to achieve its desired ends (Scicluna, 2018; Scicluna and Auer, 2019). As noted above, the ends themselves – preserving the Eurozone with its current membership and without turning it into a transfer union – have been put beyond debate by the rhetoric of necessity.

Thus, attempts at depoliticization notwithstanding, the EU has been anything but boring over the last decade. Its most recent challenge – the global spread of Covid-19 – accelerated the tendency towards executive empowerment, but with varying degrees of efficiency and legitimacy. Indeed, in our view, the pandemic raises a different, and no less important, set of questions for EU institutions and member states: namely whether they – acting alone or in concert – can effectively respond to an emergency when there is one. Indeed, this is the question that hung over the European project in 2020.

V. Even Paranoids Have Emergencies

Invoking an emergency where there is none threatens the life of democracy. Yet *not* invoking one where the danger is real threatens the lives of many citizens. 'No form of order, no reasonable legitimacy or legality can exist without protection and obedience', wrote Schmitt, to assert famously (leaning on Hobbes) that 'the *protego ergo obligo* is the *cogito ergo sum* of the state' (Schmitt, 2007, p. 52). Schmitt was no friend of liberal democracy, but we ignore his insights at our peril. Failure to protect citizens will weaken any polity, democratic or not. And, indeed, 'a Europe that protects' was perceived as a hollow promise by many Italians in March 2020, when the virus outbreak was out of control in Lombardy, and again across Europe in late 2020 and early 2021, as EU citizens faced another wave of the pandemic accompanied by delays in vaccine rollouts.[10] This is corroborated by a recent survey conducted by the European Council on Foreign Relations, which found that 'many European citizens have less confidence in EU institutions' (Dennison and Puglierin, 2021) more than a year after the outbreak of the pandemic (April 2021). High levels of dissatisfaction reached even Europe's core, including Germany, where the number of people believing that 'the EU system is broken' increased significantly (55 per cent in April 2021 compared to 44 per cent in November 2020), alongside the number of Germans expressing the view that 'EU integration has gone too far'.[11]

As a post-sovereign polity, the EU's possibilities for quick and decisive action are somewhat limited. This is a serious liability. As Machiavelli noted with respect to a 'wasting disease', in its early stages it 'is easy to cure but difficult to diagnose; after a time … it becomes easy to diagnose but difficult to cure'. It requires a prudent politician, Machiavelli argued, to live up to this challenge. In fact, deciding on what constitutes an emergency is a profoundly political act that ought not be left to a technocratic body. At the EU level, where we confront the phenomenon of 'emergency rule without a defined institutional sovereign' (White, 2019, p. 34), the difficulty is even more pronounced. Decisions are still taken in the absence a sovereign, but 'bureaucratic rule by nobody' (Arendt, 2005, p. 78) tends to replace political rule. Instead of a political decision, Hannah Arendt warned, 'we find haphazard settlements of universal procedures, settlements which are without either malice or arbitrariness because there is no will behind them, but to which there is also no appeal' (Arendt, 2005, p. 78). In other words, when power is dispersed, nobody rules and nobody is responsible.

Across the world, both politicians and experts failed to identify the seriousness of the danger that Covid-19 presented. The countries and territories that did well in suppressing the pandemic in its early stages (for example, Taiwan, Hong Kong, Vietnam, Singapore, Australia and New Zealand), did so by taking the kind of drastic action that the EU – given its unique model, which requires coordination among multiple levels and institutions of governance – could not. As late as the end of February 2020, more than a month after Wuhan was locked down, and at a time when Italy recorded 400 out of 477 Europe-wide cases of Covid-19, the Commission advised national governments against border closures, dismissing the Italian government's concerns as unfounded (Gutschker, 2020). The assertion that 'Covid-19 does not respect borders' (Laffan, 2020) became something of a platitude obfuscating the fact that stricter border controls, when implemented early, dramatically reduced the spread of the virus. Indeed, having failed to craft a coordinated response on borders and other virus suppression measures, most European states ended up imposing much harsher, and more haphazard, restrictions on individual freedoms, in the form of (repeated) 'lockdowns'.

The EU's vaccine procurement scheme has also demonstrated that it lacks the legitimacy resources – and arguably also the capacity – to take bold steps early. Compared

[10]53 per cent of Italians felt that 'no one' (28 per cent), or 'China' (25 per cent) was their 'country's greatest ally in the coronavirus crisis', in contrast to 10 per cent of Italians who viewed the EU as such (Dennison and Zerka, 2020, p. 7).
[11]'Forty-nine per cent of Germans claim to have less or much less confidence in the EU as a result of its vaccines policy … And 33 per cent of Germans now think that the coronavirus crisis shows that EU integration has gone too far, compared to 23 per cent in 2020' (Leonard and Puglierin, 2021).

to the UK, the Commission (to which member states delegated responsibility for procurement) signed contracts with vaccine manufacturers later, while the European Medicines Agency has been significantly slower than its UK counterpart to approve vaccines. Moreover, the main benefit of centralized procurement – avoidance of 'vaccine nationalism' – has been undermined by some member states reaching side agreements with vaccine manufacturers, as well as by the Commission's threat to impose an export ban on vaccines produced in the EU (Mussler, 2021).

Considering the high degree of interconnectedness that the EU has achieved, an effective response to the pandemic would have had to have come (also) from the supranational level. Yet, as the inability to undertake any meaningful constitutional reform over the past decade indicates, the EU as a polity does not have enough popular support to be endowed with emergency powers (cf. Kreuder-Sonnen, 2021). Consequently, democratic legitimation demands that emergency powers be located at the level of nation-states, though their effectiveness will be limited. There is no straightforward way to resolve this tension. In fact, the problem reveals the same dysfunction in EU governance that can be observed in relation to other crises. The EU has what we may call a 'sovereignty paradox': in many important areas, member states have ceded too much control to the supranational level to be able to act effectively on their own. Yet, they retain enough power to undermine common solutions.

Conclusion

In this article, we have argued that the EU's decade of emergency politics, culminating in 2020, has damaged its rule of law and undermined the legitimacy of its constitutional order. At the same time we argue that the *failure* to recognize – and act on – an emergency when one exists has also undercut the authority of the EU polity, which relies heavily on its perceived ability to deliver the goods. The overarching question that links both parts of this argument is how emergencies ought to be identified and from which level and organs of governance emergency responses ought to emanate.

In sketching an answer to this question, we have focused on the interaction between exceptionalism and the EU's constitutional order. We have suggested that the obstacles in the path of constitutionalizing 'emergency Europe' are formidable, if not insurmountable. This claim is two-fold. Firstly, in a polity without a sovereign, in which power is diffused across institutions and levels of governance, codifying a constitutional framework for the exercise of emergency powers is likely unviable. This is, in no small part, owing to the absence of EU-level actors with sufficient legitimacy to invoke, govern, and end states of emergency (cf. Kreuder-Sonnen, 2021). Secondly, and in partial explanation of the first claim, the collective inability of national governments and supranational institutions to seize the EU's constitutional moment (owing largely to domestic opposition) indicates that the EU is far from becoming the kind of democratically constitutionalized entity that could exercise such authority.

We conclude then by reiterating our reservations about the viability of constitutionalizing emergency powers at the supranational level, all the while acknowledging that such powers would be required for the EU polity to function effectively in bad times as well as good. This intractable problem reflects the dysfunction of the EU's experimental polity. Addressing it would require substantive constitutional reform, including by bringing key Euro crisis response measures within the treaty framework. In 2021, we may hope that the Conference on the Future of Europe will offer an opening to embark on such a project.

References

Arendt, H. (2005) *The Promise of Politics* (New York: Schocken).

Auer, S. (2021) 'Merkel's Germany and the European Union: Between Emergency and the Rule of Rules'. *Government and Opposition*, Vol. 56, No. 1, pp. 1–19.

Christiansen, T. and Reh, C. (2009) *Constitutionalizing the European Union* (London: Palgrave Macmillan).

Costamagna, F. (2018) 'National Social Spaces as Adjustment Variables in the EMU: A Critical Legal Appraisal'. *European Law Journal*, Vol. 24, No. 2-3, pp. 163–90.

Craig, P. (2001) 'Constitutions, Constitutionalism, and the European Union'. *European Law Journal*, Vol. 7, No. 2, pp. 125–50.

Dawson, M. (2020) 'Coping with Exit, Evasion, and Subversion in EU Law'. *German Law Journal*, Vol. 21, pp. 51–6.

Dennison, S. and Puglierin, J. (2021) 'Crisis of Confidence: How Europeans see their Place in the World'. *European Council on Foreign Relations Policy Brief*, 9 June.

Dennison, S. and Zerka, P. (2020) 'Together in Trauma: Europeans and the World after Covid-19'. *European Council on Foreign Relations* Policy Paper ECFR/328, pp. 1–68.

Everson, M. and Joerges, C. (2014) 'Who is the Guardian of Constitutionalism in Europe after the Financial Crisis?' In Kröger, S. (ed.) *Political Representation in the European Union* (London: Routledge).

Fabbrini, F. and Kelemen, R.D. (2020) 'With One Court Decision, Germany may be Plunging Europe into a Constitutional Crisis'. *Washington Post*, 8 May.

Genschel, P. and Jachtenfuchs, M. (2021) 'Postfunctionalism Reversed: Solidarity and Rebordering During the COVID-19 Pandemic'. *Journal of European Public Policy*, Vol. 28, No. 3, pp. 350–69.

Grimm, D. (1995) 'Does Europe Need a Constitution?' *European Law Journal*, Vol. 1, No. 3, pp. 282–302.

Grimm, D. (2015) 'The Democratic Costs of Constitutionalisation: The European Case'. *European Law Journal*, Vol. 21, No. 4, pp. 460–73.

Grimm, D. (2020) 'A Long Time Coming'. *German Law Journal*, Vol. 21, pp. 944–9.

Grunert, M. and Gutschker, T. (2021) 'Der Streit ums letzte Wort'. *Frankfurter Allgemeine Zeitung*, Vol., No. 9 June.

Gutschker, T. (2020) 'EU-Kommission lehnt neue Grenzkontrollen ab'. *Frankfurter Allgemeine Zeitung*, 28 February.

Herszenhorn, D. and Wheaton, S. (2020) 'How Europe Failed the Coronavirus Test'. *Politico*, April 7.

Klabbers, J. (2005) 'Two Concepts of International Organization'. *International Organizations Law Review*, Vol. 2, No. 2, pp. 277–94.

Klabbers, J. and Leino, P. (2003) 'Death by Constitution? The Draft Treaty Establishing a Constitution for Europe'. *German Law Journal*, Vol. 4, No. 12, pp. 1293–305.

Kreuder-Sonnen, C. (2019) *Emergency Powers of International Organizations: Between Normalization and Containment* (Oxford: Oxford University Press).

Kreuder-Sonnen, C. (2021) 'Does Europe Need an Emergency Constitution?' *Political Studies.* https://doi.org/10.1177/00323217211005336

Kreuder-Sonnen, C. and White, J. (2021) 'Europe and the Transnational Politics of Emergency''. *Journal of European Public Policy.* https://doi.org/10.1080/13501763.2021.1916059

Kumm, M. (2006) 'Beyond Golf Clubs and the Judicialization of Politics: Why Europe has a Constitution Properly So Called'. *American Journal of Constitutional Law*, Vol. 54, No. Fall, pp. 505–30.

Laffan, B. (2020) 'Europe in the Time of Covid-19'. *Bridges*, 2 April.

Leonard, M. and Puglierin, J. (2021) 'How to Prevent Germany from becoming Eurosceptic'. *European Council on Foreign Relations, Policy Brief*, 9 June.

Lokdam, H. (2020) '"We Serve the People of Europe": Reimagining the ECB's Political Master in the Wake of its Emergency Politics'. *Journal of Common Market Studies*, Vol. 58, No. 4, pp. 978–98.

Majone, G. (2005) *Dilemmas of European Integration: The Ambiguities and Pitfalls of Integration by Stealth* (Oxford: Oxford University Press).

Matthijs, M. (2017) 'Integration at What Price? The Erosion of National Democracy in the Euro Periphery'. *Government and Opposition*, Vol. 52, No. 2, pp. 266–94.

Mayer, F.C. (2020) 'The Ultra Vires Ruling: Deconstructing the German Federal Constitutional Court's PSPP decision of 5 May 2020'. *European Constitutional Law Review*, Vol. 16, pp. 733–69.

Monnet, J. (1978) *Memoirs* (London: Collins).

Moravcsik, A. (2008) 'The European Constitutional Settlement'. *The World Economy*, Vol. 31, No. 1, pp. 158–84.

Mussler, W. (2021) 'Europäischer Impfnationalismus'. *Frankfurter Allgemeine Zeitung*, 27 January.

Patberg, M. (2021) 'The Democratic Ambivalence of EU Disintegration: A Mapping of Costs and Benefits'. *Swiss Political Science Review*, Vol. 27, No. 3. https://doi.org/10.1111/spsr.12455

Scharpf, F. (2017) 'De-constitutionalisation and Majority Rule: A Democratic Vision for Europe'. *European Law Journal*, Vol. 23, No. 5, pp. 315–34.

Schmidt, V.A. (2020) *Europe's Crisis of Legitimacy: Governing by Rules and Ruling by Numbers in the Eurozone* (Oxford: Oxford University Press).

Schmidt, V.A. (2021) 'European Emergency Politics and the Question of Legitimacy'. *Journal of European Public Policy (forthcoming).*

Schmitt, C. (2007) *The Concept of the Political* (G. Schwab, Trans.) (Chicago: University of Chicago Press).

Schmitter, P.C. (2000) 'Federalism and the Euro-Polity'. *Journal of Democracy*, Vol. 11, No. 1, pp. 40–7.

Scicluna, N. (2015) *European Union Constitutionalism in Crisis* (London: Routledge).

Scicluna, N. (2018) 'Integration through the Disintegration of Law? The ECB and EU Constitutionalism in the Crisis'. *Journal of European Public Policy*, Vol. 25, No. 12, pp. 1874–91.

Scicluna, N. and Auer, S. (2019) 'From the Rule of Law to the Rule of Rules: Technocracy and the Crisis of EU Governance'. *West European Politics*, Vol. 42, No. 7, pp. 1420–42.

van Middelaar, L. (2021) *Das europäische Pandämonium – Was die Pandemie über den Zustand der EU enthüllt* (Berlin: Suhrkamp).

White, J. (2015) 'Emergency Europe'. *Political Studies*, Vol. 63, No. 2, pp. 300–18.

White, J. (2019) *Politics of Last Resort: Governing by Emergency in the European Union* (Oxford: Oxford University Press).

Wolf, M. (2020) 'German Court Decides to Take Back Control with ECB Ruling'. *Financial Times*, 13 May.

JCMS 2021 Volume 59. Annual Review. pp. 32–43

DOI: 10.1111/jcms.13254

The EU Institutional Architecture in the Covid-19 Response: Coordinative Europeanization in Times of Permanent Emergency

STELLA LADI[1,2] and SARAH WOLFF[1]
[1] Queen Mary University of London, London [2] Panteion University, Athens

Introduction

The European Union's (EU) reaction to the Covid-19 crisis will be discussed for a long time and will inform policy and academic debates about European integration, the relationship between EU institutions and member states, and the power struggles between member states. The outcome of the EU policies adopted in 2020–21 will also determine the Union's longevity and its role as a global actor. Decisions were made and policies were re-designed and, on some occasions, designed from scratch in areas where close cooperation pre-existed such as economic governance, competition policy and borders control but also in less developed domains such as health policy and a common vaccines strategy (Wolff and Ladi, 2020). The EU institutions had to adjust to a new form of distant work, away from Brussels and to coordinate the EU's reaction in a health crisis, which soon affected almost all EU policies. Along with key EU institutions, a previously less-known EU agency, the European Centre for Disease Prevention and Control (ECDC), found itself at the forefront of the response. Although the EU's response at the beginning looked uncoordinated and slow, it soon picked up with trust in the EU reaching its highest level since 2009 in April 2021.[1]

In this article we explore the EU's reaction to the Covid-19 crisis and we argue that a new mode of Europeanization that can be best described as coordinative Europeanization has emerged. Moving from 'coercive Europeanization' (Leontitsis and Ladi, 2018) that had characterized the Eurozone crisis with conditionality and monitoring of EU member states by EU institutions, coordinative Europeanization is defined as a bottom-up process where the member states are actively involved in the policy-making process early on in order to guarantee the highest level of implementation possible. It is a pragmatic approach to Europeanization and the channels of member states' involvement are often informal and online. The Commission has played a leading role and has offered innovative tools in this process. The new 'permanent' state of emergency caused by the Covid-19 crisis brought to the EU a realization of what interdependence really means and the need to coordinate in order to find policy solutions even if they are just 'good enough'.

The article is organized in four sections. First, we analyse how Covid-19 revealed that the state of emergency in the EU could be more permanent than temporary, how the EU institutions reacted and how the coordinative mode of Europeanization emerged. In the

[1] https://ec.europa.eu/commission/presscorner/detail/en/IP_21_1867 (accessed 7/6/21).

next two sections we go deeper by analysing two key EU policy responses: the Recovery and Resilience Facility and the coordination of freedom of movement within the EU despite Covid-19 restrictions. These two policy areas were selected to compare and contrast two responses that followed a different pace but where the coordination between member states and institutions has been central for their design and remains central for their successful implementation. The concluding section summarizes our findings and offers some ideas for further avenues for research.

I. The EU's Institutional Response to a 'Permanent' State of Emergency

The EU is confronted with what we call a 'permanent' state of emergency. The Covid-19 crisis started only a few years after the end of the Eurozone crisis and while the migration and Brexit issues were still ongoing. The EU, similar to most of its member states, is learning to deal with crises as part of its normal mode of policymaking. How have EU institutions responded and adjusted to the Covid-19 crisis compared to prior crises? In this section we first define what a permanent state of emergency is, and we then move to explore the EU's institutional response. We argue that a new mode of Europeanization has emerged. We call it coordinative Europeanization.

Crisis is a situation which threatens the high-priority goals of the decision-making unit, restricts the amount of time available for response and surprises the members of the decision-making unit by its occurrence (Hermann, 1969; Degner, 2019). Undoubtedly, the spread of Covid-19 across the globe and in Europe falls under the definition of a crisis. Covid-19 disrupted life in the continent but also the policy-making process within the EU. It was soon framed as an 'existential' crisis since EU leaders very quickly realized that if they did not rise to the challenge the EU project would once more be threatened with becoming obsolete (Russack and Blockmans, 2020). The amount of time the EU had to respond was restricted but despite early chaotic national responses including the closure of borders, it was soon followed by the mobilization of the EU's crisis instruments, swift decision-making processes and financial packages for the economy (Wolff and Ladi, 2020). It can also be said that the multifaceted character of the disruption, the geographical universality and length of the crisis took the EU by surprise. However, after the previous turbulent decade quite a few discussions had taken place about the inevitability of crises and new procedures and mechanisms had already been put in place (e.g., Pilati and Zuleeg, 2019; Rhinard, 2019). In that sense, we could claim that in the context of the Covid-19 crisis the EU was less surprised than in previous crises.

Crises, by definition, should only last for a specific, limited time and then give space to a period of 'normality'. Emergency should last for an even shorter period. However, in the case of the EU, but also globally, 'normality' does not seem to last very long. Zuleeg *et al.* (2021) call it the age of permacrisis and claim that this is the environment that the EU will need to operate in the future. We argue that if this proves to be true, which is very likely, the new 'normal' for the EU will be a state of permanent emergency where crisis decisions will need to be made more often. Crises are not new to the EU and compromise and change during crises have been thoroughly analysed in the literature (Dinan *et al.*, 2017; D'Erman and Verdun, 2018). One could argue that the European project has been developing through a series of crises. After the Second World War, the European Political Cooperation emerged from the 1970s as a result of the oil crisis, while the disintegration of Yugoslavia and the end of the permissive consensus led to the Maastricht Treaty. Competences have always expanded through crises. Although the crisis this time is transnational and trans-sectoral, it does not (yet) call for major governance or Treaty changes. Instead it seems that the current decision-making process in place had learned from previous crises and had some structures and mechanisms in place to respond to the pandemic.

However, concepts such as 'critical junctures' and 'critical moments' that have traditionally been very useful in helping us navigate through changes that occur during and after crises need to be rethought since crises are no longer short and rare events but instead take place in a continuum of time. In that sense, inter- and intra-crisis learning is more likely to take place and often the same policy entrepreneurs are faced with multiple and similar crises during their career. Ladi and Tsarouhas (2020) show the importance of the same policy entrepreneurs (e.g., Merkel, Lagarde) learning from the Eurozone crisis during the decision-making process for the Recovery and Resilience Facility (RRF) in the summer of 2020. The normalisation of the EU response to this permanent emergency seems to have been accelerated by the exceptional nature and scale of the Covid-19 crisis. Although the implications for the legitimacy of European integration and its institutions have already been explored (Kreuder-Sonnen and White, 2021; Schmidt, 2021), fewer authors have looked into what this state of 'permanent emergency' means from a European integration and governance perspective. We argue in particular that 'permanent emergency' reveals new aspects of the interdependence between member states and EU institutions and has created an increased demand for an adequate response from the EU. This new mode of interaction between member states and the EU institutions can be framed as coordinative Europeanization. We'll return to this argument at the end of this section.

The EU institutions found the Covid-19 crisis challenging to start with not only because of uncoordinated member states' actions, but also because of the changing working pattern, which did not allow for unhindered travel for meetings as in the past. Yet, they adjusted to the new reality, although each one at a different pace and not always with the same success. Nevertheless, they managed to perform and to deliver important policy outcomes such as the RRF and the EU vaccination policy. As is often the case when there is a crisis and in line with its competence (Nugent, 2017), the European Council's coordinating role has been central. From March 2020 until April 2021, the European Council met 16 times to discuss the Covid-19 emergency and 11 of these meetings were held virtually.[2] The issues that it dealt with were numerous and included the limitation of the spread of the virus, the provision of medical equipment, the socio-economic conditions, the vaccination strategy and more recently, the digital certificates. It has certainly made some historic decisions such as the 750 billion euro recovery fund during the 17–21 July Special European Council and has managed to keep member state leaders aligned despite the usual tensions. We can observe a continuity in the significance of its role similar to previous crises but this time a process of politicisation took place at the top since the crisis was perceived as 'existential' and pushed European leaders to make quick decisions (Wolff and Ladi, 2020).

---

[2]https://www.consilium.europa.eu/en/meetings/calendar/?Category=meeting&Page=1&dateFrom=2020%2F01%2F01 &dateTo=2022%2F04%2F20&filters=2031&filters=69020 (accessed 14/6/21).

Nonetheless, we do not observe a turn towards intergovernmentalism, but rather a change in the dynamics between the EU institutions and the member states. The European Commission and its President, Ursula von der Leyden, have been clearly leading the developments in Brussels. Following a pattern that started during the Eurozone crisis, the Commission's powers and de facto importance in day-to-day management continued to increase (Bauer and Becker, 2014). The strengthening of the executive during crises has been confirmed multiple times both at the European and at member state level (Moury et al., 2021). Russack and Fenner (2020) in a preliminary study of EU crisis decision-making show that the Commission was the quickest to adjust and to take advantage of pre-existing decision-making instruments, such as the inter-service consultation, and fast-track them. Yet this pattern takes on a new dimension given the obstacles to meeting in person and to travelling to Brussels. In fact, except for the European Central Bank and the European Court of Auditors where rules regarding teleconferencing, written procedures and remote voting already existed, the rest of EU institutions were ill-equipped to deal with social distancing and remote working (Bodson, 2020).

Although many raised issues of accountability and the lack of in-depth debates online, it seems that social distancing and remote working has opened the path towards a new mode of Europeanization by coordinating 'from a distance'. Innovative experiments have taken place in the everyday administration and politics of Europe through virtual meetings. Brussels was indeed a successful space of socialization for many decision-makers who suddenly had to quickly coordinate through online meetings from their national home countries. This time Brussels came to national capitals, instead of national policy-makers coming to Brussels. In this reverse coordination, EU institutions performed differently and the Commission did very well in increasing its coordinative activity not only among EU institutions but also with the member states. A new structure emerged which brought together national ministries and Directorate Generals in online meetings and created 'Commission-Capital networks'. It was the European Council that initiated this new coordinative activity of the Commission in order to design policies that would bring fast results and would effectively combat the most acute outcomes of the crisis (Russack and Fenner, 2020).

The Council of Ministers and the European Parliament both had many more difficulties in adjusting to the online meetings and subsequent decision making because of the voting procedures and the geographical disparity of their members. For the European Parliament, its size and its multilingual functioning made it even more difficult to adapt. The Council could rely on the Permanent Representatives in Brussels and a lot of the work was concluded at the COREPER meetings but it was clear that the online environment was an obstacle to negotiations and non-verbal communication (Russack and Fenner, 2020). Initially, the Council was thus 'low on output performance and throughput efficacy or accountability' (Schmidt, 2021, p. 9). However, their role does not seem to have changed significantly from previous crises since they both continued performing their tasks adequately.

The European Parliament despite all the difficulties, managed to play a key role in the negotiation of the Multiannual Financial Framework (MFF) from July 2020 when it disagreed with the European Council's proposed cuts to future-oriented programmes on climate change, digital transition, and youth among others. It also pushed for the inclusion of a mechanism to protect the budget against breaches of the rule of law.[3] An agreement was reached in December 2020 after trilateral negotiations, which was welcomed with relief since the adoption of the MFF unblocked the RRF. Important demands of the Parliament, which included the increase of funding for future-oriented programmes, were accommodated (D'Alfonso, 2020). It can be claimed that the supranational dimension of EU decision-making expressed by the European Parliament survived intact during the Covid-19 emergency.

We claim that a new mode of Europeanization has emerged from the EU's institutional response to the Covid-19 crisis that can be best described as 'coordinative Europeanization'. This new 'permanent' state of emergency in the EU brought a realization of what interdependence really means and the need to coordinate in order to find policy solutions even if they are 'good enough'. Previous modes of Europeanization that focused on the uploading of best practices in the 2000s or in coercive mechanisms during the Eurozone crisis (Boerzel, 2002; Ladi and Graziano, 2014) seemed to be inadequate in light of this new fast-spreading virus. Instead, this time the focus was on coordination with the member states at early stages and often via the Commission in order to devise policies that would work for everyone. A similar approach was successfully adopted during the Brexit withdrawal negotiations when the Commission created the Task Force 50 to guarantee unity among member states (Schuette, 2021). Our analysis reveals that this new coordinative Europeanization is characterized by discursive coordination and the persuasive power of ideas (Schmidt, 2021) and also by a swifter decision-making process facilitated by existing crisis management mechanisms developed over the past 12 years of 'crisis'. This new coordinative mode of Europeanization emerged in parallel to intergovernmental and supranational tendencies in the EU that remain the driving forces of integration. It is very much linked to what we have described as politicisation at the top (Wolff and Ladi, 2020). In the next two sections we explore this new mode of Europeanization and its mechanisms in two of the most important policy developments of the last year: the RRF and the coordination of mobility in the Schengen area. This allows us to go more in-depth to explore the role of EU institutions during this period.

II. The Recovery and Resilience Facility

The EU's initial response to the economic challenge of the spread of Covid-19 was more coordinated than in the case of border closures straight from the beginning with the EU institutions taking decisive steps and the member states largely supporting them. The European Commission evoked the flexibility and general escape clauses on the deficit and state aid rules and launched a number of funding schemes such as the 'Pandemic Crisis Support' and a temporary recovery fund (SURE). Similarly, the ECB created a 'Pandemic Emergency Purchase Programme' (PEPP) in mid-March 2020 aiming at stabilizing financial markets and the economic outlook of the Euro area. Ladi and Tsarouhas (2020) argue that this was the result of contingent learning because of the emergency of Covid-19, which led to policy learning from the Eurozone crisis experience.

[3]https://www.europarl.europa.eu/factsheets/en/sheet/29/multiannual-financial-framework (accessed 21/4/2021).

It became apparent early on that a more ambitious EU reaction would be necessary to tackle the impact of the pandemic on the European economy but also to convince European citizens that the EU was competent and could rise to the occasion. EU leaders gave the mandate to the European Commission's President Ursula von der Leyen to prepare a proposal for growth, mixing grants and loans and outlining the linkage of this fund to the Multiannual Financial Framework (MFF) (European Council, 2020a). In May 2020, France and Germany took a bold initiative and proposed the distribution of grants of 500 billion euros to member states in need. A few days after the Franco-German proposal, the Commission unveiled a recovery instrument named 'Next Generation EU' (NGEU) worth 750 billion euro (European Commission, 2020b). Central to NGEU was the proposed Recovery and Resilience Facility (RRF), with €310 billion in grants envisaged to be dispersed to member states. An agreement worth approximately €1.8 trillion was reached on 17 July after intense negotiations between the 'Frugal Four' (Austria, Denmark, Netherlands and Sweden) and the rest of the member states (European Council, 2020b). The disagreement concerned the conditionality attached to loans and grants, the actual size of the budget and the increase of rebates of the Frugal Four together with the reduction of their net contribution to the budget. Additionally, there was a debate on the content of the funding with the 'Frugal Four' arguing for R&D, digital and green investment at the expense of cohesion funds (Ladi and Tsarouhas, 2020).

Compromises were made from both sides and a historical decision was reached. For the first time ever, the Union committed itself to engage directly in a fiscal stimulus by agreeing to set up the RRF and to move from a rule-based economic governance to a mixture of rules and transfers. The total amount of the RRF was maintained at €750 billion with grants reaching €390 billion and loans of €360 billion. The Commission for the first time would borrow from the international markets, in effect realizing the Eurobond aspirations initially discussed during the Eurozone crisis (Moesen and De Grauwe, 2009). To repay the borrowing, the Council decided to increase its own resources system with a tax on non-recycled plastic from 1 January 2021 and to consider additional resources, such as a carbon tax, digital tax, and financial transactions tax (European Council, 2020b).

Some of the compromises made during the July summit haunted the process of ratification of the agreement by the European Parliament in autumn 2020 when the MFF was discussed. De Feo (2020) describes the Parliament as the 28th member state, emphasising the importance of the autumn negotiations. The Council's agreement of a total EU budget of €1.074 billion rather than €1.1 billion which was the Commission's proposal meant that cuts were proposed for the Horizon Europe and Erasmus programmes (by 6 per cent and 14 per cent respectively), as well as the Just Transition Fund and Health programme (European Parliament, 2020, p. 2). Similarly, the 'rule of law' conditionality clause, which was watered down to ensure that countries like Poland and Hungary would sign up to the final deal, was discussed once more during the MFF debate. A final agreement of the MFF after a new compromise between the Council and the Parliament was reached in December 2020 opening up the next stage of the implementation process (D'Alfonso, 2020).

Although coordination was of paramount importance during the design of the RRF, co-ordinative Europeanization can be observed more clearly during the implementation phase since EU institutions and member states alike are central to the process. Grants and loans will be paid out based on the National Recovery and Resilience Plans (NRRP) that member states submitted to the Commission. The NRRPs had to follow the European Semester priorities and focus on six major policy areas: green transition; digital transformation; smart, sustainable, and inclusive growth; social and territorial cohesion; health, economic, social, and institutional resilience; policies for the next generation, children, and youth. The Commission is responsible for assessing the NRRPs while the final decision is made by the Council. A Recovery and Resilience Task Force (RECOVER) has been created to coordinate the implementation of the RRF (Kyriakidis, 2021).[4] The aim is for 70 per cent of the funds to be directed to member states in 2021 and 2022 while the remaining 30 per cent is to be disbursed in 2023 based on members' GDP performance in 2020 and 2021 (Ladi and Tsarouhas, 2020).

The principle of the RRF implementation is not dissimilar to previous schemes such as the financial assistance programmes during the Eurozone crisis. However, there are two key differences that make the implementation of the RRF more coordinative and European and less coercive. First, the process is totally EU-based without the participation of international actors such as the International Monetary Fund (IMF). Even further, it is embedded in the European Treaties since the rules of the European Semester are followed without the need of intergovernmental tools such as the European Stability Mechanism (ESM) or bilateral agreements, as was the case during the Eurozone crisis (Kyriakidis, 2021). Second, the conditionality attached to the disbursement of funds is lighter since it has by now been realized that strict conditionality works only partially and that member states agreement is necessary for successful implementation (Moury et al., 2021). The RRF conditionality relies on sanctions when member states fail to comply (negative conditionality) and its linkage to the rule of law is certainly one of the novelties of the 2021–27 MFF (Vita, 2020). However, the process of obstructing funding is not easy. One or more member states can call for an extraordinary summit, should it consider another country's plan to significantly deviate from agreed milestones and targets. Nevertheless, it will have to do so within a three-month timeframe and obtain the consent of a qualified majority at Council in order to stop the flow of funds. With a mix of responsibilities between member states and EU institutions, it can be argued that a shift from coercive Europeanization to coordinative Europeanization is taking place.

III. The Schengen Area

Restrictions on freedom of movement in the Schengen area were at first uncoordinated across EU member states. As a result, EU institutions were left only with the possibility to react to the unilateral reintroduction of internal border controls in 17 member states. Confronted with a discourse that defined public health as a national security issue, the European Commission had initially very little leverage and prioritised the re-establishment of green lanes by calling EU member states to ease freedom of movement for goods, medical professionals, and cross-border workers (Wolff et al., 2020). It discursively mobilised a functional-solidarity frame where coordination and

---

[4]https://ec.europa.eu/info/business-economy-euro/recovery-coronavirus/recovery-and-resilience-facility_en#national-re-covery-and-resilience-plans (visited 28/5/21).

non-discrimination were key principles to contest this uncoordinated renationalisation of Schengen by EU member states. Schengen states, as a first response to the pandemic, felt comfortable to resort to an administrative territorial logic of border management rather than prioritising a coordinated response (Bigo *et al.*, 2021, p. 15). This first phase (March–August 2020) of restrictions for the freedom of movement did not lead to much contestation by the public or legislators, due to the fact that many legislatures had to adapt to the pandemic and were in the first instance relatively marginalized (Griglio, 2020). It was indeed politically costly for legislatures, including the European Parliament, to 'politicize the breaches to the freedom of movement, as it would have meant to question the discourse of 'doing everything necessary to protect citizens' in times of uncertainty' (Wolff *et al.*, 2020, p. 1129).

The second phase which started in autumn 2020 can be characterized instead as coordinative Europeanization that culminated with the adoption of a vaccination passport in spring 2021. Under the German presidency efforts were made to coordinate a response to the restriction of free movement, and a recommendation was adopted at the Luxembourg meeting of 13 October 2020 (European Commission, 2020a). Insisting on the need to improve transparency and predictability for citizens and businesses, as well as to avoid fragmentation and disruption, the recommendation focused on the idea that 'any measures restricting free movement to protect public health must be proportionate and non-discriminatory, and must be lifted as soon as the epidemiological situation allows'. The ECDC's mandate was expanded to coordinate and collect data from EU member states on the epidemiological outlook and publish a weekly colour-coded mapping of regions in Europe. Although this document is not legally binding, member states have followed its main principles, highlighting that coordinative Europeanization happens through voluntary participation and 'guidelines' rather than formal legislation. Additionally, Council recommendations call for not restricting the free movement of people coming from green areas and adds that 'member states should in principle not refuse entry to persons travelling from other member states' and could offer a quarantine or a test upon arrival. This second phase shows that although coordinative Europeanization could not be initially observed, it took place later. The European Commission managed to work closely with the member states by avoiding the debate on Schengen governance and reform, which had been highly politicised for years, and relying instead on pre-existing crisis management mechanisms and institutions such as the ECDC to coordinate a return to the freedom of movement. Thus, coordinative Europeanization was eventually made possible through the involvement of an agency that evaluates health risks and is not one of the traditional internal security actors.

The second phase has been characterized by more direct consultations between EU institutions and national stakeholders in the decisions regarding travel in Europe. The breakthrough was the involvement of ministries of health into Schengen governance. This led to a 'new Covid-19 approach' where Schengen states decided to evolve from stopping people from crossing borders and forbidding them to do so to an approach 'which dissuades people from travelling on account of the consequences' (Bigo *et al.*, 2021, p. 14). Instead of barring EU citizens from travel, the shift has been to put the onus on citizens themselves, to dissuade them from travelling and to 'create a reluctance'. This has been balanced by more measures to track and trace people's movements, whose personal data on quarantine and travel movement is increasingly subject to scrutiny. In a way instead of relying on national borders, measures of quarantine, isolation and lock-down are calling upon the sense of civic duty among people and also pushing the borders from a national level to that of people's homes (Bigo *et al.*, 2021, p. 15). This approach has left more room for health experts to enter the debate about freedom of travel.

Another example of coordination in the Schengen area is the adoption of vaccination passports. It is an interesting example of coordination, since originally the idea was not really welcomed by EU member states, who feared it would introduce some discrimination to freedom of travel. While France was originally against the idea, it seems that discursive coordination led by the European Commission led France to shift its position and to adopt in its national model the principles proposed on 17 March 2021 by President Von der Leyen. The idea of an EU-wide travel certificate was also strongly supported by Spain and Greece whose economy depends on tourism. Direct coordination between the Commission and EU member states led to the adoption by the Council on 14 April 2021 of a negotiating mandate with the European Parliament. The so-called Digital Green Certificate involves a draft legislative proposal concerning EU citizens and their families as well as third country nationals legally residing in the EU. The legislation was adopted by July 2021, illustrating that the EU has considerably evolved and adapted its decision-making procedure to governance in times of emergency. Adopting legislation in such a short time frame is after all rare in traditional EU decision-making.

Conclusions

Coordinative Europeanization has enabled EU institutions to respond to the pandemic by demonstrating that they have learned from past crises. Coordinative Europeanization is neither a supranational nor an intergovernmental mode of cooperation. Instead direct consultations with EU member states on key emergency policies have enabled the EU to find compromises and to reach outstanding achievements like the RRF. This is a change from coercive Europeanization that characterized the EU's institutional response to the Eurozone crisis and whereby 'European institutions enforce change onto the member states' (Leontitsis and Ladi, 2018, p. 772). It is also different from the idea of diffusing 'best practices' in order to achieve the best policy solutions. In the case of the pandemic we find that lessons have been learned and that the EU's institutional response has been one of direct consultation and dialogue with its member states. This was visible in our case studies. In the case of the RRF the implementation relies on the NRRPs and no appetite for harsh conditionality and Troika-like monitoring is in sight. In the case of Schengen, the focus changed from internal security and traditional Schengen governance, where EU member states and the Commission had reached a deadlock, to a more pragmatic approach with a stronger role for the ECDC and national health ministries. Interestingly, cooperation is voluntary in relation to the freedom of movement and was made possible without legislation but instead with guidelines and recommendations.

This does not necessarily mean that coercive Europeanization has disappeared. For example, in the RRF some conditionality is in place. Future research could explore further whether coordinative Europeanization is just a characteristic of periods that we describe as 'permanent emergency' or whether it is here to stay. We need to further explore whether coordinative Europeanization, namely close cooperation between EU member states' capitals and EU institutions and agencies, leads to more pragmatic policy decisions and thus more compliance. However, coordinative Europeanization took place during a period of politicization at the top, which involved agreement between European elites about the need to react to the Covid-19 emergency (Wolff and Ladi, 2020). Emergency politics strengthen executives, presenting a risk of compromising European governance legitimacy (Kreuder-Sonnen and White, 2021, p. 9). Is coordinative Europeanization only possible during emergencies and does it suffer from the same fallacies as emergency politics? Whatever the answer, the Covid-19 crisis is not just another crisis but one that will shape the EU institutional architecture and its relationship with its member states for a long time.

References

Bauer, M.W. and Becker, S. (2014) 'The Unexpected Winner of the Crisis: The European Commission's Strengthened Role in Economic Governance'. *Journal of European Integration*, Vol. 36, No. 3, pp. 213–29.

Bigo, D., Guild, E. and Kuskonmaz, E.M. (2021) 'Obedience in Times of COVID-19 Pandemics: A Renewed Governmentality of Unease?' *Global Discourse: An Interdisciplinary Journal of Current Affairs*, Vol. 11, No. 1-2, pp. 1-2.

Bodson, B. (2020) 'EU's Institutions Operational Resilience in the Time of Covid-19'. *L' Europe en Formation*, 390, 53–73.

Boerzel, T. (2002) 'Member States Responses to Europeanization'. *Journal of Common Market Studies*, Vol. 40, No. 2, pp. 193–214.

D'Alfonso, A. (15/12/ 2020) 'Parliament's Consent to the 2021–27 MFF'. European Parliamentary Research Blog, https://epthinktank.eu/2020/12/15/parliament-consent-to-the-2021-2027-mff/

De Feo, A. (2020) 'The MFF 2021–2027: A Game Changer?' In Laffan, B. and De Feo, A. (eds) *EU Financing for Next Decade* (Florence: European University Institute), pp. 323–43.

Degner, H. (2019) 'Public Attention, Governmental Bargaining, and Supranational Activism: Explaining European Integration in Response to Crises'. *Journal of Common Market Studies*, Vol. 57, No. 2, pp. 242–59.

D'Erman, V.J. and Verdun, A. (2018) 'Introduction: Integration through Crises'. *Review of European and Russian Affairs*, Vol. 12, No. 1, pp. 1–16.

Dinan, D., Nugent, N. and Paterson, W. (2017) 'Conclusions: Crisis Without End?' In Dinan, D., Nugent, N. and Paterson, W. (eds) *The European Union in Crisis* (London: Palgrave), pp. 360–75.

European Commission (2020a) 'Council Recommendation on a coordinated approach to the restriction of free movement in response to the COVID-19 pandemic'. Brussels, 4.9.2020 COM(2020) 499.

European Commission (2020b) 'Europe's Moment: Repair and Prepare for the Next Generation', https://ec.europa.eu/commission/presscorner/detail/en/ip_20_940 (accessed 25 May 2021).

European Council (2020a) 'Conclusions of the President of the European Council following the video conference of the members of the European Council, 23/4/20', https://www.consilium.europa.eu/en/press/press-releases/2020/04/23/conclusions-by-president-charles-michel-following-the-video-conference-with-members-of-the-european-council-on-23-april-2020/ (accessed 31/7/20).

European Council (2020b) Special Meeting of the European Council: Conclusions, 21 July 2020 EUCO *10/20*.

European Parliament (2020) 'Future Financing of the Union: MFF, Own Resources and Next Generation EU', 23 July. Brussels: European Parliament.

Griglio, E. (2020) 'Parliamentary Oversight under the Covid-19 Emergency: Striving against Executive Dominance'. *Theory and Practice of Legislation*, Vol. 8, No. 1–2, pp. 49–70. https://doi.org/10.1080/20508840.2020.1789935.

Hermann, C.F. (1969) 'Some Consequences of Crisis which Limit the Viability of Organizations'. *Administrative Science Quarterly*, Vol. 8, pp. 61–4.

Kreuder-Sonnen, C. and White, J. (2021) 'Europe and the Transnational Politics of Emergency'. *Journal of European Public Policy*, pp. 1–13.

Kyriakidis, A. (2021) 'The EU's Response to the Covid-19 Pandemic: Policies of Integration, Recovery and Resilience', GPSG Working Paper No. 34.

Ladi, S. and Graziano, P. (2014) 'Fast-Forward Europeanization: Welfare State Reform in Light of the Eurozone Crisis'. In Coman, R., Kostera, T. and Tomini, L. (eds) *Europeanization and EU Integration: From Incremental to Structural Change?* (Basingstoke: Palgrave), pp. 108–26.

Ladi, S. and Tsarouhas, D. (2020) 'EU Economic Governance and Covid-19: Policy Learning and Windows of Opportunity'. *Journal of European Integration*, Vol. 42, No. 8, pp. 1041–56.

Leontitsis, V. and Ladi, S. (2018) 'The Changing Nature of European Governance and the Dynamics of Europeanization'. In Ongaro, E. and van Thiel, S. (eds) *The Palgrave Handbook of Public Administration and Management in Europe* (London: Palgrave Macmillan). https://doi.org/10.1057/978-1-137-55269-3_40.

Moesen, W. and De Grauwe, P. (2009) *Gains for All: A Proposal for a Common Eurobond*. Brussels: Centre for European Policy Studies.

Moury, C., Ladi, S., Cardoso, D. and Gago, A. (2021) *Capitalising on Constraint: Bailout Politics in Eurozone Countries* (Manchester: Manchester University Press).

Nugent, N. (2017) 'The Crisis and the EU Institutions, Political Actors, and Processes'. In Dinan, D., Nugent, N. and Paterson, W. (eds) *The European Union in Crisis* (London: Palgrave), pp. 167–87.

Pilati, M. and Zuleeg, F. (2019) 'A Nimble and Responsive EU?' in *EU Priorities for 2019–2024*, EPC, Vol. 24, pp. 149–54.

Rhinard, M. (2019) 'The Crisification of Policy-Making in the European Union'. *Journal of Common Market Studies*, Vol. 57, No. 3, pp. 616–33.

Russack, S. and Blockmans, S. (2020) 'How is EU Cooperation in Tackling the Covid-19 Crisis Perceived in Member-States?' In Russack, S. (ed.) *EU Crisis Response in Tackling Covid-19. Views from the Member States*. EPIN Report, 20 April 2020, pp. 1–3.

Russack, S. and Fenner, D. (2020) 'Crisis Decision Making: How Covid-19 has Changed the Working Methods of the EU Institutions'. CEPS Policy Insight No. 2020/17, July 2020.

Schmidt, V.A. (2021) 'European Emergency Politics and the Question of Legitimacy'. *Journal of European Public Policy*, pp. 1–15.

Schuette, L. (2021) 'Forging Unity: European Commission Leadership in the Brexit Negotiations'. *Journal of Common Market Studies*, pp. 1–18.

Vita, V. (2020) 'The Reinforced Conditionality Approach of the 2021–27 MFF'. In Laffan, B. and De Feo, A. (eds) *EU Financing for Next Decade* (Florence: European University Institute), pp. 101–13.

Wolff, S. and Ladi, S. (2020) 'European Union Responses to the Covid-19 Pandemic: Adaptability in Times of Permanent Emergency'. *Journal of European Integration*, Vol. 42, No. 8, pp. 1023–40.

Wolff, S., Ripoll Servent, A. and Piquet, A. (2020) 'Framing Immobility: Schengen Governance in Times of Pandemics'. *Journal of European Integration*, Vol. 42, No. 8, pp. 1127–44. https://doi.org/10.1080/07036337.2020.1853119.

Zuleeg, F., Borges de Castro, R. and Emmanouilidis, J. (2021) 'Europe in the Age of Permacrisis', Commentary at European Policy Centre, https://epc.eu/en/Publications/Europe-in-the-age-of-permacrisis~3c8a0c (accessed at 12/4/2021).

JCMS 2021 Volume 59. Annual Review. pp. 44–55   DOI: 10.1111/jcms.13246

Fiscal Integration in an Experimental Union: How Path-Breaking Was the EU's Response to the COVID-19 Pandemic?

WALTRAUD SCHELKLE
London School of Economics and Political Science, London

I. Inauspicious Start and Surprising Turnaround

The Covid-19 pandemic could not have started worse for the EU (Herszenhorn and Wheaton, 2020). In late February 2020, Italy requested supplies of medical equipment from other member states under the EU's crisis response programme, the Civil Protection Mechanism. The Commission duly escalated it to highest alert. But there was no response. Alarmed by Italy's request, France engaged in a stock-taking exercise that did not allow trading. Czechia, Germany, and Poland introduced export controls for medical equipment. Embarrassingly, China, Cuba and Russia came to the rescue more readily than fellow-Europeans (Poggioli, 2020). Under pressure from the Commission, German controls were lifted soon after (Reuters, 2020), but support for EU membership in Italy plummeted. The prospects for collective, forward-looking crisis management were bleak. Considerable policy resources had been spent since 2008 and their replenishment did not look promising. Some interventions, especially of the Troika, had done lasting political damage. A deepening political crisis seemed imminent, dividing an already divided union even further.

Yet, over several months, the EU managed to agree on a massive support package for the anticipated long slow recovery. The breakthrough came in mid-July. This was not a Hamiltonian Moment, founding the fiscal union that some see as the panacea for all Euro Area (EA) woes (Kaletsky, 2020). But the flagship Recovery and Resilience Facility (RRF) recognizes that a preventive fiscal capacity is required to shield and support the EA's most vulnerable members. This is in stark contrast to the European Stability Mechanism (ESM), which handed out cheap rescue loans only once a government was shut out of bond markets, and imposed intrusive prescriptions for fiscal policy and institutional reforms, overseen by the Troika. The RRF adopts the principle that the promise of mutual support can prevent a panic before it spreads. This subsequently changed the political economy of Covid-19, although the public relations debacle of the Commission's vaccine procurement and the slow roll-out of the immunization programme in member states continued to test political unity.

Research for this article was supported by the European Research Council under the Synergy Grant number ERC_SYG_2018 Grant no. 810356, in the scope of the project SOLID – *Policy Crisis and Crisis Politics. Sovereignty, Solidarity and Identity in the EU post 2008*. I am grateful to members of the SOLID team, the seminar participants at LUISS and Deborah Mabbett for their constructive comments.

This article analyses what made the dynamic of the Covid-19 pandemic so different in political-economic terms. I look at this dynamic through the lens of three significant reforms, which were accompanied by a new crisis politics in which heads of state directly addressed sceptical audiences in other countries as well as their own. I provide evidence that the legacy of failure in the EA crisis spurred attempts by major protagonists to break with a path that they saw as politically disastrous for the EU polity as a whole.

This should surprise any long-term observer of EU affairs. Ever since its revival in the late 1980s, the EU has enshrined long-term commitments of its members to openness and stability (Majone, 1996). The union operates in a rule-bound, path-*dependent* way that militates against such turnarounds. This scholarship is still valid and can actually explain why fiscal integration remains difficult even though a majority of member states has already given up their national currency. I propose a historical-institutionalist argument in the tradition of Pierson (2004) that can explain potentially path-breaking (or switching) reforms in the evolution of the experimental EU polity. The argument draws on literature on the possibility, and nature, of change in path-dependent institutional development (Streeck and Thelen, 2005; Capoccia and Kelemen, 2007). The reforms of 2020 can be seen as a critical juncture in a longer process, in which the EU transcends the confines of a regulatory polity but does not commit to fiscal federalism either (Genschel and Jachtenfuchs, 2014; Kriesi *et al.*, 2021, pp. 4–6).

The next section reviews how intergovernmental contestation over the legacy of the EA crisis led to a surprising political response to the Covid-19 pandemic. The subsequent section explains the innovations in the recovery packages agreed at the EU level. The last section outlines how we can understand path-breaking in the EU polity theoretically.

II. A Surprising Response to a Multi-Dimensional Crisis

After the inauspicious start, political actors tried to shape the public conversation about the pandemic. This conversation revolved, first, around crisis interpretation: is the crisis a shock from outside the EU or is past mismanagement to blame; does it affect all or primarily vulnerable Southern Europe members? The other debate concerned the appropriate economic response by the EU: how much additional support from the EU is needed to rekindle growth in member states?

For answers, I look primarily at the public statements of five heads of state, using discourse as evidence for a political strategy of change (Schmidt, 2000). It was one of the notable features of pandemic politics that political leaders spoke directly to audiences across borders where they expected opposition. The selection of these five leaders reflects the focus of media reports on the EU's pandemic management. There are, first of all, the Prime Ministers of Italy, Guiseppe Conte, and of Spain, Pedro Sánchez, who started the conversation by calling for bold action to a pandemic that hit them first and hard. Mark Rutte, the Dutch Prime Minister, was their main opponent, representing at least three more member states (Austria, Denmark, Sweden). French President Emmanuel Macron (France) joined Italy and Spain in an initiative of nine countries calling for Eurobonds in late March and adopted the role of an interlocutor. The German Chancellor Angela Merkel kept a low profile until mid-May when she and Macron proposed a surprisingly big transfer scheme, providing an anchor for the grand bargain under the German Council Presidency in July.

What Kind of Crisis?

An early influential diagnosis can be gleaned from a transnational statement by Prime Minister Sánchez, after the first extraordinary European Council on 10 March, 2020. More clearly than the Council conclusions, Sánchez stressed the dual nature of the crisis: a global emergency with a health and an economic dimension (Sánchez, 2020). This proved to be consequential as it divided the pandemic into a fast-burning public health crisis and a slow-burning recovery crisis (Seabrooke and Tsingou, 2019). While member states and the Commission started to coordinate their public health responses from mid-March onwards, governments could afford some time to consider measures addressing the economic fallout (Truchlewski *et al.*, 2021). Conte (2020a) seconded Sánchez a week later in an interview with the FT, stressing that this was a global, not a Southern European, emergency.

An open letter to Council President Michel signed by nine member states[1] was based on this distinction but had a normative thrust: 'we are all facing a symmetric external shock, for which no country bears responsibility, but whose negative consequences are endured by all' (Wilmès *et al.*, 2020). This letter, published on 25 March, would become notorious for its demand for a joint debt instrument ('Coronabonds'). The signatories included Greece and Ireland, Luxembourg and Slovenia, which had in fact very different experiences of the pandemic. Hence, this letter was a call for solidarity, directed against the narrative of the EA crisis in which those countries that needed a bailout were blamed for past failings that justified onerous corrections.

The interpretation 'symmetric shock, external cause, affecting all' was specifically directed against the Dutch government. In late March, Finance Minister Hoekstra scandalized Southern Europeans when he reportedly asked for an investigation into why Spain was fiscally not prepared for the pandemic (Euractiv, 2020). The Portuguese Prime Minister called his remarks 'repugnant'. A dozen mayors of Italian cities posted a one-page letter as an advertisement in a conservative German newspaper on 31 March, which was widely circulated in Dutch social media. In this letter to 'dear German friends', the Dutch position is denounced as a prime 'example of a lack of ethical standards and solidarity'. The Dutch government was accused of raiding other countries' tax bases to the detriment of the poorest (Calenda, 2020, my translation). Simultaneously, Conte gave extensive interviews in the Dutch newspaper *De Telegraaf* and the German weekly *Die Zeit*, stressing that the pandemic resembles a natural catastrophe and 'Dutch citizens may need guarantees, too' (Conte, 2020b; Google translation). Hoekstra was shamed into an apology.

The symmetric character of the pandemic could be framed, however, as a reason for why nobody should make extraordinary demands on others. Three weeks before the July summit, Mark Rutte stated in an interview with an Italian weekly: 'We owe solidarity to the countries most affected by the pandemic, knowing, however, that we too have been seriously affected. This means that states that need and deserve help must also ensure that in the future they are capable of dealing with such crises on their own in a resilient way.' (Valentino, 2020, Google translation) This understanding of resilience made it into the name of the recovery fund and it stands for reform in return for grants.

---

[1] Heads of state from Belgium, France, Greece, Ireland, Italy, Luxembourg, Portugal, Slovenia, and Spain.

In her first public statement to prepare Germany's rotating Council Presidency, Merkel (2020) adopted a multi-faceted diagnosis. It distilled the agreeable essence out of the dissenting positions. The interview, simultaneously published on 20 June in six European newspapers,[2] started with what the Dutch-led coalition stressed: 'time and again it has been shown that Europe is not yet sufficiently resistant to crises'. But she also highlighted the point Southern European leaders had made: 'the coronavirus pandemic is confronting us with a challenge of unprecedented dimensions. It has struck us all indiscriminately'. And she expressed the shared fear of a populist backlash: 'Very high unemployment in a country can become politically explosive and thereby increase the threat to democracy. For Europe to survive, its economy needs to survive.' Merkel's speeches in 2020 expressed repeatedly the quintessential liberal concern that representative democracy depends on economic stability.

Merkel did not hide Germany's interest in the integrity of the Single Market. The Coronabonds letter had stated this appeal to enlightened self-interest early on: 'Preserving the functioning of the Single Market is essential to give all European citizens the best possible care and the strongest guarantee that there will be no shortage of any kind.' (Wilmès *et al.*, 2020) Border closures, the disruption of supply chains, and the uneven ability to benefit from the easing of state aid rules were in nobody's interest. The threat to mutually beneficial economic interdependence became the compromise diagnosis, to which all sides could sign up.

What Kind of EU Support?

The debate on what response should follow from the diagnosis was dominated by the question of what role the ESM should play. Governments changed their positions as lternativesto the ESM appeared. Coronabonds were countered with limited grant proposals. It took the 'innovative' financial design of the recovery fund to set a path to agreement.

In an early FT interview (19 March), Conte (2020a) echoed ECB President Lagarde (2020) when he stated:

> Monetary policy alone cannot solve all problems; we need to do the same on the fiscal front and [..] time is of the essence [..]. The route to follow is to open ESM credit lines to all member states to help them fight the consequences of the Covid-19 epidemic, under the condition of full accountability by each member state on the way resources are spent.

But the domestic coalition of opposites that Conte headed since 2018 was less conciliatory: both the right-wing Lega and the Five Star Movement were fiercely opposed to taking recourse to ESM loans since the ESM Treaty (Article 3) requires 'strict conditionality' for any support. Lega leader Salvini portrayed conditionality as 'an attack on our country' by 'loan sharks in Berlin and Brussels' (Khan, 2020).

By early April, after the Coronabonds letter had been published, Conte argued that precautionary ESM credit lines were not up to the task. The sensibilities that had made Conte take this turn were acknowledged by Finance Minister Scholz in an interview with German media, although he supported the activation of the ESM: 'There won't be any

[2]The Guardian, Le Monde, La Stampa, La Vanguardia, Polityka and Süddeutsche Zeitung; quotes are from the Guardian transcript.

senseless conditions as there were sometimes in the past. No troika will come into the country to tell the government how to do politics. This is about support in the crisis.' (Barfield, 2020) This last phrase acknowledged that in the EA crisis, the ESM had acted primarily as a 'firewall' for the guarantor countries; the term is often used in official documents..

The Dutch Prime Minister, by contrast, made it clear that his first preference would be for the well-off members making 'a gift' to hard hit countries (in the order of €1bn from the Netherlands). If the ESM had to be used at all, then only with the usual conditionality of structural reforms attached (Khan, 2020). Charity rather than solidarity was the gist of Rutte's proposal. Interestingly, he had implied that grants were a preferable option to loans before this was publicly discussed.

Crunch time came at a Eurogroup meeting on 8–9 April. A 14-hour all-night tele-conference ended in a standoff (Khan, 2020). The Italian and the Dutch finance ministers had clashed; the former asked for assurance that the conclusions would mention 'debt mutualisation as a tool for the economic recovery' and ESM loans would have no conditionality attached. Hoekstra categorically rejected both demands, with reference to a consensus in the Dutch parliament and his coalition government. And yet, on 9th April, the Eurogroup delivered its report on the comprehensive response to the pandemic. It contained, inter alia, crucial details of the ESM Pandemic Crisis Support which was signed off by all relevant bodies about a month later (European Council, 2020a: para. 16). Debt mutualisation was not explicitly mentioned. How was this possible? Khan (2020) reports where negotiations had broken off: '"Coronabonds has to die if we are to get a compromise," said one northern eurozone diplomat. A draft circulating in the early hours last night mentioned the use of "innovative financial instruments" — too much for the Dutch and too little for Italy.' In fact, it was enough for both. The package deal was that innovative financial instruments were to replace Coronabonds. The battle was now on for these instruments.

Shortly before the Eurogroup meeting, two liberal MEPs, Luis Garicano and Guy Verhofstadt, had proposed just such an innovation, a 'European Reconstruction Fund'.[3] On 15 April, the European Parliament passed a resolution (2020: para. 17) with the votes of the four mainstream party groupings 'calling on the European Commission to propose a massive recovery and reconstruction package [..], beyond what the European Stability Mechanism, the European Investment Bank and the European Central Bank are already doing, that is part of the new multiannual financial framework (MFF); [..] the necessary investment would be financed by an increased MFF, [..] and recovery bonds guaranteed by the EU budget; this package should not involve the mutualisation of existing debt and should be oriented to future investment.' A day later, the Commission President gave a speech in which she endorsed the novel idea: 'The European budget will be the mothership of our recovery.[..] We will use the power of the whole European budget to leverage the huge amount of investment we need to rebuild the Single Market after Corona.' (Von der Leyen, 2020).

Based on the liberal MEPs' idea, the Socialist finance minister of Spain, Nadia Calviño, proposed a €1.5tn reconstruction fund on 19 April. It would provide grants

[3]A first version circulated on 2 April, published in a popularised form as a Project Syndicate blog on 15 April. See Garicano (2020) for links to relevant documents.

financed by perpetual bonds on which the EU would have to pay interest only. It sounded too daring. Yet, a month later von der Leyen presented technical details on the recovery fund of unknown quantity to the European Parliament. This was five days before the Franco-German proposal endorsed the principle of bond finance guaranteed by the EU budget for grants only. However, it proposed a transfer volume of €500bn, to be repaid in the long term through the Commission's 'own resources'. As the Commission has no 'own resources', this must mean finding a source of tax revenue, although this cannot be said explicitly as it would require a Treaty change. Ten days later, the Commission proposal added to this €250bn in loans. It was dubbed 'Next Generation EU' and eventually combined a number of smaller programmes with the RRF of €672.5bn (of which €312.5bn are grants).

On the evening before the Commission proposal, the 'Frugal Four' coalition presented a non-paper for an 'Emergency Recovery Fund'. They reiterated the ESM principles of 'loans-for-loans'[4] and strict conditionality. But they accepted the principle of allowing the Commission to borrow within the multi-annual budget (Non-paper, 2020). This created an issue linkage between the recovery fund and budget negotiations that could be turned to their advantage. The paper was not dated and not signed, but posted on the Dutch government's website. It reads like a last-minute reminder that the four countries would have to be compensated for agreeing to anything resembling the Franco-German proposal. Compensation came in the guise of generous rebates that reduce their net contributions to the EU budget.

The Eurogroup meeting in early April had started the deliberations on the grand bargain of the EU budget and a recovery fund. The Franco-German proposal was the political signal of an emerging compromise. Merkel said as much at a pre-summit press conference with Italian Prime Minister Conte in mid-July: 'it is important [..] that [the recovery fund] is something massive, something extraordinary. [..] It has to be a special effort to show that Europe wants to be united; there is a political dimension beyond the numbers.' (Conte and Merkel, 2020, my translation) In line with Merkel's desire for a unifying gesture, the fund would apply to all EU members. This also served her goal of preventing Eurobonds that would have provided funding only to euro area members.

In contrast to the other two reforms, the 'temporary Support to mitigate Unemployment Risks in an Emergency' (SURE) was a swift and uncontroversial affair. Throughout March, member states announced massive support programmes that dwarfed their fiscal responses during the financial crisis in 2008–09 (Bruegel, 2020). Within these fiscal stimulus programmes, country after country announced relatively generous job retention schemes, obviously in the expectation that lock-downs would not last for very long. Governments in OECD countries supported around 50 million jobs, ten times as many as during the financial crisis (OECD, 2020). A re-insurance scheme for national unemployment benefits has been discussed in EU circles for a while (Vandenbroucke et al., 2020). A job insurance scheme based on low-interest-rate loans was easier to agree since it is inherently temporary. Unlike unemployment insurance, short-time and furlough schemes are not permanent programmes in national welfare states. Hence, the Commission was able to propose SURE very quickly, on 2nd April, and put it into effect on 19th May, 2020. It had a volume of €100bn, of which €75.5bn were disbursed by end-

---

[4]That is, the ESM raises funds in bond markets to finance credit for programme countries.

© 2021 The Authors. JCMS: Journal of Common Market Studies published by University Association for Contemporary European Studies and John Wiley & Sons Ltd.

of-March 2021 (European Commission, 2021). It seemed generous at the time although less so after a third wave of the pandemic rolled over the continent.

V. The Innovation of Three Reforms

How path-breaking or path-dependent were these reforms in institutional terms? Unlike many political structures, EU institutions do come with an instruction sheet, to paraphrase Blyth (2003). But political agency and historical contingencies can alter the original intentions significantly. Whether the intended innovations will materialize in years to come depends on institutional practice.

In chronological order of coming into effect, the ESM Pandemic Crisis Support was first and explicitly modelled on the ESM's Enhanced Conditions Credit Line. But under the latter programme, the 'requesting country has to sign a Memorandum of Understanding (MoU) detailing policy conditionality, aimed at addressing the remaining weaknesses' (ESM, 2020). The Pandemic Support provides support on demand of a state government, each of which is entitled to loans worth 2% of its GDP. Above all, no conditionality is imposed beyond earmarking, which requires spending to be pandemic-related, detailed in a Pandemic Response Plan (PRP), which is standardized for all ESM members.[5] The overriding purpose was to remove the stigma attached to ESM loans.

The reform as such is not innovative, indeed it ostentatiously continues an existing credit line of the ESM. But it stands for an explicit coordination of fiscal and monetary policy in that it builds a bridge between Quantitative Easing by the ECB and Troika lending to governments. The ECB can buy government bonds from banks only after a prescribed time lag, so as not to violate the prohibition of public debt monetisation under Article 123 TFEU. This means that, if financial investors shun a government's new bond issue, the ECB cannot directly step in the bank has already hovered up all qualifying bonds. Previously, such a government could only get a Troika programme. Now, it can avoid acute liquidity problems arising from the loss of market access by drawing on Pandemic Support, without the strict conditionality and lengthy negotiation of an MOU that accompanies other precautionary ESM credit lines with similar purposes.

SURE, the EU's re-insurance programme for national job-retention schemes is a relatively large labour market stabilizer, to the tune of close to 1% of EU-GDP in 2020. It encouraged member states to introduce such schemes and thus maintain employment, substituting for unemployment benefits as automatic stabilizers. Job retention schemes subsidize labour hoarding in existing businesses instead of down-sizing businesses through unemployment, allowing firms to use this time for training staff and adopting new work practices. Moreover, SURE could be used for schemes to support the self-employed, who are typically not entitled to unemployment benefits. Loans under SURE operate like an overdraft for national expenditure on job (and business) maintenance. There is no conditionality attached, beyond the member state providing evidence of costs of job retention incurred. The Commission must report back to the Council every six months on how loans have been used (Regulation 2020/672, Article 14). The programme is financed out of the EU budget but secured by explicit guarantees from member states,

[5]Non-EA members can become ESM members if they sign the Fiscal Compact.

given that it exceeds the margin ('headroom') for excess demand on budget resources (Garicano, 2020).

SURE is innovative in that it has no obvious predecessor in other EU programmes. Re-insuring job retention marks a stark contrast to EU interventions in the protracted crisis since 2008 where the maxim of structural reforms was to flexibilise labour markets. The EU's official labour market paradigm is flexicurity (European Commission, 2007), that can be summarized as 'protecting workers, not jobs.' Job retention goes directly against higher labour market turnover. At the same time, the adjective 'temporary Support' emphasizes that SURE is a programme for an extraordinary situation. If SURE became a permanent re-insurance scheme for employment and unemployment schemes in the EU, it would mark a paradigm shift towards reinforcing national automatic stabilizers rather than prioritising fiscal retrenchment that switches off automatic stabilizers.

Finally, the grant element of the RRF has affinity with a gigantic cohesion programme. Grants are allocated such that they help poorer member states more but also those harder hit economically by the pandemic, i.e. the allocation combines redistribution with insurance.[6] The grant element also required giving the Commission for the first time the power to tax. The Council authorized the Commission 'to borrow on behalf of the Union in capital markets' (European Council, 2020b, A.3). The long-term bonds are secured by the budget itself, skilfully avoiding the dead-end of the Eurobonds discussion. The RRF is procedurally tied to the European Semester (Regulation 2021/241: Preamble para 17), for the first time providing financial incentives for compliance with this process of coordinating economic policies. The European Semester also ensures that the European Parliament has a say; the legislators' insistence on the rule of law as a precondition for funding signalled that MEPs are keen to use this power.

Conditionality is minimal (and the term is avoided): payments can be suspended if recommendations to correct an excessive deficit have not been followed twice (Regulation 2021/241: Article 10). This is a minimal condition because the RRF itself should make it easier to meet the fiscal rules. Recovery and resilience plans must set out a package of reforms and public investment projects, to be implemented by 2026; over half of the requested finance must be spent on climate change and digital transition. The Commission assists in drawing up these plans to a presentable standard and the Council signs them off on a case-by-case basis. Obviously, the latter allows the sceptics in the Council to put pressure on recipient governments.

The RRF is a novel support mechanism that gives fiscal powers to the EU level that it did not have before. The Commission was allowed to 'mortgage' the EU budget in order to resist both Coronabonds and ever more contingent liabilities (guarantees) for overstretched national budgets (Garicano, 2020). Providing grants on a macroeconomic scale is another novelty and an element of fiscal federalism. Finally, member states have now an incentive to give the Commission the power to tax, a power which is likely to be exercised through a digital tax and environmental levies, which are sources that nation-states find hard to target. These are big steps and yet incremental insofar they are reversible. The RRF is a temporary measure and it applies to the EU as a whole;

---

[6] Allocation criteria are based on population size and the inverse of GDP level plus (for 70% of amount) relative unemployment rate in 2020–21 and (for 30%) change in real GDP in 2020–21 (grants (Article 11 of Regulation 2021/241, Annexes 1–3).

the link to the common currency is absent as long as not all EU members adopt the euro. The powers to tax and spend are earmarked for purposes of fighting the pandemic. Its conspicuously redistributive design makes containment and reversal somewhat more likely because better-off countries have strong incentives to pay close attention to the (mis-)use of funds by beneficiary members.

The three reforms constitute fiscal integration for an experimental polity. The EU polity provides targeted re-insurance when catastrophe or systemic destabilization overwhelms national risk pools (Schelkle, 2017, pp. 316–22). The RRF re-insures asymmetric budget risks and SURE re-insures relatively short, sharp shocks to businesses. The ESM Pandemic Crisis Support re-insures liquidity risks for sovereigns and thus prevents solvency problems. The political wisdom of these reforms lies in the fact that they allow EU governments to sit on the fence for longer as regards a common budget while providing the politically and economically called-for stabilizers. Charting a way to closer fiscal integration without firmly committing to a divisive fiscal federation was arguably the only viable decision for a union of democracies.

VI. A Historical-Institutionalist Explanation of Path-Breaking Reform

The change we have seen in the EU's latest crisis is of wider theoretical relevance. The process and the outcome of the ESM reform and massive recovery funding can be understood as a deliberate attempt to change the path of bailout funding. This path had been paved with a series of Troika programmes since 2010 and, de jure, tightened fiscal rules. They constituted a legacy of perceived failure as public statements by Conte, Macron and Sánchez made clear. Historical institutionalism can explain why established paths and legacies require deliberate, often futile, attempts at moving beyond them. Incremental change is the expected pattern of institutional evolution (Streeck and Thelen, 2005). But knowing this, actors may also try to construe crises as critical junctures in which the future is open and agency can have a disproportionate impact on the course of events (Capoccia and Kelemen, 2007, pp. 351–2; Grzymala-Busse, 2011, p. 1277).

The experimental polity of the EU lends itself to such situations.[7] Its dispersed authority empowers networks of national and supranational executives to make decisions that can change the direction of what in normal times proceeds slowly through highly codified, regularised and routinised policy processes. In this densely institutionalized polity, agents are accustomed to seizing opportunities thrown up by a massive policy challenge, and presenting them as critical junctures in which accelerated change can happen (Capoccia and Kelemen, 2007, p. 358). Fiscal integration, a major construction site of this polity, has repeatedly shown this pattern.

The publication of the Coronabonds letter is arguably evidence for such political agency. After all, proposing an institutional reform that would require lengthy negotiations was hardly an obvious response to an emergency. The pandemic was also not confined to euro area members. But the letter demonstrated the determination, especially of Italy's and Spain's governments, of resisting a replay of euro area crisis management and reverting to ESM programmes as the default option. The publication of a proposal

---

[7]Kriesi *et al.* (2021) provide a fuller exposition of the underlying theory. The term experimental union goes back to Laffan *et al.* (1999).

for €1.5trn worth of grants by the Spanish government indicated that small would not do to satisfy the promise of innovative financial instruments when Coronabonds were taken off the table. The refusal by Italy's Prime Minister to accept standard ESM treatment told those on the safe side of the firewall that they required Italy's cooperation if they wanted protection.

Following the trodden path was a distinct possibility, which is compatible with the notion of a critical juncture (Capoccia, 2015: 151). The Frugal Four, above all the Dutch government, volunteered to play the conservative force that defended a no-change scenario. But they were constantly on the back foot. Their progressive opponents not only drove the policy discussion but, above all, engaged in open-letter and interview diplomacy that captured citizens' sympathy for the plight of their European neighbours. A week after the Coronabond letter and a day after the Italian mayors' letter, the German Bild-Zeitung had on its front-page an open letter to Italian citizens. It assured them that 'We are with you! We weep with you [..]. Without you, the German economic miracle would not have been possible.' (Bild, 2020, my translation) Readers also got a translation into Italian. This from a tabloid not known for a sympathetic view of Greece's suffering during the euro crisis.

A decisive contingent factor that worked against the status quo was Germany's turn in the rotating Council Presidency, under a Chancellor who must have been concerned about her legacy. *Ferrera et al.* (2021) show in detail how Merkel used her favourable polling during the early phase of the pandemic to engage in an exercise of 'polity-maintenance'. Repeatedly, she made the case to domestic audiences that this was a crisis that warranted Germany's solidarity with other EU members, not only for its own economic good but also because a united Europe remains the foundation of the German state.

Even if, in the long-run, these reforms do not amount to a decisive permanent step to further fiscal integration, they still mark a critical juncture in 2020. They would have shown an alternative, namely targeted re-insurance of macro-risks in the EU as a whole, as a potential diversion from the path-dependent development of the EA (Capoccia, 2015, p. 160). I have indicated that the ESM and even the RRF reform have precedents and can revert to the status quo ante. But political awareness of path-dependence can also stimulate strategies that are the undoing of historical determinism. Here, this meant that the crisis narrative had to be changed and that the contestation over the appropriate response had to be forward-looking and pre-emptive. This shows understanding of a basic historical-institutionalist insight, that default options are privileged simply because they are readily available and have already established stakeholders. Blame games then tend to add insult to injury and do lasting political damage. It was the good fortune of the EU this time that just when two Southern European countries were brought again to their knees by a crisis, their governments refused to let the shadow of the past dictate the future.

References

Barfield, T. (2020) 'Germany Backs EU Bailout Fund without "Senseless Conditions" in Virus Fight'. Barron's AFP news. 3 April.

Bild (2020) Wir sind bei Euch!. *Bild*. 1 April.

Blyth, M. (2003) 'Structures Do Not Come with an Instruction Sheet: Interests, Ideas, and Progress in Political Science'. *Perspectives on Politics*, Vol. 1, No. 4, pp. 695–706.

Bruegel (2020) The fiscal response to the economic fallout from the coronavirus. Brussels. 24th November.

Calenda, C. (2020) Liebe deutsche Freunde. *Frankfurter Allgmeine Zeitung*. 31 March.

Capoccia, G. (2015) 'Critical Junctures and Institutional Change'. In Mahoney, J. and Thelen, K. (eds) *Advances in Comparative-Historical Analysis* (Cambridge: Cambridge University Press), pp. 147–79.

Capoccia, G. and Kelemen, R.D. (2007) 'The Study of Critical Junctures: Theory, Narrative, and Counterfactuals in Historical Institutionalism'. *World Politics*, Vol. 59, No. 3, pp. 341–69.

Conte, G. (2020a) 'Giuseppe Conte Calls on EU to Use Full Financial Firepower'. *Financial Times*. 19 March.

Conte, G. (2020b) 'Vriendschap blijft, maar Mark, help ons nou'. *De Telegraaf.* 1 April.

Conte, G. and Merkel, A. (2020) 'Pressekonferenz von Bundeskanzlerin Merkel und Ministerpräsident Conte'. Meseberg. 13 July.

Euractiv (2020) 'Portugal Slams Dutch Finance Minister for "Repugnant" Comment's. 30 March.

European Commission (2021) SURE. Brussels. 30 March.

European Commission (2007) Towards Common Principles of Flexicurity: More and better jobs through flexibility and security. Communication SEC(2007) 861, Brussels. https://eur-lex.europa.eu/LexUriServ/LexUriServ.do?uri=COM:2007:0359:FIN:en:PDF.

European Council (2020a) 'Report on the Comprehensive Economic Policy Response to the COVID-19 Pandemic'. The European Council, 9 April.

European Council (2020b) Conclusions – 17, 18, 19, 20 and 21 July 2020 (EUCO 10/20). Brussels.

European Parliament (2020) 'EU Coordinated Action to Combat the COVID-19 Pandemic and its Consequences (2020/2616(RSP))'. 15 April.

Ferrera, M., Miró, J. and Ronchi, S. (2021) 'Walking the Road Together? EU Polity Maintenance during the COVID-19 Crisis'. *West European Politics*, Vol. 44, Nos. 5–6, pp. 1329–52. https://doi.org/10.1080/01402382.2021.1905328

Garicano. L. (2020) 'Towards a European Reconstruction Fund'. VoxEU-CEPR blog. 5 May.

Genschel, P. and Jachtenfuchs, M. (2014) *Beyond the Regulatory Polity? The European Integration of Core State Powers* (Oxford: Oxford University Press).

Grzymala-Busse, A. (2011) 'Time Will Tell? Temporality and the Analysis of Causal Mechanisms and Processes'. *Comparative Political Studies*, Vol. 44, No. 9, pp. 1267–97.

Herszenhorn, D. and Wheaton, S. (2020) 'How Europe Failed the Coronavirus Test'. *Politico*, 7 April.

Kaletsky, A. (2020) 'Europe's Hamiltonian Moment'. *Project Syndicate*. 21 May.

Khan, M. (2020) 'Eurogroup Battles Gridlock over Pandemic Response'. *Financial Times*, 8 April.

Kriesi, H., Ferrera, M. and Schelkle, W. (2021) 'The Theoretical Framework of SOLID – A Research Agenda'. SOLID Working Paper.

Laffan, B., O'Donnell, R. and Smith, M. (1999) *Europe's Experimental Union: Rethinking Integration* (Milton Park, New York: Routledge).

Lagarde, C. (2020) Press Conference. European Central Bank. 12 March.

Majone, G.(1996) *Regulating Europe*. (London and New York: Routledge)

Merkel, A. (2020) '"For Europe to Survive, Its Economy Needs to Survive": Angela Merkel Interview in Full'., by P. Oltermann. *The Guardian*. 26 June.

Non-paper (2020) 'Non-Paper EU Support for Efficient and Sustainable COVID-19 Recovery'. Last accessed 24/4/21.

OECD (2020) 'Job Retention Schemes during the COVID-19 Lockdown and Beyond'. Paris. 12 October.

Pierson, P. (2004) *Politics in Time: History, Institutions, and Social Analysis* (Princeton, NJ: Princeton University Press).

Poggioli, S. (2020) 'For Help on Coronavirus, Italy Turns to China, Russia and Cuba'. *NPR. Org*, 25 March.

Reuters (2020) 'Reuters Exclusively Reports ECB's Lagarde Asked Euro Zone Ministers to Consider One-off "coronabonds" Issue'. *Reuters News Agency*, 25 March.

Sánchez, P. (2020) Press conference by President of the Government after extraordinary European Council on coronavirus. Non-official translation, Government of Spain. 10 March.

Schelkle, W. (2017) *The Political Economy of Monetary Solidarity: Understanding the Euro Experiment* (Oxford: Oxford University Press).

Schmidt, V.A. (2000) 'Values and Discourse in the Politics of Adjustment'. In Scharpf, F.W. and Schmidt, V.A. (eds) *Welfare and Work in the Open Economy* (Vol. 1) (Oxford: Oxford University Press), pp. 229–309.

Seabrooke, L. and Tsingou, E. (2019) 'Europe's Fast- and Slow-Burning Crises'. *Journal of European Public Policy*, Vol. 26, No. 3, pp. 468–81.

Streeck, W. and Thelen, K. (eds) (2005) *Beyond Continuity* (Oxford: Oxford University Press).

Truchlewski, Z., Schelkle, W. and Ganderson, J. (2021) 'Buying Time for Democracies? European Union Emergency Politics in the Time of Covid-19'. *West European Politics*, Vol. 44, Nos. 5–6, pp. 1353–75. https://doi.org/10.1080/01402382.2021.1916723

Valentino, P (2020) 'Cara Italia, impara a farcela da sola'. *Corriere della Sera* Weekly Newsmagazine '7', 3 July, 14–19.

Vandenbroucke, F., Andor, L., Beetsma, R. M., Burgoon, B., Fischer, G., Kuhn, T., Luigjes, C. and Nicoli, F. (2020) 'The European Commission's SURE Initiative and Euro Area Unemployment Re-insurance'. *VoxEU blog*. 6 April.

Von der Leyen, U. (2020) Speech by President von der Leyen at the European Parliament Plenary on the EU coordinated action to combat the coronavirus pandemic and its consequences. Brussels. 16 April.

Wilmès, S., Macron, E. Mitsotakis, K., Varadkar, L., Conte, G., Bettel, X., Costa, A., Janša, J. and Sánchez, P. (2020) [Letter to European Council President Charles Michel]. 25 March.

JCMS 2021 Volume 59. Annual Review. pp. 56–68   DOI: 10.1111/jcms.13259

The EU Response to COVID-19: From Reactive Policies to Strategic Decision-Making

REBECCA FORMAN[1] and ELIAS MOSSIALOS[1,2]
[1]London School of Economics and Political Science, London, UK [2]Institute of Global Health Innovation, Imperial College London, London, UK

Introduction

Like every region in the world, the EU struggled in its response to COVID-19 – particularly in 2020 when much was still unknown about the disease. The Global Health Security Index ranked several European Union (EU) countries – the Netherlands, Sweden, Denmark, Finland, France, Germany and Spain – among the 15 countries with the highest health security capabilities to respond to infectious disease outbreaks (Nuclear Threat Initiative and Johns Hopkins Bloomberg School of Public Health, 2019). Similarly, much of Western Europe received the best scores on the Epidemic Preparedness Index published early in 2019 (Oppenheim et al., 2019). But just a few months into 2020 it was clear these index predictions were wrong.

COVID-19 policy making has involved significant uncertainties – about the nature of the disease, its transmission, and behavioural responses – and our understanding of the current and past trajectory of the pandemic has been limited by this (Manski, 2020). Thus, the EU was not alone in facing challenging choices.

Even before COVID-19 hit, it was widely acknowledged that the world was underprepared. But many assumed that given the resources at its disposal, the EU would be better equipped to fight infectious outbreaks. After all, it is home to some of the highest performing health systems and scientific institutions in the world. Additionally, several institutions designed to support collective European response to communicable diseases were well established before COVID-19.

However, there was limited consideration of globalization, geography and governance in the abovementioned measures – including gaps in analysis of regional and international organizations and the need to coordinate efforts between sub-national, national and global entities (Baum et al., 2021). Additionally, predictions about Europe's health security capabilities made the flawed assumption that just because European intergovernmental institutions were established, they had decision-making power, authority and adequate financing, they served the entire European region, and they had strong coordination with national and local-level efforts within countries.

This was a significant oversight for the EU, where countries are highly interdependent and where healthcare systems and associated decision-making power lies with national governments rather than international policy bodies. As of 2017, 19 of the 25 most connected countries in the world and five of the world's 20 busiest airports were in Europe (Pan-European Commission on Health and Sustainable Development, 2021). Thus, an infectious agent emerging anywhere in the world can quickly pass into Europe and become a threat, and vice versa. Additionally, while Europe's global connectivity is a strength in many ways, disruptions in global trade and supply chains can prove catastrophic because of its interdependent nature.

In this paper, instead of focusing on the individual national strategies that were so often split across Europe (Dergiades *et al.*, 2020), we examine how the EU responded to the COVID-19 crisis and the interplay between the EU and its member states. Throughout, we consider the legal, institutional and political restrictions that may have influenced the boundaries of EU policy decisions.

We begin with a background on the constraints on EU health (care) policy and then describe how these led to a series of knee-jerk reactions in initial COVID-19 management efforts which were exacerbated by the rise of nationalism among and lack of coordination between Member States. We then discuss how this was followed by elements of more strategic decision-making with the refinement of vaccination policies, the announcement of a new European health emergencies response agency and considerations on how to expand and strengthen infectious disease control at the European level. Finally, we conclude with suggestions on how the EU can continue taking strategic approaches towards pandemic planning and response, including through globally collaborative mechanisms and efforts.

I. Background on EU Health (Care) Policy

Health policy in the EU has a fundamental contradiction at its core (Mossialos and McKee, 2002). On the one hand, the Treaty on the Functioning of the EU (TFEU), as the definitive statement on the scope of EU law, states explicitly that healthcare is the responsibility of the Member States (Official Journal of the European Union, 2012.[†]). On the other hand, Member State health systems involve interactions with people (patients and staff), goods (pharmaceuticals and devices) and services, which are all granted freedom of movement across borders by the same Treaty. Furthermore, many national health activities are in fact subject to EU law and policy.

EU health policies are influenced by what Scharpf terms the 'constitutional asymmetry' between EU policies to promote market efficiency and those to promote social protection (Scharpf, 2002; Permanand and Mossialos, 2005). The EU has a strong regulatory role in respect of the former, but weak redistributive powers as requisite for the latter. The asymmetry can be ascribed to the Member States' interest in developing a common market while seeking to retain social policy at the national level. However, while welfare and solidarity remain national-level prerogatives, many issues affecting the daily life and collective prosperity of individuals are dependent on EU-level actions (Tsoukalis, 2005).

In the health arena, we see that the asymmetry is exacerbated by a dissonance between the Commission's policy-initiating role in respect of single market free movement concerns and the Member States' right to set their own social priorities. As a result, health policy in the EU has, in large part, evolved within the context of the economic aims of the single market programme (McKee *et al.*, 1996; Wismar *et al.*, 2002). This has led to a situation in which the Member States have conceded the need for the EU to play a role in health, even if only a limited one, and in ill-defined circumstances.

[†]https://eur-lex.europa.eu/legal-content/EN/TXT/HTML/?uri=CELEX:12012E/TXT

Furthermore, since the 1992 Maastricht Treaty, the EU has been required to 'contribute to the attainment of a high level of health protection' for its citizens. This is an understandable and important objective in its own right, and there is compelling evidence that access to timely and effective healthcare makes an important contribution to overall population health. But, notwithstanding the EU's commitment to various important public health programmes and initiatives, how are EU policymakers to pursue this goal of a high level of health attainment when they lack Treaty-based competences to ensure that national health systems are providing effective care to their populations?

This is in stark contrast to environmental protection, an area of EU policy where the EU is given explicit competence over measures affecting water resources, land use (with the exception of waste management) and energy choices and supplies under Title XX of the TFEU (Consolidated versions of the Treaty on European Union and the Treaty on the Functioning of the European Union, 2012). This is not to equate health and social policy with environmental policy; rather, it simply highlights that a greater policy mandate for areas outside (though related to) the single market could be accorded to the EU via the Treaties if desired, and that the asymmetry need not be as clear or as limiting as it appears to be for health. This suggests a redefinition or, at least, a reorganization and re-prioritization of health at the EU level is needed.

Before considering the initial COVID-19 response, we must take stock of the legal framework in which these institutions were situated, and the governance challenges posed by transboundary health threats. While health policy in the EU is dominated by national policies, some transboundary emergency response capabilities have increasingly been delegated to EU bodies in the last decade (Schomaker *et al.*, 2021). Article 168 of the TFEU, referring to 'normal' non-emergency situations, stipulates that a 'high level of human health protection shall be ensured in the definition and implementation of all Union policies and activities' (Consolidated versions of the Treaty on European Union and the Treaty on the Functioning of the European Union, 2012). EU actions could include 'monitoring, early warning of and combating serious cross-border threats to health'.

The European Commission (EC) was responsible for the initial COVID-19 responses mainly through the Directorate-General for Health and Food Safety (DG-SANTE) which has a broad scope to protect public health and build a strong European Health Union and the Directorate-General for Research and Innovation (DG-RTD) which coordinates and allocates funding towards health research and innovation – including preparedness for pandemics through the research and development (R&D) of medical countermeasures and diagnostics.

EU agencies involved in the management of the crisis included the European Centre for Disease Control (ECDC) (Regulation (EC) No *851/2004,* 2004) which aims to strengthen the European defence to infectious diseases through the identification, assessment, and communication of current and emerging infectious threats to human health and the European Medicines Agency (EMA), which works to 'foster scientific excellence in the evaluation and supervision of medicines, for the benefit of public and animal health in the EU' (European Medicines Agency, 2020). The EU Civil Protection Mechanism which was established to boost cooperation on civil protection matters and improve prevention, preparedness and response efforts for environmental emergencies and disasters also played an important role in managing COVID-19. The mechanism includes the Emergency Response Coordination Centre (ERCC) responsible for coordinating assistance to countries (both inside and outside the EU) affected by disasters as well as rescEU, responsible for enhancing the protection of EU citizens from disasters and managing emerging risks, mainly through reserves of resources and stockpiles of medical equipment.

Furthermore the Health Security Committee (HCS), based in DG-SANTE and the Early Warning and Response System (EWRS) hosted by the ECDC, granted the EU some additional capacity to coordinate policy responses (*Decision No 1082/2013/EU*, 2013).

Thus, going into the COVID-19 crisis there was an institutional and legal basis for the EU to operate; albeit other policy areas, such as humanitarian aid, had a much larger remit and more organizations supporting them in crisis responses (Schomaker *et al.*, 2021)

II. Initial Management of the COVID-19 Response in Europe

In the first months of 2020, much of the bloc was conducting business as usual and failed to take threats of the virus seriously. From as early as January 2020, the Commission sounded the alarm on the novel coronavirus and called for coordinated responses. But without the buy-in of all member states, its influence was severely limited. By the time attention shifted towards the virus, it was far too late: at the end of the first quarter, COVID-19 had spread to most countries in Europe and forced decision-makers to take knee-jerk reactions in policy response.

On 9 January 2020, DG-SANTE opened an alert notification through the ECDC's EWRS and the ECDC released a Threat Assessment Brief which reported that a novel coronavirus had been the causative agent for 15 of 59 cases of pneumonia in Wuhan, China (European Centre for Disease Prevention and Control, 2020a). Soon after, the ECDC published a rapid risk assessment and the EU held its first coronavirus-related conference call on 17 January to discuss measures to prevent the virus from entering Europe. However, only 12 of the 27 member states (and the UK) attended the call (Boffey *et al.*, 2020), and those who did disagreed about the main matter in question – recommendations for border measures in advance of Chinese New Year celebrations. Very little was known about the illness, its mode of transmission and infectiousness, and many leaders made the flawed assumption that this was like previous outbreaks and would mostly stay confined to Asian borders (as with the SARS outbreak in 2003).

On 22 January the ECDC updated its rapid risk assessment from low to moderate likelihood of case importation to EU/European Economic Area (EEA) countries (European Centre for Disease Prevention and Control, 2021). Days later, the first confirmed cases of COVID-19 appeared in France and Germany on 24 and 28 January respectively. The EU Civil Protection Mechanism was activated for the repatriation of EU citizens on 28 January (European Commission, 2020a) and by 30 January, the WHO declared the outbreak of what is now called SARS-CoV-2 a public health emergency of international concern (PHEIC). Efforts continued into February and on 7 February, the ECDC published a report on the need for personal protective equipment (PPE) in healthcare settings in preparation of an increase in infectious patients. Additionally, on 10 February, the ECDC released guidelines for non-pharmaceutical interventions (NPIs) to delay and mitigate the impacts of the illness (European Centre for Disease Prevention and Control, 2021).

Despite the above, many EU country leaders did not consider the threat of the virus to be serious enough to warrant event cancellations or shifts to teleworking and online learning. These were unprecedented moves at the time, and likely to be considered wildly undemocratic by constituents who also did not understand the gravity of the COVID-19 situation.

But by late February, clusters of positive COVID-19 cases in four regions of Italy had emerged, and individual cases continued to pop up across European countries. On 2 March 2020, EC President Ursula von der Leyen established a Coronavirus response team at the political level, but the virus was already spreading rapidly throughout Europe (European Commission, 2020b). In Spring 2020, Italy replaced Wuhan as the epicentre of the pandemic.

COVID-19 Exposes the Limitations European Health Institutes Must Work with

Throughout the pandemic, DG SANTE has undertaken the negotiation of contracts for the procurement of medicines, vaccines and PPE via the EU Joint Procurement Agreement (JPA) (Anderson *et al.*, 2021). DG-SANTE monitors national compliance with laws and policies, but it is the responsibility of national, regional, and local governments to apply the laws, recommendations, and policies that DG-SANTE adopts on public health (European Commission, n.d.).

While DG-SANTE, through the ECDC, began sounding the alarm on the novel coronavirus on 9 January 2020, COVID-19 quickly exposed the weaknesses of these institutions. Despite having 'European' in its title, the ECDC did not have remit beyond the EEA. Furthermore, the ECDC was severely limited by its human resource and financial capacity at the start of the pandemic (Anderson and Mossialos, 2020). Additionally, the institution could only issue scientific advice, which restricted its authority to implement prevention measures.

This is not to say that the ECDC did not provide useful contributions to early COVID-19 response efforts. After the establishment of a network of major CDCs in June 2019, the ECDC attended regular meetings (every 4–8 weeks) at the start of the pandemic to exchange information, expertise and best practices with the Chinese, US, Canadian, African Union, Caribbean, Korean, Israeli, and Singaporean CDCs (European Court of Auditors, 2021). It also established a COVID-19 network which met on a weekly basis, published a COVID-19 surveillance strategy, and collected COVID-19 data through the EWRS and European Surveillance System (TESSy) (European Centre for Disease Prevention and Control, 2020b). However, the heterogeneity between member states' data quality and methods of collection, and the limited remit and powers of the ECDC proved significant challenges in managing the start of the COVID-19 crisis.

In addition to the limits of the ECDC, the European response was significantly weakened by nationalistic decisions taken by Member States to secure scarce resources for their own populations, rather than distributing these around Europe based on need (Anderson *et al.*, 2020). Despite a virtual European Council meeting on 10 March 2020 where members discussed solidarity and cooperation and identified four priorities (reducing transmission, promoting research, mitigating socioeconomic consequences, and providing medical equipment) for mitigating the impacts of COVID-19, several European countries quickly introduced export bans on PPE when severe shortages were occurring elsewhere (Anderson *et al.*, 2020). When the pandemic first began, rescEU hosted a list of resources from member states that could be supplied in times of emergency (rather than controlling the resources themselves), and was underprepared to handle a situation where multiple member states were dealing with the same emergency and in need of the same supplies (Brooks *et al.*, 2021). This hindered countries' abilities to secure access to PPE for their medical workers and general populations. In attempt to fix these issues, in the first half of 2020 the Commission began to strengthen and reinforce the system by providing rescEU more funding and creating more stockpile locations across member states (European Commission, 2020c). At present, a strategic rescEU medical reserve (including ventilators and PPE) has been established with the stockpile hosted by nine EU member states.

Furthermore, the legal obstacles, especially regarding data sharing, of cross-border efforts to tackle infectious outbreaks were exposed. This was heightened by Brexit, which occurred just as the virus was beginning to circulate around the bloc. Additionally, there was not adequate investment for R&D at this stage in the pandemic – in March 2020, only €140 million had been committed to 17 R&D projects; whereas €25bn were committed to efforts to mitigate economic impacts of COVID-19 to health systems, enterprises and labour markets (Anderson *et al.*, 2020).

Interplay between the European Commission, Member States and the Role of International Organizations

The early weaknesses in the pandemic response seemed to trigger a process of, what some experts termed, 'failing forward' whereby diverse member states which face problems participate in intergovernmental bargaining and agree to lowest common denominator solutions (Brooks *et al.*, 2021).

Early in 2020, in response to the virus, the EU established a Crisis Coordination Committee. It sounded the alarm on COVID-19 on 29 January and in the same week issued calls to strengthen healthcare capacity in preparation of the virus' inevitable havoc. But media coverage and most public attention within Europe focused on the Brexit vote (Boffey *et al.*, 2020). Similar disregard of and lack of urgency around other international advice was seen: on 25 January, the WHO Regional Office for Europe called for the region to prepare for the virus and 'act as one' (Kluge, 2020), but at this time, most member states failed to heed to these warnings and address their depleted stockpiles of PPE, to plan for an influx of infectious patients in health and long-term care facilities, and to begin implementing non-pharmaceutical interventions (NPIs) such as social distancing requirements and mask wearing. This led to the situation in March when infections spiralled and ICUs swelled beyond capacity, countries introduced export bans, border closures were imposed, economies were shut down, and education systems were (*de facto*) halted.

And so the cycle of failing forward began. After such a clear demonstration of lacking solidarity was seen in Europe in the spring of 2020, and as desperation to source equipment rose, Member States' attitudes shifted and support for an earlier idea to jointly procure equipment grew. But even this was slow: governments were delayed in sending necessary information about the equipment they needed, and by the time they did, global stocks were limited. Then in the scramble to secure supply, countries individually contacted Chinese manufacturers and created additional competition for PPE. Ultimately, it took until early June for the first shipment of masks to be delivered under the scheme (Boffey *et al.*, 2020).

When it saw that the joint procurement scheme was inadequate, the European Commission introduced emergency legislation that allowed for a central stockpile through rescEU – once again creating positive changes in the aftermath of initial patchy responses (European Commission, 2020c). By this point, appetite for designating more decision-making power to European institutions in times of crisis was increasing.

III. Vaccination Efforts Get off to a Rough Start in the Bloc in the Latter Half of 2020

By the second half of 2020, incredible scientific progress had already been made in the development of COVID-19 vaccines. In summer 2020, there were several promising candidates, and ultimately, a few COVID-19 vaccines were developed, produced, authorized, distributed, and administered in parts of the world by the end of the year – in record time. Despite the lessons learned from experiences with COVID-19 in the first half of 2020, challenges continued with vaccines in the latter half of the year and into 2021.

In June 2020, Member States approved the European Commission Vaccine Plan (European Commission, 2020d) which included a joint procurement mechanism they hoped would avoid the competition and lack of solidarity in Europe that was seen with PPE early in the pandemic. While joint procurement may have been a sensible idea in theory, the EC was inexperienced with such a process, and rather than treating it as an emergency negotiation for essential products, it opted for lower prices over conditions for speedy deliveries. By 1 May, the UK had secured a contract to supply its entire population with one jab, and enough for half its adult population to receive a second. Similarly, on 20 May the US agreed a contract guaranteeing them 300 million doses of a COVID-19 vaccine (Ovaska and Kumar Dutta, 2021). The EU did not strike its first vaccine agreement until mid-August; by which point, the UK and the US had secured enough vaccines from multiple pharmaceutical companies to fully vaccinate their entire populations more than once over. So while the EU may have gotten a better financial deal on vaccine doses, there were unintended consequences: in early 2021, vaccine manufacturers faced severe delays and shortages, and while deliveries to Europe stalled, they continued in countries which had negotiated stricter delivery conditions in their contracts (Ovaska and Kumar Dutta, 2021). This quickly set the EU far behind countries such as the UK and the US in the beginning of its inoculation programme.

Lack of coordination and inconsistent communication also continued during early vaccination efforts. On 2 December 2020, the UK was the first country to approve a COVID-19 vaccine (Pfizer/BioNTech) (Mahase, 2020). The US and Canada followed suit shortly after. The EMA bluntly criticised the UK's regulatory agency – the MHRA – for being hasty in its authorization decision and claimed that the EMA approval procedure was more thorough (Guarascio, 2020). However, three weeks later, the EMA recommended emergency authorization for the same vaccine with similar guidelines to that of the MHRA. Of course, the EMA is not solely responsible for these divergent responses, and efforts to improve harmonization between these bodies is needed from all sides. The current lack of international coordination will only lead to more challenges and complexities as the pandemic response continues; for example, which proof of vaccine evidence is accepted as borders reopen for tourist travel.

While the EMA makes authorization recommendations to the EC, the ultimate decisions about use of vaccines lie with Member State governments. This led to divergences across the EU countries in which vaccines were made available, who was prioritized and advised to receive them, and the time-gap recommended between first and second jabs. Even before any vaccines were authorized, surveys indicated high levels of vaccine hesitancy in several countries in the bloc (Boyon, 2020). The mixed messaging and differences in vaccine policies around the EU and globally created further confusion and, for some, increased reservations about the safety and effectiveness of the jabs – particularly with regards to AstraZeneca's Vaxzevria vaccine (Forman et al., 2021).

IV. Future Direction and Conclusions

New Institutions to Tackle Future Health Emergencies: The Health Emergency Response Agency (HERA)

To address the gaps in fighting COVID-19 in 2020, and to prevent similar occurrences from arising in the future, in autumn 2020, the EC announced that a new EU Health Emergency Preparedness and Response Authority (HERA) (formerly referred to as EU-BARDA) would be established (European Parliament, n.d.). The exact scope of the agency has not yet been formally agreed or announced, but it is expected to be similar to the US Biomedical Advanced Research and Development Authority (BARDA) and its broad objectives will include scanning the horizon for major health threats, funding R&D for potential medical countermeasures, supporting manufacturing capacity, and stockpiling essential medical supplies and equipment (Anderson et al., 2021). Importantly, the establishment of HERA reflects the re-prioritization of health at the EU level and the willingness of the EC to transition to a more hands-on approach to its member states' health systems during times of emergency.

HERA will join a complex landscape for emergency preparedness planning and response in Europe. Thus, its success and legitimacy will not only hinge upon achieving its objectives, but also on how it operates within this space and cooperates with existing EC agencies and institutions to build EU capacity to prepare for, respond to, and recover from health threats, rather than simply reinventing the wheel (Anderson et al., 2021; FEAM and Wellcome, 2021). HERA could play a key coordination role: it has the potential to coordinate infrastructure development to support mid- to large-size clinical trials in collaboration with the EMA; to coordinate various funding programmes for health across the bloc – potentially collaborating with DG-RTD; to coordinate with DG-SANTE to support the maintenance of medical countermeasure stockpiles; to coordinate with the EU Civil Protection Mechanism to arrange the delivery of the goods in these stockpiles; and to coordinate with international partners and contribute to international initiatives such as the COVID-19 Vaccines Global Access (COVAX) scheme (Anderson et al., 2021). This may be easier said than done though, and its early outcomes will be largely dependent on clear definitions of its objectives, its relationships with existing agencies, and its allocated funding.

Expanding the Role of the ECDC

There is also an opportunity to strengthen European infectious disease control. The ECDC was established in 2005 in the wake of the 2003 SARS outbreak in 2003, with the mission to boost the European defence to infectious diseases through the identification, assessment and communication of current and emerging infectious threats to human health. It has several coordination mechanisms for disease response, collaborates closely with the WHO and additionally hosts an early warning and response system that connects countries and allows them to share data quickly and effectively. However, the ECDC has suffered historically from a number of issues including understaffing, under-resourcing, limited geographical scope and legislative barriers that have severely restrained its ability to achieve its objectives (Anderson and Mossialos, 2020). This was evident in the early stages of the pandemic when the ECDC's remit was mainly limited to offering advice and coordinating with national public health agencies on surveillance efforts.

Recent increases in funding to the EU4Health programme may represent a chance to invest additional funding into the ECDC and expand its role to collaborate and co-invest with countries to increase surveillance capacities (European Commission, 2021). It could also contribute to workforce planning efforts and capacity-building by coordinating and subsidising educational programmes to train infectious disease nurses, physicians and epidemiologists (Anderson and Mossialos, 2020). However, an expanded role of the ECDC would require changes to legislation and extension of its geographic scope. Current legislative barriers such as data protection/sharing rules and the voluntary nature of surveillance mechanisms may need to be amended. (Anderson and Mossialos, 2020).

Learning from the Early Management of the Pandemic

Beyond the introduction of HERA and the expanded role of the ECDC, there is still a lot of work to do and ground to recover in this pandemic, and in better preparing for the next one. The EU and member states must learn lessons from their experience with COVID-19 (Forman *et al.*, 2020) and make efforts to strengthen the capacity of its institutions to prevent, respond to and recover from health threats.

In 2021, after a rough start to the EU vaccination campaign, Europe refined its vaccine procurement strategy and is predicted to catch up with, and even surpass, US and UK vaccination rates by the end of summer 2021 (McEvoy, 2021). Early in 2021, amidst supply shortages and unmet vaccine deliveries and pauses on the administration of Vaxzevria after rare cases of blood clots occurred, Europe fell behind on its rollout. But by May, Europe was regaining ground: EC president Ursula Von der Leyen agreed a contract with Pfizer and BioNTech for over 1.8 billion doses of their vaccine to the EU by 2023 (Cokelaere, 2021). And even while it struggled to sort its own vaccine campaign challenges, the EU exported vaccine doses and supported the COVAX initiative with billions of euros in late 2020 and early 2021.

This demonstrates progress, but there are still many important challenges which need to be addressed to improve pandemic preparedness and response in Europe. Investments in social and microbial epidemiology could enable better predictions of where, when and how infectious disease threats will (re-)emerge in the coming decades. The development of mechanisms to understand and exploit genomic 'big data' spanning entire viral families could transform future biomedical countermeasures and enable quicker identification and response to future outbreaks. Social and behavioural changes could also be made to prevent the risk of spill-over and spread of zoonotic threats, to slow or stop outbreak/epidemic transmission at early stages and to mitigate the impacts of 'infodemics' on infectious disease response. Furthermore, challenges related to health and healthcare can be tackled, and broader definitions and policies of 'hygiene' and 'preventable healthcare measures' and better preparedness plans to identify and respond (and evaluate response) to the next pandemic may be created, tested and scaled.

Given these challenges and need for change, the EU should develop an integrated pandemic response strategy for Europe which considers the strategic plans of and the interactions between DGs, EU agencies, mechanisms, Member States, as well as international organizations such as the World Health Organization. The EU must also take a One Health approach (Anderson *et al.*, 2019) in its strategy design in recognition of and preparation for the looming threats of climate change and antimicrobial resistance (Pan-European Commission on Health and Sustainable Development, 2021). Afterall, we know that European health is not just dependent on national health systems, but also relies on well-functioning education, environmental, economic and global governance systems (Pan-European Commission on Health and Sustainable Development, 2021).

It is crucial that the EU also works at the forefront of global planning efforts. Pandemics are global by definition, and thus they necessitate international responses which are well-prepared, coordinated and coherent. The EU should continue in its work towards and support of a Pandemic Treaty which creates legally binding norms and responsibilities for states to abide to under pandemic circumstances, taking stock of what has and has not worked with existing arrangements like COVAX and the International Health Regulations (Pan-European Commission on Health and Sustainable Development, 2021). Additionally, the EU should not only continue efforts to boost its own COVID-19 vaccination campaigns, but it can also play a central role in the development of a Global Vaccine Policy for Pandemics. This global policy should set out the rights and responsibilities of all those involved in the vaccine development, deployment and distribution processes, and it should reward innovation while also ensuring that high levels of vaccine protection are achieved rapidly under pandemic circumstances (Pan-European Commission on Health and Sustainable Development, 2021).

Conclusions

The constitutional asymmetry inherent in the EU healthcare policy system has exacerbated challenges in the first year of the COVID-19 crisis and going forward, the EU must learn from these experiences and take an increasingly central role in efforts to deal with cross-border threats to health. This will likely require amendments to the TFEU that grant the EU temporary competencies under extraordinary circumstances. While this may have been controversial among Member States in the past, the appetite for it has likely increased since the COVID-19 crisis has demonstrated the importance of European strategy, coordination and solidarity in cross-border emergency responses.

References

Anderson, M., Cecchini, M. and Mossialos, E. (eds) (2019) *Challenges to Tackling Antimicrobial Resistance: Economic and Policy Responses* (Cambridge: Cambridge University Press).

Anderson, M., Forman, R. and Mossialos, E. (2021, forthcoming) *Navigating the Role of the European Union (EU) Health Emergency Preparedness* and Response Authority (HERA) in Europe and Beyond (Europe: The Lancet Regional Health).

Anderson, M., Mckee, M. and Mossialos, E. (2020) 'Covid-19 Exposes Weaknesses in European Response to Outbreaks'. *BMJ*, m1075. https://doi.org/10.1136/bmj.m1075

Anderson, M. and Mossialos, E. (2020) 'Time to Strengthen Capacity in Infectious Disease Control at the European Level'. *International Journal of Infectious Diseases*, Vol. 99, pp. 263–5. https://doi.org/10.1016/j.ijid.2020.08.005

Baum, F., Freeman, T., Musolino, C. *et al.* (2021) 'Explaining Covid-19 Performance: What Factors Might Predict National Responses?' *BMJ*, Vol. 372, n91. https://doi.org/10.1136/bmj.n91

Boffey, D., Schoen, C., Stockton, B. and Margottini, L. (2020) 'Revealed: Italy's Call for Urgent Help Was Ignored as Coronavirus Swept through Europe'. *The Guardian*. https://www.theguardian.com/world/2020/jul/15/revealed-the-inside-story-of-europes-divided-coronavirus-response

Boyon, N. (2020) COVID-19 Vaccination Intent is Decreasing Globally. Ipsos. https://www.ipsos.com/en/global-attitudes-covid-19-vaccine-october-2020 (accessed 8.5.21).

Brooks, E., de Ruijter, A. and Greer, S.L. (2021) 'The European Union Confronts COVID-19: Another European Rescue of the Nation-state?' In *Coronavirus Politics: The Comparative Politics and Policy of COVID-19* (Ann Arbor: University of Michigan Press).

Cokelaere, H. (2021) 'EU Seals Contract for 1.8 Billion BioNTech/Pfizer Vaccines'. *POLITICO*. https://www.politico.eu/article/eu-seals-contract-for-1-8-billion-biontech-pfizer-vaccines/

Consolidated versions of the Treaty on European Union and the Treaty on the Functioning of the European Union (2012) 2012/C 326/01. *OJ C 326, 26.10.2012.* https://eur-lex.europa.eu/legal-content/EN/TXT/?uri=celex%3A12012E%2FTXTDecision No. 1082/2013/EU of the European Parliament and of the Council of 22 October 2013 on serious cross-border threats to health and repealing Decision No. 2119/98/EC Text with EEA relevance. https://eur-lex.europa.eu/legal-content/EN/TXT/?uri=celex%3A32013D1082

Dergiades, T., Milas, C., Mossialos, E. and Panagiotidis, T. (2020) *Effectiveness of Government Policies in Response to the COVID-19 Outbreak' (SSRN Scholarly Paper No. ID 3602004)* (Rochester, NY: Social Science Research Network).

European Centre for Disease Prevention and Control (2020a) 'Threat Assessment Brief: Pneumonia Cases Possibly Associated with a Novel Coronavirus in Wuhan, China'. https://www.ecdc.europa.eu/en/publications-data/pneumonia-cases-possibly-associated-novel-coronavirus-wuhan-china

European Centre for Disease Prevention and Control (2020b) 'EU Level Surveillance of COVID-19'. European Centre for Disease Prevention and Control. https://www.ecdc.europa.eu/en/covid-19/surveillance (accessed 8.2.21).

European Centre for Disease Prevention and Control (2021) 'Timeline of ECDC's Response to COVID-19. European Centre for Disease Prevention and Control'. https://www.ecdc.europa.eu/en/covid-19/timeline-ecdc-response (accessed 8.2.21).

European Commission (2020a) 'Coronavirus: EU Civil Protection Mechanism Activated for the Repatriation of EU Citizens'. https://ec.europa.eu/commission/presscorner/detail/it/IP_20_142

European Commission (2020b) Remarks by President von der Leyen at the joint press conference with Commissioners Lenarčič, Kyriakides, Johansson, Vălean and Gentiloni at the ERCC ECHO on the EU's response to COVID-19. https://ec.europa.eu/commission/presscorner/detail/en/statement_20_368

European Commission (2020c) 'COVID-19: Commission Creates First Ever RescEU Stockpile'. https://clustercollaboration.eu/news/european-commission-creates-first-ever-resceu-stockpile-medical-equipment

European Commission (2020d) 'Coronavirus: Commission Unveils EU Vaccines Strategy'. https://ec.europa.eu/commission/presscorner/detail/en/ip_20_1103

European Commission (2021) 'Questions and Answers: EU4Health Programme 2021–2027'. https://ec.europa.eu/commission/presscorner/detail/en/qanda_21_1345 (accessed 8.5.21).

European Commission (n.d.) What we do – Health and Food Safety. https://ec.europa.eu/info/departments/health-and-food-safety/what-we-do-health-and-food-safety_en (accessed 8.2.21).

European Court of Auditors (2021) 'The EU's Initial Contribution to the Public Health Response to COVID-19' (No. 01/2021). European Court of Auditors, Luxembourg. https://www.eca.europa.eu/en/Pages/DocItem.aspx?did=57722

European Medicines Agency (2020) 'What We Do'. https://www.ema.europa.eu/en/about-us/what-we-do (accessed 8.5.21).

European Parliament (n.d.) 'Legislative Train Schedule: Legislative Proposal to Establish a European BioMedical Research and Development Agency (BARDA)/European Health Emergency Preparedness and Response Authority (HERA)'. https://www.europarl.europa.eu/legislative-train/theme-promoting-our-european-way-of-life/file-european-biomedical-research-and-development-agency (accessed 8.2.21).

FEAM and Wellcome. (2021) 'How Should the EU Prepare and Respond to Future Cross Border Health Threats?' https://www.feam.eu/wp-content/uploads/2021_Wellcome-FEAM-HERA-report.pdf

Forman, R., Atun, R., McKee, M. and Mossialos, E. (2020) '12 Lessons Learned from the Management of the Coronavirus Pandemic'. *Health Policy*, Vol. 124, pp. 577–80. https://doi.org/10.1016/j.healthpol.2020.05.008

Forman, R., Jit, M. and Mossialos, E. (2021) 'Divergent Vaccination Policies Could Fuel Mistrust and Hesitancy'. *The Lancet*, Vol. 397, p. 2333. https://doi.org/10.1016/S0140-6736(21)01106-5

Guarascio, F. (2020) 'EU Criticises "Hasty" UK Approval of COVID-19 Vaccine'. *Reuters*. https://www.reuters.com/article/us-health-coronavirus-britain-eu-idUSKBN28C1B9

Kluge, H. (2020) 'Statement – Novel Coronavirus Outbreak: Preparing Now as One'. https://www.euro.who.int/en/media-centre/sections/statements/2020/statement-novel-coronavirus-outbreak-preparing-now-as-one

Mahase, E. (2020) 'Covid-19: UK Approves Pfizer and BioNTech Vaccine with Rollout Due to Start Next Week'. *BMJ*, Vol. 371, m4714. https://doi.org/10.1136/bmj.m4714

Manski, C.F. (2020) 'Forming COVID-19 Policy Under Uncertainty'. *Journal of Benefit-Cost Analysis*, Vol. 11, pp. 341–56. https://doi.org/10.1017/bca.2020.20

McEvoy, J. (2021) 'The EU Just Hit its 70% Vaccination Target – Here's How it Overcame a Slow Start and Passed The US'. *Forbes*. https://www.forbes.com/sites/jemimamcevoy/2021/07/27/the-eu-just-hit-its-70-vaccination-target-heres-how-it-overcame-a-slow-start-and-passed-the-us/

McKee, M., Mossialos, E. and Belcher, P. (1996) 'The Influence of European Law On National Health Policy'. *Journal of European Social Policy*, Vol. 6, pp. 263–86. https://doi.org/10.1177/095892879600600401

Mossialos, E. and McKee, M. (2002) *The Influence of EU Law on the Social Character of Health Care Systems, Work & Society* (Brussels: P.I.E. – Peter Lang).

Nuclear Threat Initiative, Johns Hopkins Bloomberg School of Public Health. (2019) 'Global Health Security Index'. Nuclear Threat Initiative. https://www.ghsindex.org/wp-content/uploads/2019/10/2019-Global-Health-Security-Index.pdf

Oppenheim, B., Gallivan, M., Madhav, N.K., Brown, N., Serhiyenko, V., Wolfe, N.D. and Ayscue, P. (2019) 'Assessing Global Preparedness for the Next Pandemic: Development and Application of an Epidemic Preparedness Index'. *BMJ Global Health*, Vol. 4, e001157.

Ovaska, M. and Kumar Dutta, P. (2021) Europe's Vaccine Hesitancy. *Reuters*. https://graphics.reuters.com/HEALTH-CORONAVIRUS/EU-VACCINES/qmypmrelyvr/

Pan-European Commission on Health and Sustainable Development (2021) *Rethinking Policy Priorities in the light of Pandemics – Final Report* (Copenhagen: World Health Organization).

Permanand, G. and Mossialos, E. (2005) 'Constitutional Asymmetry and Pharmaceutical Policy-Making in the European Union'. *Journal of European Public Policy*, Vol. 12, pp. 687–709. https://doi.org/10.1080/13501760500160607

Regulation (EC) No 851/2004 of the European Parliament and of the Council (2004) 'Establishing a European Centre for Disease Prevention and Control'. https://eur-lex.europa.eu/legal-content/EN/ALL/?uri=celex%3A32004R0851

Scharpf, F.W. (2002) 'The European Social Model: Coping with the Challenges of Diversity' (MPIfG Working Paper No. 02/8). Max Planck Institute for the Study of Societies.

Schomaker, R.M., Hack, M. and Mandry, A.-K. (2021) 'The EU's Reaction in the First Wave of the Covid-19 Pandemic between Centralisation and Decentralisation, Formality and Informality'. *Journal of European Public Policy*, Vol. 28, pp. 1278–98. https://doi.org/10.1080/13501763.2021.1942153

Tsoukalis, L. (2005) *What Kind of Europe?* (Oxford: Oxford University Press).

Wismar, M., Busse, R. and Berman, P.C. (2002) 'The European Union and Health Services – The Context'. In *The European Union and Health Services: The Impact of the Single European Market on Member States* (Amsterdam: IOS Press).

JCMS 2021 Volume 59. Annual Review. pp. 69–80   DOI: 10.1111/jcms.13218

Social Perspectives on Brexit, COVID-19 and European (Dis) Integration

LINDA HANTRAIS
London School of Economics and Political Science, UK

Introduction

The on-going trade negotiations between the UK and the EU, in combination with the impact of the COVID-19 pandemic, created a perfect storm for Europe in 2020. For observers of the social scene, 2020 was a year when the debates, controversies, dilemmas and compromises that had characterized the European project during the previous seven decades moved centre-stage. Latent dissension in the social arena during the Brexit negotiations and COVID-19 pandemic were foreshadowed in earlier conflicts over economic and social trade-offs; the balance between national sovereignty and international solidarity; the distribution of EU and national public health competences; and policies to support inter- and intra-European social cohesion. The social domain played a determining role as the process of implementing the Political Declaration unfolded between 1 February and 31 December 2020, and the two parties compromised on a 'thin' deal in the area of trade. Underlying social disunity between member states resurfaced during the COVID-19 pandemic, with its amplifying effects on existing socio-economic inequalities both between member states and within societies.

I. Setting the Scene for European Social (Dis)Integration

From the 1950s when the European Economic Community was established, the social dimension was a controversial, though necessary, component of European integration, simultaneously supporting and competing with economic objectives (Hantrais, 2019). Diverse welfare traditions, approaches to social protection, political ideologies and national interests among the founding member states meant that it would be difficult to achieve a level playing field in the social domain.

The six founding member states shared a commitment to social progress. They accepted that certain common principles and standards should be adopted in their social protection systems to facilitate the free movement of workers across national borders, and to avoid unfair competition, social dumping and welfare tourism. They disagreed not only about which areas of social policy to include in the EEC Treaty, but also about the distribution of competences between 'supranational' institutions and national governments. Social policy was initially identified as an area of shared and supporting competence, with the Commission's role limited to proposing legislation, and monitoring and reporting on the progress made.

As the Union expanded to 28 member states, each wave of enlargement brought further culturally determined conceptions of social protection, distinct socio-demographic, economic and policy environments for formulating social policies, and differing financial resources for delivering social services. The latent conflicts inherent in the relationships between economic and social progress and between European institutions and member states, embedded in the 1957 EEC Treaty, resurfaced periodically in later years as the treaty's field of action progressively spilled over into other social and labour market areas (Leibfried and Pierson, 1995). The same issues became increasingly contentious during the UK's membership of the EU, making the initial objectives of achieving centrally regulated European social harmonisation ever more distant.

In recognition of the controversial nature of social affairs within the EU's regulatory toolkit, an attempt was made to clarify the distribution of competences between the Commission and EU member states in the Treaty on the Functioning of the European Union (TFEU, arts. 2–3). Public health had been given its own clear, albeit limited, legal basis in the Maastricht Treaty (art. 129). TFEU article 168 unambiguously established the distribution of competences specifically in the area of public health. Together the treaties reaffirmed the supportive, complementary or supplementary roles that the EU should play during the pandemic through its monitoring, coordinating, promotional and public health protection activities, while acknowledging that member states should remain responsible for defining, organising and delivering health services and medical care.

The launch of Jean-Claude Juncker's European Pillar on Social Rights in 2017 coincided fortuitously, if not opportunistically, with the UK's decision to leave the EU. The aim of the Pillar was to improve the lives of European citizens by advocating a more pro-active approach to future European social policy. Recognizing that not all member states would want, or be in a position, to pursue his objectives at the same pace, Juncker sought to engineer a compromise between champions of the social dimension and its critics. His two-speed social Europe, with the eurozone countries constituting the core group, was designed to respect cultural differences and national specificities in the social domain, in compliance with the principle of subsidiarity while ensuring greater involvement of civil society and the social partners.

Paradoxically, by losing sight of the single-track regulatory harmonised European social union of Delors' vision in the 1990s, the Pillar set the parameters for a two-speed, or differentially integrated, social Europe post-Brexit, which the UK had long been advocating and practising through its opt-outs. EU27 reactions to Juncker's proposals provided further evidence of the fragility of social union, even without the UK (European Economic and Social Committee, 2017). They cast doubt on the likelihood that the UK's withdrawal would substantially alter the nature of the contribution of social policy to European integration in the short or longer term. Rather, they could be seen as presaging the tensions and recriminations that would simultaneously characterize the acrimonious relationships between the EU and the UK during the Brexit negotiations, and between the Commission and EU27 member states during the pandemic in 2020. Just as the provisions of the EEC and EU Treaties had led inexorably to spillover, the field was left open, post-Brexit, for 'mission and scope creep' (Green, 2016). Social affairs had always been controversial at EU level and would become even more so in the pandemic's management toolkit.

II. The Impact of Brexit and the Pandemic on Social (Dis)Integration

The provisions made in the treaties for the distribution of competences between EU institutions and member states had laid the ground rules for the stalemate that ensued when the
Withdrawal Agreement and the Political Declaration were being negotiated. Legislation
on workers' rights, freedom of movement and state aid were identified at the outset as
areas of potential disagreement between the UK and EU institutions in negotiating the
Brexit settlement. Boris Johnson's version of the Withdrawal Agreement expunged
Theresa May's conciliatory provisions for non-regression of labour and social standards.
The reference to 'building on the level playing field arrangements' provided for in May's
draft Withdrawal Agreement (HM Government, 2018, §79) was replaced by a statement
indicating that 'the Parties should uphold the common high standards applicable in
the Union and the United Kingdom at the end of the transition period' (HM
Government, 2019, §77). The implication was that any truce agreed in the Political
Declaration would be of short duration.

In February 2020, the EU and UK embarked on the next phase of negotiations – the
11-month transition or implementation period – as mapped out succinctly in the Political
Declaration accompanying the Withdrawal Agreement. Neither party anticipated the
global threat to public health that would be posed by the COVID-19 pandemic nor its
longer-term impact on EU and UK social policy. During the year, public health, privacy
and data protection, together with state support for industry, workers and their families,
assumed a prominent position among the issues to be addressed, making it difficult to un-
tangle the negative effects of Brexit and the pandemic not only for the political economy
but also for social life.

Brexit and EU Social (Dis)Integration

In early 2020, the EU was recovering from the economic and immigration crises of the
first two decades of the 21st century. The incoming president of the European Commission, Ursula von de Leyen, had placed the European Green Deal and digital society at
the top of her political agenda (see Eckert, 2021 in this issue). The UK Conservative
government with its recently acquired substantial parliamentary majority was prematurely
celebrating having 'got Brexit done' by the deadline of 31 January 2020 (Hantrais, 2020).
The negotiations over the Trade and Cooperation Agreement (TCA) were reminiscent of
debates in earlier years about the extent to which European integration depended on the
balance between economic and social integration to ensure a level playing field and fair
competition (see Usherwood, 2021 in this issue). Perennial issues about living and
working conditions, access to employment and social protection for (mobile) workers
and their families, equivalence of qualifications and educational exchanges were blocking
progress, since they called into question the common rights and standards – *acquis
communautaire* – that member states had been required to transpose into their national
legislation as a condition of membership.

In a speech in London on 8 January, Von der Leyen (2020) laid down the EU's red
lines: no trade deal without a level playing field; no Brexit deal unless the four freedoms
(of movement, goods, persons, services and capital) were respected; and no state aid to
prop up failing industries. In a written statement to parliament on EU–UK relations issued on 3 February 2020, Johnson (2020) made explicit his own red lines: the UK

government would not countenance 'any regulatory alignment, any jurisdiction for the CJEU over the UK's laws, or any supranational control in any area, including the UK's borders and immigration policy'. By subordinating social policy issues to market exigencies and wider political concerns, the vexed issues of state aid and the level playing field threatened to derail the negotiations, portending a hard Brexit or no-deal.

Although EU27 member states continued to maintain a united front under the relentless stewardship of Michel Barnier, at the European Council's meeting on 21–2 February 2020, the heads of state or government failed to reach agreement over the long-term budget for 2021–27, providing renewed evidence of underlying divisions (Boucart, 2020). The 'frugal' member states – Austria, Denmark, Finland, Germany, the Netherlands and Sweden (later the 'frugal four' when Finland and Germany changed their approach) – advocated capping the budget at 1 per cent of EU gross domestic product and focusing on more 'modern' (economic) policy priorities. By contrast, the 17 'friends of cohesion' group of countries – essentially the southern, central and eastern European member states – sought reassurances that they would not be left on the periphery, as implied in Juncker's proposal for the European Pillar of Social Rights (subsequently Macron's concentric circles). They advocated continuing support for cohesion policy if the EU wanted to achieve greater economic and social convergence by levelling up across member states.

Within the friends of cohesion group, Czechia, Hungary, Poland and Slovakia, the four Central and East European countries, previously known as the Visegrád Group, adopted a 'semi-frugal' position in the 2021–27 European budget discussions (Ehl, 2020). They had been less affected by COVID-19 than the southern European member states during the first wave of the pandemic and wanted to avoid jeopardising their cohesion status and access to EU funds, since their economies had been severely affected by their early and stringent lockdown.

On 25 February, the Council of the European Union (2020, §10) issued directives for negotiating a new partnership with the UK; they reaffirmed that the EU was seeking 'a level playing field that will stand the test of time' and that, as a non-Schengen third country, the UK would not be subject to the same obligations. But nor would it enjoy the same benefits. In addition to social and employment standards, the areas targeted encompassed public health, social services and education, with provision to include 'additional areas or to lay down higher standards over time' (Council of the European Union, 2020, §95).

The Brexit negotiations stalled as Barnier contracted COVID-19 on 19 March and then Johnson on 27 March. With Europe at the epicentre of the pandemic, Brexit was eclipsed, although the 31 December 2020 deadline for closing the deal was not postponed. At EU and national levels, attention focused on measures to control the spread of the virus and mitigate economic damage. The UK did not join the EU-level effort to procure personal protective equipment (PPE) and ventilators in April 2020, despite still being entitled to do so (Brunsden et al., 2020). Nor did the UK participate in the European Commission's scheme for Support to mitigate Unemployment Risks in an Emergency (SURE), announced on 2 April, having by then launched its own Coronavirus Job Retention Scheme and other measures to protect incomes. To all intents and purposes, the UK was already exercising its autonomy by resorting to state aid on an unprecedented scale to support hard-hit sectors of the economy.

The final version of the TCA was eventually signed off on 24 December 2020 by the UK government and European Council, albeit too late to be ratified by the

European Parliament before the formal deadline. As in the EEC and TFEU Treaties, trade, labour and social standards remained inextricably linked. Other topical priorities were added to the list of issues that had been dealt with in the EEC Treaty. The TCA recognized:

> ...the Parties' respective autonomy and rights to regulate within their territories in order to achieve legitimate public policy objectives such as the protection and promotion of public health, social services, public education, safety, the environment including climate change, public morals, social or consumer protection, animal welfare, privacy and data protection and the promotion and protection of cultural diversity, while striving to improve their respective high levels of protection. (EUR-Lex, 2020, Preamble)

A section (EUR-Lex, 2020, Chapter 6) was devoted to labour and social standards, including articles on non-regression from levels of protection, enforcement and dispute settlement. The two parties retained the right to set their own policies, priorities and allocation of resources in these areas, provided they did not 'weaken or reduce' the labour or social levels of protection in place at the end of the transition period in a way that would affect trade or investment (EUR-Lex, 2020, art. 6.2). They were required to respect the provisions of the Council of Europe's 1961 European Social Charter, the counterpart of the European Convention on Human Rights in the sphere of economic and social rights. These provisions covered working conditions, health and safety at work, non-discrimination for migrant workers and social dialogue. By stopping the EU's Charter of Fundamental Rights of the European Union from having effect post-Brexit, the UK could, however, reduce the protection of human rights if it decided to amend its Equality Act (Dawson, 2019).

Two-thirds of the 165 references in the TCA to social security were contained in a dedicated Protocol on Social Security Coordination (EUR-Lex, 2020). Some of the most stringent and far-reaching EEC legislation – most notably Regulations Nos 3/58 and 4/58 on the coordination of social security systems – had been implemented even before the UK joined the European Communities to support free movement of people and the level playing field, thereby over-ruling national competence in this area. The TCA protocol covered every conceivable aspect of social security, as amended over the years, together with exemptions that had been negotiated by and between individual countries including the UK. Annex SSC-1 listed bilateral arrangements for reimbursements of costs for benefits and treatments, illustrating innumerable differences in national systems. Long-term care benefits were subject to lengthy national exemptions, demonstrating the diversity of conceptual approaches and financial resources devoted to this area of social policy.

During the transition phase, EU law continued to apply to the UK, even though it was no longer represented at the decision-making table. Early in the withdrawal process, the government had begun 'domesticating' EU law (Cowie, 2018). EU retained legislation covered three categories: legislation implementing or related to former EU obligations, such as the UK's Working Time Regulations; EU legislation directly applicable in the UK without implementing legislation, such as the EU's General Data Protection Regulation; and other rights and principles in EU law that had direct effect in the UK, for example the right not to be discriminated against on grounds of nationality, as provided for in the TFEU.

Tensions due to the 'interdependence between States and the independence of States' are known to re-emerge during times of crisis (De Witte, 2018, p. 478). The Brexit shock was no exception. Interpretations of the possible implications of Brexit for European social integration reflected longstanding debates among academics and politicians about the need for more flexibility in EU policy regulation and implementation (Schimmelfennig et al., 2015; Schmidt, 2019). For EU institutions, Brexit was expected to remove the threat of the UK using its blocking tactics, and also to weaken the coalition of opponents to closer social union (Oliver, 2018). Optimists continued to argue that European social union would be strengthened by the incentive to pursue a more proactive EU social policy to counter the growing populism and euroscepticism accompanying widespread disillusionment with European supranationalism (Donoghue and Kuisma, 2020).

For the UK, as argued by the leave campaign, sovereignty in the form of parliamentary control over social affairs would be restored, and the UK would no longer be constrained by the level playing field in the social domain. The immediate impact of Brexit on UK social legislation at the end of the transition period appeared to be mitigated. However, the thin deal agreed on 24 December provided for the EU to sanction the UK if it was found to have infringed the TCA by reducing its employment and social standards to gain an unfair competitive advantage. In other social areas too, it was clear that the UK would not be allowed to serve as an example to remaining member states that non-compliance with EU standards would be met with impunity.

The Challenge of COVID-19 for European Social Integration

Public health was not given prominence in the EEC Treaty since attention focused primarily on health and safety at work. Due to institutional prescience, the distribution of competences in the area of public health, mooted in the Maastricht Treaty in 1992 and clarified in the 2009 Lisbon Treaty, had prepared the ground for the pandemic that hit the EU in 2020. This latest crisis demonstrated that membership of the European Council conferred on heads of state or government a dual, and potentially incompatible, role. Their responsibility for taking decisions at EU and national levels, based on proposals and evidence supplied by the Commission in the area of public health policy, meant that, together, the Commission and national leaders were faced with the almost intractable dilemma of finding a balance between their conflicting competences. National and European institutions were confronted with the additional challenge of achieving a mutually supportive relationship between economic and social outcomes without losing sight of their political objectives.

On 10 March 2020, EU heads of state or government collectively recognized the situation as a policy crisis emergency (see Auer and Scicluna, 2021 in this issue), justifying a coordinated and coherent response both within the EU and between the social and economic impacts of the pandemic. Despite the apparent unity expressed in the summit's conclusions, national leaders disagreed over how to contain the pandemic without causing irreparable damage to economic and social life. COVID-19 revealed deep-seated latent divisions, both between and within societies, that had been momentarily concealed during the Brexit negotiations. EU27 unity quickly dissipated as national interests overruled the European Commission's faltering attempts to exercise its monitoring and coordinating roles. As public health rose to the top of the EU's agenda, the pandemic illustrated the reasons why social policy had remained such a contentious issue throughout the construction of the European Union. It also showed how the UK's departure did not make the situation any easier to manage (Hantrais, 2020).

With the Commission reluctant to acknowledge the seriousness of the outbreak, and the European Council unable to agree on a concerted collective approach, initially national governments reacted unilaterally, at varying speeds and with different degrees of stringency (Hantrais and Letablier, 2021). One of the core conditions for EU membership – free movement of citizens – on which the EU had remained adamant in the Brexit negotiations – was the first red line to be crossed. Without waiting for instructions from Brussels, by mid-March 2020 member states had seized the initiative and closed land borders to prevent the spread of the virus, whereas the UK and Ireland, both non-Schengen countries, kept their borders open. Amid growing criticism of its lack of EU leadership, on 16 March the Commission began unveiling its own proposals based on the summit's conclusions. Citizens of non-Schengen EU countries, as well as the UK, were invited to apply restrictions on non-essential travel from non-EU countries in the hope that this would ease bans within the EU.

The European Commission struggled to assert its authority for carrying out its treaty remit for coordinating actions. Its failure to do so exacerbated conflicts between member states over the distribution of medical goods, with some member states unilaterally seeking to procure personal protective equipment (PPE) and ventilators from outside the EU. Other measures, such as bans on public events and gatherings, closure of workplaces and schools, were introduced progressively and differentially as the pandemic progressed. In March, the European Centre for Disease Prevention and Control (ECDC, 2020, p. 6) reminded both EU and national institutions that: 'Restrictive public health measures must always respect existing national legislation, as well as international legal and ethical principles'. The ECDC gave as an example that quarantine 'should not differentiate between social or economic groups in a population'.

In March–April, deaths from COVID-19 spiked in several of the larger member states and the UK as governments lost control over the virus. Commission pronouncements came with increasing frequency. In response to actions taken by national governments, state aid – another of the EU red lines – was recognized as an essential source of social support for furloughed workers and their families at risk of poverty. The SURE scheme, which relaxed rules on state aid and suspended strict regulations on budget deficits, deployed the EU's structural funds to assist short-time workers in eurozone countries. The Commission used its shared public health competence to advocate direct emergency support for national healthcare sectors and for the manufacturing capacity of industry using fiscal incentives, state aid and flexibility in public procurement.

While guidelines on medicines were being drawn up, the Commission circulated its lockdown exit plan to national officials before making it public on 7 April 2020. Within governments, ministers of finance and health were struggling with conflicting interests and pressures in planning their own exit strategies and rejected interference from Brussels. In recognition of national specificities and sensitivities, the European roadmap towards lifting COVID-19 containment measures focused on key principles or pre-conditions for easing lockdown rather than prescriptive policy measures (European Commission, 2020a). Acting in accordance with its limited public health mandate, the Commission stressed the need for a coordinated exit strategy, leaving member states to exercise their responsibility by taking and implementing decisions concerning the delivery of public health policies in accordance with national interests and legal competences.

After a further acrimonious summit, the European Commission released its recovery plan, Next Generation EU on 27 May 2020, alongside the budget settlement for 2020. The plan again illustrated the difficulties of reaching agreement across 27 national governments, casting further doubt not only on the viability of the Commission's call for European unity and solidarity but also on the EU's intention to comply with its own red lines. The economic recovery fund was designed to 'power a fair socio-economic recovery, repair and revitalise the Single Market, [and] to guarantee a level playing field' (European Commission, 2020b). This compromise solution involved full flexibility in budgetary and state-aid rules to repair the economic and social damage resulting from the crisis. By highlighting social and territorial cohesion, together with health and resilience, education and skills, the plan was designed to galvanise solidarity between member states.

The UK was not party to the plan when it was agreed on 21 July 2020 and, like many EU member states, continued to pursue its own measures unilaterally. The European Parliament and Council eventually adopted Regulation (EU) 2021/241, thereby formally establishing the Recovery and Resilience Facility (RRF) on 12 February 2021. The actions taken to prop up national economies were hailed as a success for European solidarity, but were overshadowed by the debacle in early 2021 regarding the approval, procurement and distribution of vaccines, where national interests (vaccine nationalism) again trumped European social unity.

A year earlier, to avoid intra-European competition, EU member states had agreed to task the European Commission with negotiating block orders of vaccines on their behalf with American, British and other competitors for the production of a European vaccine (Deutsch and Wheaton, 2021). By May/June 2020, when EU 27 health minister were finalising a Commission plan to purchase bulk supplies, France, Germany, the Netherlands and Italy broke rank to form an Inclusive Vaccines Alliance, with the option of extension to countries such as Spain. Leaving aside smaller countries, they were using their significant buying power to leverage low-cost purchases of vaccines from leading pharmaceutical industries, including AstraZeneca (UK−Swedish) and Pfizer-BioNTech (Germany and US), in the hope that manufacturing would be located in Europe.

After some relief in the summer, it became clear that a second and more virulent strain was spreading across Europe. Many of the EU member states that escaped the worst social-economic and epidemiological effects of the first wave, most notably Bulgaria, the Czech Republic, Hungary, Lithuania and Slovakia, were hardest hit by the second and third waves in the autumn and winter, suggesting that national governments had not learnt from the experience of their neighbours or from the widely available shared international scientific knowledge base (Hantrais and McGregor, 2021). Council agreed that the Commission should repurpose the Emergency Support Instrument enabling the Commission to approve and purchase vaccines directly, and distribute them to member states according to population size rather than on the basis of criteria such as resources and need. Further disputes arose between member states over the selection of vaccines and companies, and their approval, thereby delaying completion of purchasing deals.

The advantage gained from 'wielding the market power and moral authority of 27 sovereign nations − with different budgets and perspectives on risk − mean[t] moving more slowly than the one-and-done competition' (Deutsch and Wheaton, 2021). Having declined to join the EU's purchasing programme, the UK was able to move fast to authorise the Pfizer and AstraZeneca vaccines for emergency use, enabling vaccinations to begin on 6 December, three weeks before the Commission's proposed start date of 27 December. Hungary, Germany and Slovakia defied the Commission by delivering their first vaccinations on 26 December. Recriminations against the Commission followed swiftly with Italy and Poland threatening legal action against the EU for the lack of supplies.

At the same time as the EU was celebrating its successful recovery fund in February 2021, the EU became embroiled in a 'public feud' with AstraZeneca, as well as a 'diplomatic emergency' with the UK over vaccine export controls to Northern Ireland. This 'blunder' was quickly retracted. Then, France and Germany, followed by other member states, declined to use the AstraZeneca vaccine for its population aged over 65 as a precautionary measure. A few weeks later, several EU member states suspended use of the AstraZeneca vaccine, on grounds that it might be associated with a small number of cases of blood clots. WHO and European Medicines Agencies were quick to refute such a link, but were too late to prevent fuelling EU vaccine hesitancy (Hockley, 2021).

The Commission's use of the EU's size to leverage the best possible deal for European consumers raised questions about the Commission's overall governance of the vaccine programme, and its role as a 'strategic actor' in a competition with other states (Chryssogelos, 2021). Its mishandling of the procurement and rollout of vaccinations supplies exacerbated the tensions that had surfaced earlier in the year due to the sharing of competences for public health (Herszenhorn and Deutsch, 2021). The European Commission and Council were pilloried for their failure to invest in producing a European vaccine. National government were criticised for the delay in approving, procuring and delivering vaccines for their own populations and for offloading responsibility to the Commission for procurement. While it was still considered as a member of the EU during the first wave of the pandemic, the UK had been branded as one of the worst performers in terms of the lethality of the virus and for its mismanagement of the public health crisis. From outside the EU, in February 2021, the UK was enjoying a morale boost not only for its success in producing and procuring supplies of efficacious vaccines, but also for its administrative efficiency in delivering vaccinations to its most vulnerable citizens within a year of the disease being declared a pandemic.

The Combined Impact of Brexit and the Pandemic on Socio-Economic Inequalities

In combination, the TCA negotiations and the attempts to deal with fallout from the pandemic at EU and national levels revealed entrenched divisions within and between European societies. The full force of the controversies, dilemmas and compromises that had characterized the social dimension of the European project resurfaced in 2020, calling into question the relationship between member states and European institutions. First Brexit then the pandemic exposed the underlying hostility towards EU control over the social domain as well as the deep fault lines within societies.

With its 'collective and solidarity-based model of governance', it has been argued that the EU should have been 'uniquely qualified' to resolve the health crisis (Wallaschek and Eigmüller, 2020, p. 64). The pandemic should have provided an opportunity for the EU to strengthen social solidarity and advance social integration. But the legal basis and the cumbersome machinery of European governance complicated and delayed responses to the public health emergency at EU level. By leaving member states to exercise their treaty responsibility for defining their health policies and for organising and delivering health services and medical care in accordance with their own resources, the risks for societies with poorly resourced and administered health services were heightened.

The pandemic amplified existing regional, social and economic inequalities due to its disproportionate effects on certain groups within societies. Socio-demographic and economic data, and epidemiological studies, showed unequivocally that some population groups in some regions accumulated advantages and disadvantages (Hantrais and Letablier, 2021). In managing the pandemic, initially the odds were stacked against large, densely populated, internationally connected countries, with high old-age dependency ratios and urban concentrations. Severe cases of the disease and high COVID-19 mortality rates were associated underlying health conditions, poor living and working environments, differential access to health services and vaccines, online schooling and working, and financial support, reinforcing evidence that the pandemic was contributing to social disintegration at European and societal levels.

The pandemic presented greater challenges for policymakers in regions where these conditions were associated with poorly resourced public healthcare services, underdeveloped technological infrastructures, inherent socio-economic and political divisions, unstable or dysfunctional governments, sceptical electorates and hostile media. Although the acceleration of the digital revolution was being harnessed to support public health responses, the development and adoption of these technologies at scale and speed not only raised legal, ethical and privacy concerns, but also intensified risks for disadvantaged communities, thereby further widening the digital divide (Schwab and Malleret, 2020).

The unprecedented resources made available at national and European levels to support economies were, it was argued, 'short-term fixes'; they failed to address deeply embedded inequalities (Donoghue and Kuisma, 2020, p. 4). In the aftermath of Brexit, and as the pandemic entered its second year, evidence was growing of an enhanced awareness among European governments that social and economic policies were inextricably linked. They were realising that investment in health as a public good was a global concern dependent on international cooperation, demanding a rethinking and reimagining of policy priorities to strengthen resilience and ensure sustainable development and social cohesion worldwide (World Health Organisation, 2021).

References

Auer, S. and Scicluna, N. (2021) The Impossibility of Constitutionalising Emergency Europe, *Journal of Common Market Studies*, 59(S1).

Boucart, T. (2020) 'EU Budget: The Rule of 'Deadlock as Usual', *New Federalist*, 2 March. https://www.thenewfederalist.eu/eu-budget-the-rule-of-deadlock-as-usual?lang=fr

Brunsden, J., Foster, O. and Parker, G. (2020) 'Brussels says UK was Fully Aware of PPE Procurement Plans', *Financial Times*, 22 April. https://www.ft.com/content/58f5f476-7a85-4785-81bd-0806ff7c6ded

Chryssogelos, A. (2021) 'The EU's Vaccine Debacle Has Revealed its Limitations as a Strategic Actor', *LSE EUROPP Blog*, 18 February. https://blogs.lse.ac.uk/europpblog/2021/02/18/the-eus-vaccine-debacle-has-revealed-its-limitations-as-a-strategic-actor/

Council of the European Union (2020) 'Annex to Council Decision Authorising the Opening of Negotiations with the United Kingdom of Great Britain and Northern Ireland for a New Partnership Agreement', 5870/20 ADD 1 REV 3, 25 February. https://www.consilium.europa.eu/media/42736/st05870-ad01re03-en20.pdf

Cowie, G. (2018) 'The Status of "Retained EU Law"', *House of Commons Library: Research Briefing*, 08375, 30 July. https://commonslibrary.parliament.uk/research-briefings/cbp-8375/

Dawson, J. (2019) 'How Might Brexit Affect Human Rights in the UK?', *House of Commons Library: Insight*, 17 December. https://commonslibrary.parliament.uk/how-might-brexit-affect-human-rights-in-the-uk/

De Witte, F. (2018) 'Interdependence and Contestation in European Integration'. *European Papers*, Vol. 3, No. 23, pp. 475–509. https://doi.org/10.15166/2499-8249/244

Deutsch, J. and Wheaton, S. (2021) 'How Europe Fell behind on Vaccines', *Politico*, 27 January. https://www.politico.eu/article/europe-coronavirus-vaccine-struggle-pfizer-biontech-astrazeneca/

Donoghue, M. and Kuisma, M. (2020) 'Introduction'. In Donoghue, M. and Kuisma, M. (eds) *Whither Social Rights in (Post-) Brexit Europe? Opportunities and Challenges* (Berlin and London: Social Europe Publishing and Friedrich Ebert Stiftung), pp. 1–6.

Eckert, S. (2021) The European Green Deal and the EU's Regulatory Power in Times of Crisis, *Journal of Common Market Studies*, 59(S1).

Ehl, M. (2020) 'The other Frugal Four: The V4 Closely Watches the EU Budget Discussion', *Visegrad Insight*, 27 May. https://visegradinsight.eu/the-other-frugal-four-v4-eu-budget/

EUR-Lex (2020) 'Trade and Cooperation Agreement between the European Union and the European Atomic Energy Community, of the One Part, and the United Kingdom of Great Britain and Northern Ireland, of the Other Part'. *L 444, OJ*, Vol. 63, 31 December, pp. 14–62. https://eur-lex.europa.eu/legal-content/EN/TXT/?uri=OJ:L:2020:444:TOC

European Centre for Disease Prevention and Control (2020) 'Considerations Relating to Social Distancing Measures in Response to COVID-19 – Second Update', Technical Report, 23 March. https://www.ecdc.europa.eu/sites/default/files/documents/covid-19-social-distancing-measuresg-guide-second-update.pdf

European Commission (2020a) 'Coronavirus: European Roadmap Shows Path Towards Common Lifting of Containment Measures', Press Release, 15 April. https://ec.europa.eu/commission/presscorner/detail/en/IP_20_652

European Commission (2020b) 'Europe's Moment: Repair and Prepare for the Next Generation', Press release, 27 May. https://ec.europa.eu/commission/presscorner/detail/en/ip_20_940

European Economic and Social Committee (2017) White Paper on the Future of Europe: National Consultations of Organized Civil Society, May–June. https://www.eesc.europa.eu/sites/default/files/resources/docs/white-paper-on-the-future-of-europe---compilation---en.pdf

Green, K. (2016) 'Power to Modify Retained Direct EU Legislation Relating to Social Security Co-ordination', UK Parliament Public Bill Committee, 16 June. https://www.theyworkforyou.com/pbc/2019-21/Immigration_and_Social_Security_Co-ordination_%28EU_Withdrawal%29_Bill/05-0_2020-06-16a.154.1

Hantrais, L. (2019) *What Brexit Means for EU and UK Social Policy* (Bristol: Policy Press).

Hantrais, L. (2020) 'Afterword' to What Brexit Means for EU and UK Social Policy (Bristol: Policy Press). https://policy.bristoluniversitypress.co.uk/asset/8562/hantrais-online-afterword.pdf

Hantrais, L. and Letablier, M.-T. (2021) *Comparing and Contrasting the Impact of the Covid-19 Pandemic in the European Union* (Abingdon: Routledge).

Hantrais, L. and McGregor, S. (2021) 'Incorporating Complexity into Policy Learning: The Case of Covid-19 in Europe', LSE EUROPP Blog, 22 February. https://blogs.lse.ac.uk/europpblog/2021/02/22/incorporating-complexity-into-policy-learning-the-case-of-covid-19-in-europe/

Herszenhorn, D.M. and Deutsch, J. (2021) 'Brussels Gives Vaccine Strategy an Injection', *Politico*, 17 February. https://www.politico.eu/article/european-commission-coronavirus-vaccine-strategy-boost-ursula-von-der-leyen-stella-kyriakides-thierry-breton/

HM Government (2018) Political Declaration Setting Out the Framework for the Future Relationship between the European Union and the United Kingdom, 22 November. https://ec.europa.eu/info/publications/political-declaration-setting-out-framework-future-relationship-between-european-union-and-united-kingdom_en

HM Government (2019) Political Declaration Setting Out the Framework for the Future Relationship between the European Union and the United Kingdom, 19 October. https://assets.publishing.service.gov.uk/government/uploads/system/uploads/attachment_data/file/840656/Political_Declaration_setting_out_the_framework_for_the_future_relationship_between_the_European_Union_and_the_United_Kingdom.pdf

Hockley, T. (2021) 'The Brexit Vaccine War is a Failure of Empathy', LSE Brexit Blog, 24 March. https://blogs.lse.ac.uk/brexit/2021/03/24/the-brexit-vaccine-war-is-a-failure-of-empathy/

Johnson, B. (2020) 'Statement to Parliament', 3 February. Statement UIN HCWS86. https://questions-statements.parliament.uk/written-statements/detail/2020-02-03/HCWS86

Leibfried, S. and Pierson, P. (1995) 'Semisovereign Welfare States: Social Policy in a Multitiered Europe'. In Leibfried, S. and Pierson, P. (eds) *European Social Policy: Between Fragmentation and Integration* (Washington DC: The Brookings Institution), pp. 43–77.

Oliver, T. (2018) *Understanding Brexit: A Concise Introduction* (Bristol: Policy Press).

Schimmelfennig, F., Leuffen, D. and Rittberger, B. (2015) 'The European Union as a System of Differentiated Integration: Interdependence, Politicization and Differentiation'. *Journal of European Public Policy*, Vol. 22, No. 6, pp. 764–82. https://doi.org/10.1080/13501763.2015.1020835

Schmidt, V. (2019) 'The Future of Differentiated Integration: A "Soft-Core" Multi-Clustered Europe of Overlapping Policy Communities'. *Comparative European Politics*, Vol. 17, No. 2, pp. 294–315. https://doi.org/10.1057/s41295-019-00164-7

Schwab, M. and Malleret, T. (2020) *Covid-19: The Great Reset* (Geneva: World Economic Forum).

Usherwood, S. (2021) "Our European friends and partners"? Negotiating the Trade and Cooperation Agreement, *Journal of Common Market Studies*, 59(S1).

Von der Leyen, U. (2020) 'Old Friends, New Beginnings: Building another Future for the EU-UK Partnership', Speech at the London School of Economics, 8 January. http://www.lse.ac.uk/Events/Events-Assets/PDF/2020/01-LT/20200108-Speech-by-President-von-der-Leyen-at-the-London-School-of-Economics.pdf

Wallaschek, S. and Eigmüller, M. (2020) 'Never Waste a Good Crisis: Solidarity Conflicts in the EU'. In Donoghue, M. and Kuisma, M. (eds) *Whither Social Rights in (Post-) Brexit Europe? Opportunities and Challenges* (Berlin and London: Social Europe Publishing and Friedrich Ebert Stiftung), pp. 60–8.

World Health Organisation (2021) 'A Call to Action: National Governments and the Global Community Must Act Now', 16 March. https://www.euro.who.int/en/health-topics/health-policy/european-programme-of-work/pan-european-commission-on-health-and-sustainable-development/rethinking-policy-priorities-in-the-light-of-pandemics-a-call-to-action

JCMS 2021 Volume 59. Annual Review. pp. 81–91   DOI: 10.1111/jcms.13241

The European Green Deal and the EU's Regulatory Power in Times of Crisis

SANDRA ECKERT[1,2]
[1] Aarhus Institute of Advanced Studies, Aarhus [2] Goethe University Frankfurt/Main (on leave of absence), Frankfurt

Introduction

It was by the end of 2019 that the incoming European Commission with its new President Ursula von der Leyen had formulated its policy agenda for the years to come. The top priority was the European Green Deal committing to carbon neutrality which von der Leyen announced as 'Europe's man on the moon moment' (von der Leyen, 2019b). The agenda built on the global momentum around the climate emergency, such as the warning issued by the Intergovernmental Panel on Climate Change in 2018 (IPCC, 2018) that the world needed to reach net zero emissions by 2050 to avoid a climate catastrophe, and the societal mobilization triggered by the Friday's for Future movement the same year. The European Green Deal (EGD) is an encompassing regulatory agenda and the new growth strategy of the EU, comprising 50 actions to be achieved by 2050. The green transition is supposed to break with an economic model based on fossil fuels and pollution while leaving no one behind. The EGD ambition is nothing less than a fundamental transformation of the economy and strives to bring all EU policies in line with the climate neutrality pledge. In short, with the EGD the EU aims to be a 'global standard setter' (von der Leyen, 2019c) and seeks to mobilize its regulatory capacity and power (Bradford, 2015, 2020) to that end.

The EGD, first presented on 11 December 2019, has been followed up with a variety of policy proposals and measures throughout 2020. The bulk of EGD related agenda setting and policy formulation throughout the last year has been overshadowed by the Covid-19 pandemic, which was recognized as an emergency on the European continent since March 2020. Based on experience from previous crises, when environmental policy goals risked to be sidelined by the pressing need to secure economic recovery and social cohesion (Howarth, 2009; Gravey and Jordan, 2016; Lenschow et al., 2020), we might expect the economic hardship caused by the pandemic to negatively affect the realization of the EGD. This article analyses how the European Commission has sought to claim a global leadership role in the green transition, and discusses the ways in which EGD-related policy formulation has interacted with the unfolding Covid-19 crisis over the course of the past year. To that end, I will address the following research question: *To what extent has Europe's ambition to lead the global green transition been disrupted (or strengthened) by the Covid-19 crisis?*

To prepare the ground for the discussion of this research question, the paper will first address EGD's ambition as it was formulated by the European Commission, briefly engaging with the broader discussion on the EU as a global actor. Following this, I will

[Correction added on 21 October 2021, after first online publication: Level of headings and sub-headings have been corrected.]

revisit the major events in 2020 regarding the EGD process. In doing so I will discuss the attempts by some policymakers and industry representatives to weaken the EGD agenda, and will also analyse how the European Commission and EGD supporters have sought to capitalize on the momentum to link the issues of green transition and economic recovery.

I. The EU as a Global Standard Setter

The proposal of the incoming von der Leyen Commission takes inspiration from Franklin D. Roosevelt's 'New Deal' growth package issued in the 1930s in the United States. Moreover, it builds on a plethora of ideas around a 'Green New Deal' generated both at national and international levels in the aftermath of the 2007–08 economic and financial crisis (Luke, 2009; Pettifor, 2020). The Global Green New Deal agenda issued by the United Nations Environment Programme (UNEP) in 2008 is probably the most visible international policy agenda in this context (Barbier, 2010). The EGD is the EU's new growth strategy 'where there are no net emissions of greenhouse gases in 2050 and where economic growth is decoupled from resource use' (European Commission, 2019, p. 2). With the EGD the incoming Commission has furthermore formulated the EU's ambition to be 'the first climate neutral continent in the world by 2050' (von der Leyen, 2019a) and to be a global standard setter (von der Leyen, 2019c). Moreover, the Green Deal is advocated as a policy agenda which allows European businesses 'to innovate and to develop new technologies while creating new markets', to benefit from 'a competitive advantage' and 'to ensure a level playing field' (von der Leyen, 2019c). The EU thus seeks to be a first mover in global regulatory competition around the green transition, but also wants to lead by example and diffuse its environmental norms. It can therefore be argued that the European Commission seeks to capitalize on both the EU's normative and regulatory power. At the same time, however, the EGD as the EU's new growth and industrial strategy has a strong inward-looking component as it seeks to protect both European (environmental) values and economic interests. These latter aspects are more in line with what has been discussed as the EU's geopolitical and geoeconomic role more recently, and befits von der Leyen's idea of a 'geopolitical Commission' (von der Leyen, 2019c). In view of these considerations, it is worth revisiting these concepts of the EU's role as a global actor, and reflect on how the Covid-19 crisis might affect their realization.

Normative, Market and Regulatory Power

In his article published in this journal in 2002, Ian Manners introduced the idea of the EU being a normative power in contrast to established international relations categories such as civilian and military power (Manners, 2002). While Manners argued that the EU as a supranational polity through its very nature incorporates normative power, his reflections on intentional norm diffusion are more relevant for the EGD context. Relevant norms are environmental – climate neutrality, zero pollution and a circular economy – but also social, given that a 'just transition' both inside the EU and globally is a declared goal of the EGD. A decade later Chad Damro argued that the EU, while certainly incorporating normative aspects, is above all a big market and by that means can externalize its policies effectively. While market power draws on effects of scale, the concept of regulatory power draws attention to the fact that being a big market does not suffice to set standards globally. Rather, the capacity to formulate and enforce rules is required. Building on this notion of regulatory power Manu Bradford coined the emblematic term 'Brussels effect' (Bradford, 2020) in analogy to David Vogel's work on the 'California effect' (Vogel, 1997). The remarkable feature of these processes of rule export is that they involve an upward rather than a downward regulatory dynamic. With the aspiration to set standards globally, the European Commission seeks to mobilize this Brussels effect intentionally. If the EGD proves successful in this regard, we could see both a *de facto* and *de jure* effect, as described by Bradford: companies operating internationally could choose to adhere to the standards beyond the EU's remit; other jurisdictions could adopt rules similar to those introduced by the EU. Finally, the discussion of the EU as a geopolitical actor cannot be disregarded, not in the least because the Commission president in office adheres to this notion. The discussion of the concept is complex and manifold, with a political and a more economic angle (Dodds, 2004; Meunier and Nicolaidis, 2019). Contrary to the notion of normative power, the geopolitical orientation is more about protecting rather than diffusing norms, and often is linked to domestic economic interests. The new international context, where norms of multilateralism and liberalism have been challenged, has significant ramifications for the EGD, which in many aspects is an EU-centred industrial and growth strategy. The most eminent example of this is the Commission's intention to introduce a carbon border adjustment mechanism, which has fuelled criticism and allegations of protectionism by the EU's major trading partners such as China and the United States. Moreover, the perceived priority given to EU interests may hamper its goal of being a global standard setter as well as an advocate of a globally just transition – with negative implications for its normative power.

Crises and Integration Dynamics

How could the Covid-19 crisis potentially affect the realization of these aspects of EU global power through the EGD? The discussion around crisis and institutional change and, for that matter, integration dynamics in the EU context is long-standing, but worthwhile revisiting in the current context. Crises are major, unexpected, non-routine, disruptive occurrences that may allow for change, and the pandemic surely qualifies as such. We have seen a flourishing literature on how the previous crises over the last two decades have affected European integration dynamics (see also Auer and Scicluna, 2021 in this issue). Drastic shifts during times of crisis, such as deeper integration resulting from the Eurozone crisis have been described as 'a leap forward' (Grossman and Leblond, 2011) and stand out in comparison to stagnation and deadlock which resulted from the migration crisis (Schimmelfennig, 2018). Such a differential impact also shows that the relationship between crisis and (more) European integration should not be taken for granted (see also Niemann and Zaun, 2018). The least we can expect is that a crisis constitutes a window of opportunity both for supporters as well as opponents of a policy agenda. On the side of the advocates of the EGD, issue linkage between the green transition and economic recovery is an appealing option. From this viewpoint a green recovery constitutes the way out, very much in line with Monnet's dictum that 'Europe will be forged in crises, and will be the sum of the solutions of those crises' (Monnet, 1978, p. 417). Crises such as Covid-19 or the climate emergency, in essence, would provide such challenges soliciting new, European solutions. On the other hand, however, economic hardship following continued periods of lockdown could be used as an argument to put on hold ambitious policy agendas in order to give priority to crisis management and economic recovery instead.

II. The European Green Deal in the Shadow of Covid-19

Let us now consider the interplay of the Covid-19 crises and the implementation of the EGD tabled in December 2019, shortly before the outbreak of the pandemic on the European Continent. To that end, the policy proposals issued by the European Commission will be briefly discussed, as well as the policy formulation process involving the European Parliament and national governments. Positions both in favour and in opposition to the EGD agenda will be considered. Figure 1 provides an overview of the key events in 2020.

Formulating the Green Deal Agenda in a Context of Crisis

In January 2020, both the European Green Deal Investment Plan (EGDIP) and the Just Transition Mechanism (JTM) were proposed. The EGDIP shall mobilize EU funding of at least €1 trillion of sustainable investments over the next decade, facilitate public and private investment and lend support to implement relevant projects. The JTM aims at addressing socioeconomic ramifications of the transition, focusing on the regions, industries and workers who will face the greatest challenges, and mobilizing at least €150 billion. Importantly, both the GDIP and the JTM target the green transition in the EU member states and at regional level, but do not address global aspects of economic development and climate justice. By contrast, there is mention of international cooperation to promote sustainable finance globally, for instance through the International Platform on Sustainable Finance, and an aspiration 'to make European industry a global leader in these clean

Figure 1: The European Green Deal in 2020. [Colour figure can be viewed at wileyonlinelibrary. com]

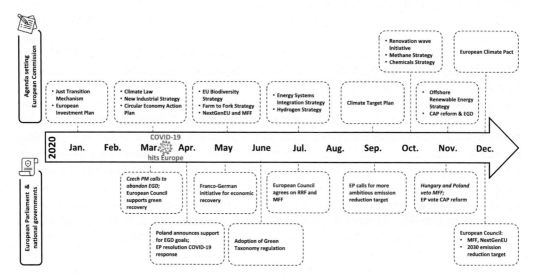

technologies' (European Commission, 2020a, pp. 7, 10). This would speak in favour of the EU as a regulatory rather than a normative power.

Shortly before the outbreak of the Covid-19 pandemic and virtually at the same time when some of the member states started to enter lockdown, the European Commission came up with key EGD proposals, namely for a European Climate Law (4 March), a New Industrial Strategy (10 March) and a New Circular Economy Action Plan (11 March). The Climate Law enshrines the net zero greenhouse gas emissions by 2050 in binding law, and commits to an interim goal for 2030. In September 2020, the Commission followed up on the proposal suggesting to increase the 2030 emission reduction target to at least 55 per cent compared to 1990 levels in its Climate Target Plan – a proposal which was backed up by a political agreement of the European Council in December 2020. Institutional agreement on the climate law was reached in June 2021. The New Industrial Strategy (NIS) makes an important contribution to the EGD's growth ambition. The previous strategy for economic growth, Europe2020, aimed at 'smart, sustainable and inclusive growth' (European Commission, 2000, p. 12), following up on the unsuccessful Lisbon Strategy, issued in 2000. The NIS commits to decarbonizing energy-intensive industries while supporting green ones and to secure the supply of low-carbon energy as well as critical raw materials. With the EGD's Climate Law the EU has moved its commitment to international climate goals (see also Dupont et al., 2020, pp. 1099–100; Oberthür and Groen, 2017) to the next level by enshrining them into binding legislation. Climate action has started to take centre stage in the EU since 2010, when a dedicated policy portfolio and Commissioner post was established. Compared to an observed trend of a reduced level of activity in European environmental policy (Knill and Liefferink, 2013) as well as a process of (subtle) policy-dismantling (Gravey and Jordan, 2020; Lenschow et al., 2020), climate action goals stand out in that they have continued to be on top of the policy agenda (Lenschow, 2020, pp. 298–300). The industrial strategy, as mentioned before, bears witness to a geopolitical orientation. The Commission situates the NIS in a context of 'moving geopolitical plates which affect the nature of competition. The need for Europe to affirm its voice, uphold its values and fight for a level playing field is more important than ever. This is about Europe's sovereignty' (European Commission, 2020c, p. 1). In this context, the proposal refers to global competition, protectionism, market distortions, trade tensions and challenges to the rules-based system (European Commission, 2020c, p. 3). In a nutshell, the Commission advocates a somewhat geopoliticised version of a global leadership role, which at the same time capitalizes on market power: 'The EU should continue leading by example, but it must also use its leverage to promote a global change in economic incentives in support of the low-carbon transition taking into account changing geopolitical and geoeconomic realities' (European Commission, 2020d, p. 23).

Promoting a Green Recovery

As soon as the Covid-19 emergency reached Europe, many policy-makers engaged in issue linkage with the EGD. By the end of March 2020 member states in the European Council lent support to simultaneously strive for economic recovery and a green transition (Simon, 2020a). Similarly, the European Parliament in a resolution issued in April 2020 backed the Commission's Green Deal and called for its implementation despite the crisis context (European Parliament, 2020). In May 2020, the European Commission formulated additional proposals to implement the EGD, such as the EU Biodiversity Strategy and the Farm to Fork Strategy, which had been slightly delayed due to Covid-19 (Sánchez Nicolás, 2020). The issue of biodiversity gained salience with Covid-19, because it was argued that the pandemic has its root causes in biodiversity loss (European Commission, 2020b, pp. 1, 3, 22). Issue linkage can also be retraced in the way in which the policy agenda has been formulated. A word frequency analysis of the 18 EGD proposals issued by the European Commission illustrates how there was a shift towards promoting green recovery: in the six documents issued pre-Covid – the initial EGD Communication and the March 2020 proposals being included – the noun 'climate' (55.59 per cent of documents) and the adjective 'circular' (16.97 per cent of documents) are the EGD keywords most frequently mentioned; by contrast, in the 12 documents issued since April 2020, economic 'recovery' (19.29 per cent, 213 times) emerges as a new keyword and is the term most frequently mentioned after 'climate' (44.57 per cent, 492 times).

The most important step to link the EGD agenda with the concept of recovery, however, was taken with the Next Generation EU (NextGenEU) and the Multiannual Financial Framework (MFF). While the EGD from the outset highlighted the need for investment, both from public and private sources, the level of EU funding generated in the context of crisis was significantly higher. Pre-crisis it was estimated that with an additional annual green investment of €260bn the 2030 climate and energy targets could be achieved (European Commission, 2019, p. 15). The outgoing Juncker Commission had proposed an Action Plan on Financing Sustainable Growth in March 2018 (European Commission, 2018). The most tangible measure adopted in June 2020 is the Green Taxonomy (regulation (EU) 2020/852). On the side of public funding, in 2020 a Franco-German initiative closely coordinated with the European Commission paved the way for NextGenEU, resulting in a proposed recovery instrument of €750bn and an expansion of the EU's budget for 2021–27. The European Council adopted the regulation establishing the Recovery and Resilience Facility (RRF) in February 2021 (European Council, 2021). Together, the MFF for 2021–27 and the recovery instrument mobilize an unprecedented 1.8 trillion euros. Member states need to spend at least 37 per cent of their national recovery and resilience plans in support of the green transition, and all plans should respect the 'do no significant harm' principle.

The trajectory of the EGD agenda illustrates that overall the Covid-19 crisis has been skilfully used by EU policymakers as a window of opportunity to link economic recovery and green transition. This linkage, however, was not uncontested, as some EU member states and industry branches sought to use the Covid-19 emergency to derail the EGD agenda or at least slow it down.

Attempts to Disrupt the Green Deal Agenda

The Visegrad group of countries consisting of the Czech Republic, Hungary, Poland and Slovakia have been particularly vocal opponents of an ambitious green transition. Poland, heavily relying on coal, was the only EU country that in December 2019 did not endorse the EGD commitment to climate neutrality. At that time, the Czech Republic and Hungary, despite being sceptical, were brought on board in return for concessions (Rankin, 2019). Following the outbreak of Covid-19 in Europe, an early and spectacular call to abandon the EGD altogether was issued in March 2020 by the Czech government leader Andrej Babiš, who argued that priority had to be given to fighting the pandemic instead (Sánchez Nicolás, 2020). Similarly, officials from Poland urged the EU to scrap its emission trading scheme or to exempt Poland from the scheme in order to generate additional funds to fight the pandemic (Barteczko, 2020). Such visible resistance to climate neutrality goals did not last long, and by April 2020 the Polish government moved a step closer to commit to the EU's 2050 climate neutrality goal when its environment minister delivered a public statement to that end (Simon, 2020b). The Hungarian and Polish vetoes to the EU budget and recovery fund – which put at risk the funding scheme of the EGD, although motivated by proposed EU measures against democratic backsliding – were overcome by an accommodating deal in the European Council in late December 2020. At the time of writing the four Visegrad countries back the green transition idea, probably also with a view to mobilize the NextGenEU funds. Doubts as to these countries' genuine political commitment to transformative change, however, remain (Zachová et al., 2020).

Besides member state reluctance to commit to green goals there was also significant industry lobbying to suspend, delay or withdraw EGD measures. After a short interrupting effect of the pandemic, businesses soon stepped up lobbying activities to influence the Commission's packed policy agenda (Bayer, 2021). EU policymakers were faced with demands from cross-sectoral alliances as well as powerful industry branches affected by the EGD regulatory agenda (Lazarus, 2020). As early as in March 2020, European car manufacturers joined forces to ask the European Commission to relax CO_2 targets for cars alongside further regulatory relief (ACEA et al., 2020). By April 2020 the umbrella group BusinessEurope requested to delay the EGD agenda in a letter addressed to Commissioner Timmermans, calling to 'extend all non-essential environment and climate-related consultations' as well as 'deadlines to implement EU legislation' for which examples such as the European Climate Law are listed in the letter's Annex (BusinessEurope, 2020). Similarly, the European association of Plastic Converters addressed a letter to the Commission to call for postponed implementation of the Single-Use Plastics Directive, a central legislative piece of the Circular Economy strategy, and to 'lift all bans on some of the single-use plastics items' (EuPC, 2020). All of these calls, however, have been dismissed by the European Commission.

Provisional evidence thus points to a situation where blatant calls for the suspension or removal of environmental regulation proved unsuccessful. Policy-makers have overall successfully engaged in linking the green transition with the economic crisis caused by the Covid-19 pandemic. That said, a significant bulk of the EGD agenda still needs to go through policy formulation and once adopted will be followed by a lengthy and costly process of implementation.

Conclusion

EGD agenda-setting and policy formulation in 2020 has coincided with the outbreak and consequences of the Covid-19 pandemic. Contributing to existing literature on the effects of crisis on the EU's environmental policy (Howarth, 2009; Gravey and Jordan, 2016; Lenschow et al., 2020), the article has analysed the extent to which the EGD agenda has been disrupted (or strengthened) by the Covid-19 crisis. Moreover, it has sought to situate the significance of the EGD with respect to the rich debate about the EU as a global actor, in the realm of climate policy (see also Oberthür and Dupont, 2021) and beyond (see Manners, 2002; Damro, 2012).

The discussion of the major events in 2020 regarding the EGD process has shown that the European Commission was able to put forward its policy proposals practically as planned, and that the European Parliament and most national governments backed the issue linkage between the green transition and the economic recovery from the crisis. The past year has also seen major attempts by some member states and business lobbies to suspend, postpone or even abandon the EGD policy agenda, yet with limited success. Overall, the EGD has proven resilient despite the crisis context, and its proponents have managed to push through its realization. Additional funding generated in the context of economic recovery has even strengthened the EGD rationale and has added a fiscal layer and conditionality to a regulatory policy.

With respect to the role of the EU as a global standard setter the novelty of the Green Deal is that it makes a binding commitment to carbon neutrality and seeks to mainstream climate considerations into a range of policy areas, including the financial sector. The EGD could thus reinforce the 'Brussels effect' (Bradford, 2020) in the realm of global climate and environmental policy. Given that the real challenge will lie in the implementation of the EGD goals (see also Bloomfield and Steward, 2020; Dupont *et al.*, 2020) it is at this stage too early to tell whether the EU can live up to its ambition to lead the global green transition.

Acknowledgements

The article was researched and written during a COFUND-AIAS fellowship (European Union Horizon 2020 Research and Innovation Programme Marie Sklodowska-Curie grant agreement no. 754513 and Aarhus University Research Foundation) awarded by the Aarhus Institute of Advanced Studies (AIAS). I would like to express my gratitude for the helpful comments and guidance provided by the editors of the Annual Review. Moreover, I thank Amber Davis for providing excellent proofreading services (for which financial support by the Johanna Quandt Young Academy at Goethe is gratefully acknowledged), as well as Kamila Duraj and Henry Hempel for their invaluable research assistance.

References

ACEA, CLEPA, ETRma and CECRA (2020) 'Joint Letter to President Ursula von der Leyen', 25 March 2020. https://www.acea.be/uploads/news_documents/COVID19_auto_sector_letter_Von_der_Leyen.pdf

Auer, S. and Scicluna, N. (2021) 'The Impossibility of Constitutionalising Emergency Europe'. *Journal of Common Market Studies*, Vol. 59, this issue.

Barbier, E. (2010) 'How is the Global Green New Deal Going?' *Nature*, Vol. 464, No. 7290, pp. 832–3.

Barteczko, A. (2020) 'EU Should Scrap Emissions Trading Scheme, Polish Official Says'. *Reuters*, 17 March 2020. https://www.reuters.com/article/us-health-coronavirus-poland-ets-idUSKBN2141RC

Bayer, L. (2021) 'Brussels Lobbying Business Picks Up Despite Pandemic'. *Politico*, 10 March 2021. https://www.politico.eu/article/brussels-lobbying-business-picks-up-despite-coronavirus-pandemic

Bloomfield, J. and Steward, F. (2020) 'The Politics of the Green New Deal'. *Political Quarterly*, Vol. 91, No. 4, pp. 770–9.

Bradford, A. (2015) 'Exporting Standards: The Externalization of the EU's Regulatory Power via Markets'. *International Review of Law and Economics*, Vol. 42, pp. 158–73.

Bradford, A. (2020) *The Brussels Effect. How the European Union Rules the World* (Oxford: Oxford University Press).

BusinessEurope (2020) 'Letter of the Director General to Frans Timmermans', 10 April 2020. https://www.businesseurope.eu/sites/buseur/files/media/public_letters/iaco/2020-04-10_businesseurope_letter_environment_and_climate_consultations_and_regulations_-_executive_vp_timmermans.pdf

Damro, C. (2012) 'Market power Europe'. *Journal of European Public Policy*, Vol. 19, No. 5, pp. 682–99.

Dodds, K. (2004) *Global Geopolitics. A Critical Introduction* (London: Routledge).

Dupont, C., Oberthür, S. and von Homeyer, I. (2020) 'The Covid-19 Crisis: A Critical Juncture for EU Climate Policy Development?' *Journal of European Integration*, Vol. 42, No. 8, pp. 1095–110.

EuPC (2020) 'COVID19 – Request for a Recast or Postponement of the Single-Use Plastics Directive', 9 April 2020. https://pieweb.plasteurope.com/members/pdf/p244923b.PDF

European Commission (2000) Communication from the Commission. Europe 2020. A Strategy for Smart, Sustainable and Inclusive Growth. COM (2010) 2020 (Brussels: European Commission).

European Commission (2018) Communication from the Commission to the European Parliament, the European Coucil, the Council, the European Economic and Social Committee and the Committee of the Regions. Action Plan: Financing Sustainable Growth. COM (2018) 97 final (Brussels: European Commission).

European Commission (2019) Communication from the Commission to the European Parliament, the European Coucil, the Council, the European Economic and Social Committee and the Committee of the Regions. The European Green Deal. COM (2019) 640 final (Brussels: European Commission).

European Commission (2020a) Communication from the Commission to the European Parliament, the European Council, the Council, the European Economic and Social Committee and the Committee of the Regions. Sustainable Europe Investment Plan. European Green Deal Investment Plan. COM (2020) 21 final (Brussels: European Commission).

European Commission (2020b) Communication from the Commission to the European Parliament, the Council, the European Economic and Social Committee and the Committee of the Regions. EU Biodiversity Strategy for 2030. Bringing nature back into our lives. COM (2020) 380 final (Brussels: European Commission).

European Commission (2020c) 'Making Europe's Businesses Future-Ready: A New Industrial Strategy for a Globally Competitive, Green and Digital Europe', 10 March 2020. https://ec.europa.eu/commission/presscorner/detail/en/ip_20_416

European Commission (2020d) 'Proposal for a Regulation of the European Parliament and of the Council Establishing the Framework for Achieving Climate Neutrality and Amending Regulation (EU) 2018/1999 (European Climate Law) COM (2020) 80 final', 4 March 2020.

European Council (2021) 'A Recovery Plan for Europe'. Available at https://www.consilium.europa.eu/en/policies/eu-recovery-plan

European Parliament (2020) *Resolution of 17 April 2020 on the Climate and Environment Emergency* (Brussels: European Parliament).

Gravey, V. and Jordan, A. (2016) 'Does the European Union Have a Reverse Gear? Policy Dismantling in a Hyperconsensual Polity'. *Journal of European Public Policy*, Vol. 23, No. 8, pp. 1180–98.

Gravey, V. and Jordan, A.J. (2020) 'Policy Dismantling at EU Level: Reaching the Limits of "an Ever-Closer Ecological Union"?' *Public Administration*, Vol. 98, No. 2, pp. 349–62.

Grossman, E. and Leblond, P. (2011) 'European Financial Integration: Finally the Great Leap Forward?' *Journal of Common Market Studies*, Vol. 49, No. 2, pp. 413–35.

Howarth, D. (2009) 'Greening the Internal Market in a Difficult Economic Climate'. *Journal of Common Market Studies*, Vol. 47, No. S1, pp. 133–50.

IPCC (2018) Global Warming of 1.5°C. An IPCC Special Report on the Impacts of Global Warming of 1.5°C Above Pre-industrial Levels and Related Global Greenhouse Gas Emission Pathways (Geneva: United Nations International Panel on Climate Change).

Knill, C. and Liefferink, D. (2013) 'The Establishment of EU Environmental Policy'. In Jordan, A. and Adelle, C. (eds) *Environmental Policy in the EU: Actors, Institutions and Processes* (London: Routledge), pp. 13–29.

Lazarus, A. (2020) '5 Ways Opportunistic Lobbyists are Using Coronavirus to Attack EU Environmental Law'. European Environmental Bureau, 16 April 2020. https://meta.eeb.org/2020/04/16/5-ways-opportunistic-lobbyists-are-using-coronavirus-to-attack-eu-environmental-laws

Lenschow, A. (2020) 'Environmental Policy. Contending Dynamics of Policy Change'. In Wallace, H., Pollack, M.A. and Young, A.R. (eds) *Policy-Making in the European Union* (Oxford: Oxford University Press), pp. 297–320.

Lenschow, A., Burns, C. and Zito, A. (2020) 'Dismantling, Disintegration or Continuing Stealthy Integration in European Union Environmental Policy?' *Public Administration*, Vol. 98, No. 2, pp. 340–8.

Luke, T.W. (2009) 'A Green New Deal: Why Green, How New, and What is the Deal?' *Critical Policy Studies*, Vol. 3, No. 1, pp. 14–28.

Manners, I. (2002) 'Normative Power Europe: A Contradiction in Terms?' *Journal of Common Market Studies*, Vol. 40, No. 2, pp. 235–58.

Meunier, S. and Nicolaidis, K. (2019) 'The Geopoliticization of European Trade and Investment Policy'. *Journal of Common Market Studies*, Vol. 57, No. S1, pp. 103–13.

Monnet, J. (1978) *Memoirs* (London: Doubleday).

Niemann, A. and Zaun, N. (2018) 'EU Refugee Policies and Politics in Times of Crisis: Theoretical and Empirical Perspectives'. *Journal of Common Market Studies*, Vol. 56, No. 1, pp. 3–22.

Oberthür, S. and Dupont, C. (2021) 'The European Union's International Climate Leadership: Towards a Grand Climate Strategy?' *Journal of European Public Policy*, Vol. 28, No. 7, pp. 1095–114.

Oberthür, S. and Groen, L. (2017) 'Explaining Goal Achievement in International Negotiations: The EU and the Paris Agreement on Climate Change'. *Journal of European Public Policy*, Vol. 25, No. 5, pp. 708–27.

Pettifor, A. (2020) *The Case for the Green New Deal* (London: Verso Books).

Rankin, J. (2019) 'European Green Deal to Press Ahead Despite Polish Targets Opt-Out'. *The Guardian*, 13 December 2019.

Sánchez Nicolás, E. (2020) 'Will Coronavirus Torpedo the Green Deal?'. *EU Observer*, 20 March 2020. https://euobserver.com/coronavirus/147815

Schimmelfennig, F. (2018) 'European Integration (Theory) in Times of Crisis. A Comparison of the Euro and Schengen Crises'. *Journal of European Public Policy*, Vol. 25, No. 7, pp. 969–89.

Simon, F. (2020a) 'EU Leaders Back "green transition" in Pandemic Recovery Plan'. *Euractiv*, 27 March 2021. https://www.euractiv.com/section/energy-environment/news/eu-leaders-back-green-transition-in-pandemic-recovery-plan

Simon, F. (2020b) 'Warsaw Says 'Committed' to EU's Climate Neutrality Goal'. *Euractiv*, 9 November 2020. https://www.euractiv.com/section/energy-environment/news/warsaw-says-committed-to-eus-climate-neutrality-goal

Vogel, D. (1997) *Trading Up. Consumer and Environmental Regulation in a Global Economy* (Cambridge, MA: Harvard University Press).

von der Leyen, U. (2019a) 'Presentation of the European Green Deal', 11 December 2019. https://ec.europa.eu/info/strategy/priorities-2019-2024/european-green-deal_en

von der Leyen, U. (2019b) 'Press Remarks by President von der Leyen on the Occasion of the Adoption of the European Green Deal Communication', 11 December 2019. https://ec.europa.eu/commission/presscorner/detail/en/speech 19_6749

von der Leyen, U. (2019c) 'Speech in the European Parliament Plenary Session. Ursula von der Leyen. President-elect of the European Commission', 27 November 2019.

Zachová, A., Wolska, A., Hudec, M. and Szicherle, P. (2020) 'Green Recovery after COVID-19: Last Chance for V4 to Climate Transition?' *Euractiv*, 27 November 2020. https://www.euractiv.com/section/climate-environment/news/green-recovery-after-covid-19-last-chance-for-v4-to-climate-transition

JCMS 2021 Volume 59. Annual Review. pp. 92–102   DOI: 10.1111/jcms.13258

Immigration, Refugees and Responses

JANE FREEDMAN
Université Paris 8, Paris

Introduction

In 2020, the situation of refugees arriving, or attempting to arrive, in the EU was often largely overshadowed by the wider Covid-19 pandemic. However, reform of EU migration policies and the attempt to arrive at a consensus on these issues amongst Member States remained a priority for the European Commission who on 23 September 2020 presented its New Pact on Migration and Asylum (European Commission, 2020a). Whilst the New Pact was promoted by the Commission as a foundation for a 'predictable and reliable' (European Commission, 2020b) migration management system, it did not overcome the pre-existing divisions on these issues. As a matter of fact, it can be seen as a move to strengthen cooperation only in those areas on which there is already broad agreement amongst Member States (namely tightening border controls, increasing returns, and further cooperation with Third Countries), whilst failing to find a consensus on the issue of greater intra-European solidarity with regard to 'burden sharing' in refugee reception. At both national and European levels, the Covid-19 pandemic was used to justify further tightening of border controls, through the representation of refugee arrivals as a health 'threat'. In many cases this supposed threat and the associated state of emergency introduced at national levels allowed States to sidestep international and European law for the protection of the human rights of refugees. This notion that refugees were a threat to European health compounded established securitizing discourse that construct refugee flows as a 'crisis' and a threat to European security. However, the various measures of border control and lockdown taken both by individual Member States and by the EU as a whole did not reduce the 'threat' of Covid-19 to EU populations, and only served to reinforce the insecurities faced by the refugees themselves, both in their journeys to Europe, and on arrival. In this article I will discuss the various measures taken to control migration and to restrict the movements of refugees in Europe, and the impacts that this has had on the refugees themselves, adopting an intersectional gender perspective to understand the specific impacts on women, for example. I will then go on to discuss the new Pact on Migration and its probable implications for the future of refugee protection in Europe.

I. Continuing Refugee Arrivals

The Covid-19 pandemic provided further justification at both at national and EU level for increasing border controls and closures, thus increasing difficulties for refugees aiming to reach the EU. A general closure of the EU's borders to Third Country Nationals was accompanied by various national level measures which rendered journeys to the EU even more complex and dangerous. However, despite this, the arrival of refugees via the various Mediterranean land and sea routes continued with the UNHCR estimating that 95,031 refugees arrived in Italy, Spain, Greece, Cyprus and Malta in 2020 (UNHCR, 2020). Although a decrease on previous years, this is still a significant number of arrivals, considering the major barriers created by Covid-19 related restrictions. 1401 refugees are estimated to have died in their attempt to reach the EU (UNHCR, 2020), although again it is important to note that this figure probably underestimates the number of deaths and does not take into consideration the many refugees who die crossing the Sahara or whilst in Libya. The majority of the refugees arriving on these routes are men, but there are also increasingly many women attempting the journey. NGOs working with refugees have noted a specific increase in women migrating alone, or alone with their children. Single women may be particularly at risk of sexual and gender-based forms of violence on these migration routes (Freedman, 2016) and are amongst those groups who are often singled out as 'vulnerable' both within EU policy frameworks and by NGOs working in the field (Freedman, 2019). Whilst the frequency of SGBV and the publicization of this through various media and NGOs reports has made this a widely acknowledged risk for this migrant population, the public discourses on protection of these 'vulnerable' populations are generally trumped in reality by the desire to control migration and to limit the number of those who are arrive in Europe, or who are granted asylum once they do arrive.

II. Border Closures and Pushbacks: Making Journeys Increasingly Insecure

As noted above, the Covid-19 pandemic provided justification for the closure of national and European borders, thus reinforcing a trend towards border closure and restriction which had already been accelerated since the so-called European refugee 'crisis' from 2015 onwards in what Kriesi et al. (2021) describe as a process of rebordering as 'defensive integration'. On 17 March 2020 the EU Schengen border was closed to non-residents (Ní Ghráinne, 2020; Ramji-Nogales and Goldner-Lang, 2020). Moreover, individual Member States also began to introduce their own border restrictions so that by July 2020, seventeen States had re-introduced controls on their intra-Schengen borders (European Commission, 2020c). The pandemic thus led to a real infringement on the free movement which has been a core part of EU integration. Whilst the Schengen Border Code does not include any previsions for closing intra-Schengen borders as a public health measure, these individual decisions were accepted by the Commission on the grounds that the risk posed by Covid-19 could be equated to an internal security threat (Ramji-Nogales and Goldner-Lang, 2020; European Commission, 2020d). The 'threat' of refugees spreading Covid-19 which underlay the decisions to close borders was clearly articulated by some leaders. For instance, in March 2020 Viktor Orbán justified the transfer of refugees into Hungary's transit zones (rather than letting them enter the territory directly) by claiming and clear link between Covid-19 and 'illegal migration' (Hungary Today, 2020).

The Covid-19 crisis was in fact an opportunity for the EU to further securitize asylum and migration policies, using the supposed 'risk' of migrants and refugees 'importing' Covid-19 into Europe to justify new border closures and restrictions. But the results of this increased securitization of migration were in fact to increase various insecurities both for EU populations and for the migrants and refugees attempting to enter Europe. As UNHCR argues (UNHCR and IOM, 2020):

> In the absence of protection-sensitive border management which would enable regular means to enter at the borders of States – subject to health checks and quarantine where needed – migrants, asylum seekers and refugees might be forced to resort to irregular and often dangerous movements to access assistance and international protection, often facilitated by smugglers, which increases the risk of human trafficking, exploitation and abuse.

These border securitization measures can thus be seen as counterproductive in that they increase insecurities and risks on the one hand for migrants and refugees who are forced to resort to more dangerous and more expensive routes, and are increasingly dependent on smugglers and traffickers. And on the other hand these measures also increased health risks of Covid-19 spreading as in their attempts to avoid border checks, these migrants and refugees also avoided any kind of Covid-19 testing or quarantine measures that Member States had put in place. As such they can be understood as another step in what Andersson (2016) labels as the EU's 'failed fight' against migration. Ultimately, by using the ongoing public health crisis to justify further securitizing migration, Member States thus increased both the insecurity of migrants and refugees and of European populations who they were claiming to protect.

Border closures resulting in the inability of a refugee to gain access to a country in order to claim asylum therefore can be seen to be in contradiction of the 1951 Refugee Convention of which all EU Member States are signatories. The European Commission did issue a recommendation that border closures should contain an exemption for those who had an essential need to travel, including those people who had an essential need to cross borders in order to claim international protection as refugees (Marin, 2020). However, many States seemed to ignore this recommendation and several reports point to an increase in refoulement of refugees by various EU Member States. These included mass 'pushbacks' at the Greek-Turkish border which followed an announcement by the Turkish government on 28 February 2020 that it would open its land border with Greece and freely allow (even encourage) refugees to cross (Cortinovis, 2021). Turkey was reported to be facilitating this movement by providing free buses for refugees to arrive at the Evros border and encouraging them to walk towards the Evros River (Cortinovis, 2021). Officially the Turkish government justified this decision on humanitarian grounds with reference to the difficult living conditions in refugee camps in Turkey due to new arrivals from Idlib in Syria, however it can be seen as a political move to put pressure on the EU and to highlight the EU's failure to live up to its commitments under the EU-Turkey Statement of March 2016 (Border Violence Monitoring Network, 2020). As the refugees attempted to cross the border, Greece deployed large numbers of police and armed forces and engaged in what many NGOs and human rights organizations decried as indiscriminate violence to push them back to Turkey (Human Rights Watch, 2020). Some accused Greece of using the new 'crisis' at the borders to openly break its own asylum laws (Souli, 2020). The EU was in turn criticised in turn for its failure to condemn the violence of the Greek reaction, and indeed its support for Greece in its role as a 'protector' or 'shield' of the EU borders (Cortinovis, 2021).

The pandemic was also used to justify further restrictive measures over sea arrivals, both by Greece and other Mediterranean countries, and a scaling down even further of European search and rescue operations in the Mediterranean. As Müller and Slominski (2020) argue, since the 2012 Hirsi judgement of the ECtHR, EU States have been increasingly 'orchestrating' intermediaries in the Central Mediterranean to reduce their involvement in rescuing refugees without breaking the law. The circumstances of Covid-19 have given States an excuse to further reduce their involvement in search and rescue and to go further towards direct refoulement of refugees, invoking health risks to deny disembarkation to boats carrying rescued refugees. Italy, Malta and Cyprus all cited Covid-19 related health risks to justify closing their ports to nearly all boats, including those boats which were carrying refugees rescued at sea. The Italian government declared that its ports were 'unsafe' for the disembarkation of refugees who had been rescued at sea during the duration of the Covid-19 public health crisis (Carrera and Luk, 2020). Malta even resorted to using private boats to detain refugees at sea or to return them directly to Libya (Ghezelbash and Tan, 2020: Kingsley, 2020). The closure of ports led to incidences of refugees being stranded on boats at sea for long periods, provoking death in various cases (Tazzioli and Stierl, 2021) or being returned to countries on the other side of the Mediterranean. Disembarkations in Libya increased by 60 per cent in the first five months of 2020 compared with the same period in 2019, despite the deteriorating political situation and IOM's call to suspend the return of refugees to the country (Schöfberger and Rango, 2020). At the same time, NGO search and rescue operations in the Mediterranean were completely suspended from April to June 2020, again increasing the dangers of the crossing. The Covid-19 pandemic and states of emergency thus allowed EU Member States to sidestep their obligations under international and European law. By proclaiming that their ports were 'not safe' because of the health risks of Covid-19, for example, they could carry out refoulements without breaking international law which requires States to disembark people rescued at sea where they are safe (Keller *et al.*, 2020).

III. Lockdowns and Quarantine: Differential Treatment for Refugees

The lockdowns imposed in most EU countries as an attempt to control the spread of Covid-19 had specific impacts on many refugees, exacerbating the forms of structural violence and discrimination to which they had been exposed during pre-Covid times, exposing them to direct health risks, and also restricting their access to support, especially from various NGOs and civil society organizations who were forced to suspend or massively scale back their activities during lockdown. For those refugees living in informal camps or squats in other locations throughout Europe, the Covid-19 lockdowns also brought serious deteriorations in living conditions and exacerbation of the conditions of structural violence and neglect in which they had been living (Davies *et al.*, 2017).

Many refugee camps and accommodation centres were subjected to strict quarantine measures during the Covid-19 pandemic, often with restrictions that were harsher than those for the general population in each country. In these camps and centres, overcrowding and communal living conditions made it impossible to comply with social distancing or other hygiene measures that were widely adopted to control the spread of Covid-19. Limited access to running water and washing facilities, for example, make regular handwashing difficult, and refugees are often forced to share cooking and living facilities with other people from outside of their family groups thus making it impossible to limit social contacts. In some of the Greek islands hostpots, for example, it was reported in April 2020 that there was one shower for every 500 people and one toilet for every 160 people (Greek Council for Refugees and Oxfam, 2020). Refugees within these camps were thus exposed to increased risk of contracting and spreading Covid-19, all the while access to medical resources remained scarce. When the Covid pandemic reached Greece, the government closed off the camps. Residents were prohibited from leaving except to buy necessities at the local shops, informal schools inside the camps were closed and non-essential visitors were forbidden from accessing the camps, thus restricting the activities of many NGOs. The Moria Camp fire in September 2020 illustrate the dire conditions that refugees have been subjected to. The destruction of the camp by the fire did not lead to the rehousing of refugees in better conditions. In fact, reported conditions in the temporary camps that were put in place to replace Moria were reportedly even worse (Ozguc, 2021).

In Italy the policy of confining refugees for their own 'protection' during the pandemic resulted in the installation of quarantine ships in which all those arriving by boat were immediately detained. Some refugees from mainland reception centres were also transferred to these ships, even some of those who had tested positive for Covid-19, revealing that the logic of 'confining to protect' (Tazzioli, 2020) was primarily concerned with the protection of European populations and neglected the health and well-being of refugees themselves. Similar measures of forced confinement of refugee populations occurred in other EU States with Cyprus, for example, forcing refugees living in independent accommodation to move into the Pournara camp where they were held in lockdown even after national restrictions were eased (Bennett, 2020).

In France, NGOs working with migrants and refugees sent an open letter to the government, denouncing the conditions of refugees in informal camps in the Calais region and in and around Paris. They called for urgent measures to provide shelter, access to water and hygiene facilities, and mobile medical services for refugees living in these camps. But although the Mayor of Paris did open up some extra places in gymnasiums and other communal spaces to provide temporary accommodation to refugees during the Covid lockdowns, these places were clearly insufficient to meet the needs of all those who had been sleeping in informal camps in the city. In Calais, on the contrary, no special services were opened for refugees, and their situation worsened as places where they had been able to go to wash or get food during the day were closed down. This means that they were left with access to one water point, nowhere to charge their telephones, and very little information or access to medical help (Secours Catholique, 2020).

Along with lockdowns and quarantines of refugee camps and 'hotspots', many EU States temporarily suspended all asylum procedures during the first wave of the Covid-19 pandemic (FRA, 2020). The UNHCR argued that these suspensions in addition to the border closures put in place were putting the 'core principles' of international refugee protection to the test (Meer *et al.*, 2021). This suspension created an additional source of insecurity for asylum seekers. The time of waiting for a decision on an asylum application is a time of constant stress and uncertainty, a limbo in which the violence of the refugee regime reveals itself through 'chronic waiting', a waiting which can be understood as a disciplining mechanism to control 'unwanted' mobilities (Chattopadhyay and Tyner, 2020). Further, the suspension of normal asylum procedures included a suspension of the processes which were in place to identify 'vulnerable' refugees and offer them specific protections. This contributed to the increasing risks of gender-based violence and further limited support for survivors of violence.

IV. Vulnerability and Violence

Lockdown and confinement measures increased situations of violence and insecurity for refugees but did not affect all equally. In what was named by UN Women as a 'shadow pandemic' (UN Women, 2020), there was a general increase in gender-based violence, and specifically intimate partner violence during Covid-19 lockdowns, with women confined with violent partners, and in many cases unable to leave and seek support. This was also the case for refugee populations. As has previously been shown, refugees are at increased risk of sexual and gender-based violence at all stages of their migratory journey (Freedman, 2016) and these structural vulnerabilities have been exacerbated by the Covid-19 pandemic and subsequent lockdown measures.

The reduced registration procedures and suspension of many refugee support services across Europe meant that many 'vulnerable' refugees including those who have suffered from sexual and gender-based forms of violence were left without any specialist services (Erskine, 2020). Under EU regulations, refugees' reception and registration procedures should include a vulnerability assessment to ensure that those who are in situation of particular vulnerability and risk should gain special support. The integration of vulnerability as a central concept in international and European asylum procedures has been criticised for the ways in which is considered in an essentialised manner, categorizing certain groups as 'naturally' vulnerable. And there have also been criticisms of the ways in which vulnerability assessments have been carried out, with insufficient means to ensure that the complex and often hidden situations of vulnerability are identified (Freedman, 2019). The suspension of asylum procedures during Covid-19 meant in many cases also a suspension of the identification procedures for vulnerable refugees, leaving these people, including victims of violence without increased protection.

There were also reports of increased incidents of gender-based violence whilst refugee reception centres and camps were facing lockdowns. For example, reports show that during the lockdown in the Moria camp on Lesvos, incidences of sexual assault and violence against women increased (Pallister-Wilkins et al., 2020). At the same time, services available to refugees were restricted. For refugees in the Moria camp, for example, external referrals to psychological and psycho-social support services became unavailable, as the NGOs which had been providing these services prior to the pandemic were forced to suspend their operations (Pallister-Wilkins et al., 2020). A report by the Diotima NGO which focuses on SGBV reported that survivors of GBV remained trapped on Lesvos and have extremely limited protection which has been further limited by the Covid-19 restrictions. They give an example of a case where a woman from the camp wished to report domestic violence to the police but was prevented from doing so because 'this was not considered a sufficient reason for travel' (DIOTIMA, 2020).

V. The New Pact on Migration and Asylum

The securitization of migration and attempts to block refugee arrivals during the Covid-19 pandemic was not a new phenomenon but a continuation of ongoing trends in EU migration and refugee policies. This trend continued with the publication of the New Pact on Migration and Asylum in September 2020. The Pact was heralded by some as a new beginning for EU asylum and immigration policies (Dimitriadi, 2020) following the failure of the previous EU Commission to reach agreement on the reform of the Common European Asylum System (CEAS) or the Dublin Regulation. But the failure to oppose further securitization and to agree on any measures which would permit more inclusive measures for refugees, has led to a Pact which emphasises the need for border control, and which plans for accelerated decision-making on whether an individual has the right to enter EU territory at external border points, and expedited return procedures for those who are not deemed eligible to enter the EU (Carrera, 2021). Several researchers have underlined the fact that this New Pact should in fact be viewed overall as a pragmatic solution to the almost impossible task of agreeing on reform and of a status quo which 'has been locked in for decades' (Hadj-Abdou, 2021). The Dublin Regulation is symptomatic of this. It is worth reiterating her ethat it has been a long-standing point of contention, placing as it does the responsibility for treating asylum claims on the first country of entry, and thus largely on countries such as Italy and Greece. The New Pact promises to replace the Dublin Regulation. However, although in theory Dublin is gone, its main principle remains and responsibility for processing asylum claims remains with the first country of entry, even though various other criteria, such as the existence of close family networks in other countries within the EU, should be taken into account. Further, the Commission has abandoned the seemingly futile quest to get all Member States including the Visegrád countries, to agree to obligatory relocation quotas for refugees, and has instead introduced the idea of solidarity measures whereby instead of agreeing to accept relocated refugees, a Member State can 'sponsor' a refugee return, or 'help' receiving states with expertise or practical help such as the organization of reception centres. The mechanisms of how these solidarity measures would actually be put into practice remain fuzzy, and it can be argued that the Visegrád group have succeeded in 'cross-loading' their policy preferences (Aggestam and Bicchi, 2019), and that the attainment of any real and meaningful forms of solidarity in refugee reception in the EU is thus further away than ever. Instead, the security agenda within migration and refugee policy is further strengthened with proposals for compulsory screening of all asylum seekers at the external borders of the EU, strengthening of the Eurodac database, and quicker and more efficient returns of all those whose asylum applications are likely to be unsuccessful through accelerated procedures and new agreements with Third Countries. The organization of these would be reinforced by the creation of a new post of European coordinator for returns under the aegis of Frontex (Bloj and Buzmaniuk, 2020).

Conclusions

As the Covid-19 pandemic hit Europe, many proclaimed it as a 'great leveller', impacting all layers and categories of society. But it was quickly shown that the contrary was in fact true and that Covid-19 and the subsequent measures put in place to contain the pandemic had far worse impacts on those who were already marginalised in society through the intersection of racialised and gendered structures of inequality and violence, including refugees (Crawley, 2021). There were some glimpses of hope for improvement in the conditions for refugee reception, such as Portugal's decision to grant full citizenship rights to all migrant and refugees for the duration of the pandemic in order to ensure that they could freely access healthcare, testing and vaccination, or the Spanish government's decision to release detainees from migrant detention centres where they were at risk of catching Covid-19 (Libal *et al.*, 2021), and these policies showed that there are other less securitized means of promoting health without marginalising migrant and refugee populations. However, these types of decisions unfortunately remained the exception as most EU States used the pandemic to justify tightening border controls and exclusionary measures aimed at refugees. From both a public health and a human rights approach, there are strong arguments to suggest that the securitized management of migration adopted by the EU was both ineffective in containing infection and damaging to the human rights and well-being of migrants and refugees. And it seems that the precedents set during the Covid-19 pandemic are set to continue with the implementation of the New Pact on Migration, which can be seen as a 'pragmatic' solution to the realities of Member States policy priorities on migration, but at the same time promises a continuing exclusion and marginalisation of refugees, and a diminishing respect for migrant and refugee rights in Europe.

References

Aggestam, L. and Bicchi, F. (2019) 'New Directions in EU Foreign Policy Governance: Crossloading, Leadership and Informal Groupings'. *Journal of Common Market Studies*, Vol. 57, pp. 515–32.

Andersson, R. (2016) 'Europe's Failed 'Fight' Against Irregular Migration: Ethnographic Notes on a Counterproductive Industry'. *Journal of Ethnic and Migration Studies*, Vol. 42, No. 7, pp. 1055–75.

Bennett, C. (2020) 'Migrants Forced to Stay in Cyprus Camp Despite Easing of Covid-19 Lockdown'. France 24, 26th May. Available at: https://observers.france24.com/en/20200526-cyprus-migrants-camp-pournara-covid-19

Bloj, R. & Buzmaniuk, S. (2020) 'Understanding the New Pact on Migration and Asylum'. European Issues No. 577, Fondation Robert Schuman.

Border Violence Monitoring Network (2020) 'Border Violence Monitoring Reports'. Available at: https://www.borderviolence.eu/violence-reports/

Carrera, S. (2021) 'Whose Pact? The Cognitive Dimensions of the EU Pact on Migration and Asylum'. CEPS No. 2020-22.

Carrera, S. and Luk, N. C. (2020) 'In the Name of COVID-19: An Assessment of the Schengen Internal Border Controls and Travel Restrictions in the EU'. Policy Department for Citizens' Rights and Constitutional Affairs, Directorate-General for Internal Policies, PE.

Chattopadhyay, S. and Tyner, J.A. (2020) 'Lives in Waiting'. *Geopolitics*, pp. 1–26. https://doi.org/10.1080/14650045.2020.1819247

Cortinovis, R. (2021) Pushbacks and lack of accountability at the Greek-Turkish borders. CEPS Paper in Liberty and Security in Europe, (2021-01).

Crawley, H. (2021) 'The Politics of Refugee Protection in a (Post)COVID-19 World'. *Social Sciences*, Vol. 10, No. 3, p. 81. https://doi.org/10.3390/socsci10030081

Davies, T., Isakjee, A. and Dhesi, S. (2017) 'Violent Inaction: The Necropolitical Experience of Refugees in Europe'. *Antipode*, Vol. 49, No. 5, pp. 1263–84.

Dimitriadi, A. (2020) 'Looking for a bridge over troubled waters: The forthcoming New Pact on Migration and Asylum'. ELIAMEP| Policy Brief.

DIOTIMA (2020) Unprotected Victims of Domestic Violence in Moria. Available in Greek at: https://diotima.org.gr/deltio-typoy-aprostateyta-ta-thimata-endooikogeneiakis-vias-sth-moria/ (Accessed 18 March 2021).

Erskine, D. (2020) 'Double Jeopardy: The European Refugee and Migrant Crisis and COVID-19: Insights into the Emerging Impacts on Women and Girls'. GBV AoR Help Desk. Available at: https://gbvguidelines.org/en/documents/double-jeopardy-the-european-refugee-and-migrant-crisis-and-covid-19-insights-into-the-emerging-impacts-on-women-and-girls/. Accessed 5 April 2021.

European Commission (2020a) Communication from the European Commission to the European Parliament, the Council, the European Economic and Social Committee and the Committee of the Regions on a New Pact on Migration and Asylum COM/2020/609 final.

European Commission (2020b) Statement by President Von der Leyen on the New Pact on Migration and Asylum, 23 September 2020, Available at: https://ec.europa.eu/commission/presscorner/detail/en/statement_20_1727. Accessed 15 March 2021.

European Commission (2020c) Member States'Notifications of the Temporary Reintroduction of BorderControl at Internal Borders Pursuant to Article 25 and 28 et seq. of the Schengen Borders Code. Available at: https://ec.europa.eu/home-affairs/sites/homeaffairs/files/what-we-do/policies/borders-and-visas/schen-gen/reintroduction-border-control/docs/ms_notifications_-_reintroduction_of_border_control_en.pdf

European Commission (2020d) COVID-19 Guidelines for border management measures to protect health and ensure the availability of goods and essential services, C(2020) 1753 final, 16.3.2020.

European Union Agency for Fundamental Rights (FRA) (2020) 'Coronavirus Pandemic in the EU-Fundamental Rights Implications, Bulletin No.2'. Available at: https://fra.europa.eu/sites/default/files/fra_uploads/fra-2020-coronavirus-pandemic-eu-bulletin-may_en.pdf

Freedman, J. (2016) 'Engendering Security at the Borders of Europe: Women Migrants and the Mediterranean "Crisis"'. *Journal of Refugee Studies*, Vol. 29, No. 4, pp. 568–82.

Freedman, J. (2019) 'The Uses and Abuses of "vulnerability" in EU Asylum and Refugee Protection: Protecting Women or Reducing Autonomy?' *Papeles del CEIC, International Journal on Collective Identity Research*, Vol. 2019, No. 3, p. 204.

Ghezelbash, D. and Tan, N.F. (2020) *The End of the Right to Seek Asylum?: COVID-19 and the Future of Refugee Protection*'. EUI RSCAS, 2020/55, Migration Policy Centre (Florence: European University Institute).

Greek Council for Refugees and Oxfam (2020) 'Lesbos COVID-19 Briefing: Update on the EU "Hotspot" Moria by the Greek Council for Refugees and Oxfam'. Available at: https://www.gcr.gr/en/news/press-releases-announcements/item/1420-oxfam-gcr-briefing-for-lesvos-amidst-the-coronavirus. Accessed 2 April 2021.

Hadj-Abdou, L. (2021) 'From the Migration Crisis to the New Pact on Migration and Asylum: The Status Quo Problem'. BRIDGE Network Working Paper No. 11.

Human Rights Watch (2020) 'Greece: Violence Against Asylum Seekers at Border Detained, Assaulted, Stripped, Summarily Deported'. Available at: https://www.hrw.org/news/2020/03/17/greece-violence-against-asylum-seekers-border. Accessed 2 April 2021.

Hungary Today. (2020) 'Orban to EU Counterparts: Clear Link between Coronavirus and Illegal Migration'. Available: https://hungarytoday.hu/orban-to-eu-counterparts-clear-link-between-coronavirus-and-illegal-migration/. Accessed 5 April 2020.

Keller, V. M., Schöler, F. and Goldoni, M. (2020) 'Not a Safe Place? Italy's Decision to Declare Its Ports Unsafe under International Maritime Law'. Verfassungsblog on Matters Constitutional. https://verfassungsblog.de/not-a-safe-place/

Kingsley, P. (2020) 'Latest Tactic to Push Migrants from Europe? A Private, Clandestine Fleet'. *New York Times*, 30 April 2020. https://www-nytimes-com.acces-distant.sciencespo.fr/2020/04/30/world/europe/migrants-malta.html. Accessed 8 April 2021.

Kriesi, H., Altiparmakis, A , Bojar, A. and Oana, I.E. (2021) 'Debordering and Re-bordering in the Refugee Crisis: A Case of "Defensive Integration"'. *Journal of European Public Policy*, Vol. 28, No. 3, pp. 331–49.

Libal, K., Harding, S., Popescu, M., Berthold, S.M. and Felten, G. (2021) 'Human Rights of Forced Migrants During the COVID-19 Pandemic: An Opportunity for Mobilization and Solidarity'. *Journal of Human Rights and Social Work*, Vol. 6, pp. 148–60. https://doi.org/10.1007/s41134-021-00162-4

Marin, L. (2020) 'The COVID-19 Crisis and the Closure of External Borders: Another Stress-Test for the Challenging Construction of Solidarity within the EU?' European Papers, European Forum, Insight. October 28, pp. 1–16.

Meer, N., Hill, E., Peace, T. and Villegas, L. (2021) 'Rethinking refuge in the time of COVID-19'. *Ethnic and Racial Studies*, Vol. 44, No. 5, pp. 864–76.

Müller, P. and Slominski, P. (2020) 'Breaking the Legal Link but not the Law? The Externalization of EU Migration Control through Orchestration in the Central Mediterranean'. *Journal of European Public Policy*, Vol. 28, No. 6, pp. 801–20.

Ní Ghráinne, B. (2020) 'Covid-19, Border Closures, and International Law'. Available at SSRN: https://ssrn.com/abstract=3662218 (Accessed 22 March 2021).

Ozguc, U. (2021) 'Three Lines of Pandemic Borders: From Necropolitics to Hope as a Method of Living'. *Critical Studies on Security*, pp. 1–4. https://doi.org/10.1080/21624887.2021.1904361

Pallister-Wilkins, P., Anastasiadou, A. and Papataxiarchis, E. (2020) 'Protection in Lesvos during Covid-19: A crucial failure'. ADMIGOV Interim Report (deliverable 4.1), Mytilene: University of the Aegean. Available at http://admigov.eu

Ramji-Nogales, J. and Goldner-Lang, I. (2020) 'Freedom of Movement, Migration, and Borders'. *Journal of Human Rights*, Vol. 19, No. 5, pp. 593–602.

Schöfberger, I. and Rango, M. (2020) *COVID-19 and Migration in West and North Africa and across the Mediterranean* (Geneva: IOM).

Secours Catholique (2020) Calais: « Avec la crise du Covid-19, la situation des personnes exilées a empiré ». https://www.secours-catholique.org/actualites/calais-avec-la-crise-du-covid-19-la-situation-des-personnes-exilees-a-empire. Accessed 4 April 2021.

Souli, S. (2020) 'Greece's "New Tactic" of Migrant Expulsion from Deep Inside its Land Borders'. *The New Humanitarian*, 7 October 2020.

Tazzioli, M. (2020) 'Confine to Protect: Greek Hotspots and the Hygienic-sanitary Borders of Covid-19'. Border Criminologies Blog. https://www.law.ox.ac.uk/research-subject-groups/centre-criminology/centreborder-criminologies/blog/2020/09/confine-protect. Accessed 4 April 2021.

Tazzioli, M. and Stierl, M. (2021) 'Europe's Unsafe Environment: Migrant Confinement under Covid-19'. *Critical Studies on Security*, pp. 1–5. https://doi.org/10.1080/21624887.2021.1904365

UN Women (2020) 'Violence against Women and Girls: The Shadow Pandemic'. April 2020. Available at: https://www.unwomen.org/en/news/stories/2020/4/statement-ed-phumzile-violence-against-women-during-pandemic. Accessed 5 April 2021.

UNHCR (2020) 'On this Journey, No One Cares If You Live or Die. Abuse, Protection, and Justice along Routes between East and West Africa and Africa's Mediterranean Coast'. Available at: https://www.unhcr.org/5f2129fb4. Accessed 18 March 2021.

UNHCR and IOM (2020) 'COVID-19: Access Challenges and the Implications of Border Restrictions'. 9 May 2020. Available at: https://reliefweb.int/report/world/covid-19-access-challenges-and-implications-border-restrictions. Accessed 22 March 2021.

JCMS 2021 Volume 59. Annual Review. pp. 103–114   DOI: 10.1111/jcms.13275

Towards a Reading of Black Lives Matter in Europe

JEAN BEAMAN
University of California, Santa Barbara, USA

Introduction

In June 2020, the Parliament of the European Union voted to proclaim 'Black Lives Matter', a statement that also included how it 'strongly condemns the appalling death of George Floyd'.[1] This was a few weeks after Derek Chauvin, a white police officer in Minneapolis, killed George Floyd, a 46 year-old Black American man, by putting his knee on the Floyd's neck until he was no longer breathing. Darnella Frazier, a 17 year-old Black American woman, captured the almost nine minute video of his killing, including Floyd's last words, 'I can't breathe', which has since been shared worldwide.

In the immediate wake of Floyd's death, in the midst of a global pandemic which disproportionately affected Black individuals,[2] mass protests and demonstrations occurred proclaiming Black Lives Matter, not just in Minneapolis, but throughout the United States, as well as in much of Europe and the world, including in the United Kingdom, Germany, and Belgium. One example is Assa Traoré, a French activist of Malian origin, who led a massive demonstration outside the High Court in Paris of more 20,000 protestors against police violence, including the death of her own brother, Adama Traoré, by the police four years prior in the banlieue of Beaumont-sur-Oise, for which she and her family have still not received justice (Collins, 2020). This demonstration also invoked Floyd's murder. Several protests signs invoked Black Lives Matter and 'I Can't Breathe', the last words of both Floyd and Adama Traoré. In a later interview with the French magazine, *Antidote*, Assa said, 'When George Floyd died, that's our brother. They [Floyd and Traoré] died the same way. I recognize myself in Black Lives Matter, we are all Black Lives Matter. Our common issue is racial discrimination. Here as over there, it is the Blacks, the non-whites, who are being killed' (Rhrissi, 2020).

Later that same month, I served as panelist and moderator for a virtual panel discussion, 'Do Black Lives Matter in Europe?', for the Council for European Studies in conversation with political scientist Terri Givens and historian Kennetta Hammond Perry.[3] We had over 300 registrants for this webinar, indicating wide interest in this question. The question was not, 'should Black Lives Matter', but rather why and how Black Lives are not *seen* to matter, and historically *seen* not to have mattered, in Europe, despite the long and continued presence of Black individuals across the continent.

The EU Parliament declaration, as well as protests such as this one in Paris, suggest the relevance and importance of Black Lives Matter in Europe. But what does such a declaration mean in the face of documented racism and discrimination against Black

---

[1] https://www.dw.com/en/eu-declares-black-lives-matter-condemns-racism/a-53878516
[2] In fact, Floyd's autopsy revealed that he was positive for COVID-19 (Neuman, 2020).
[3] https://councilforeuropeanstudies.org/do-black-lives-matter-in-europe/

individuals across Europe?[4] How is Black Lives Matter relevant in the context of Europe? What shape does the Black Lives Matter take outside of the United States? How should we make sense of the resonance and connection between Black Lives Matter in the United States with long-standing anti-racist struggles across Europe?

One of the questions Floyd's death and the subsequent protests throughout 2020 raise, which we also pondered during our CES webinar, was 'why now?' In other words, Floyd's death was not the first police killing of a Black American man, in either the US or in Europe (nor the most recent), and anti-racist mobilization and activism has a long history throughout Europe (ENAR, 2014; Bryan *et al.*, 2018; Florvil, 2020). What does it mean to see these mass protests in Europe in solidarity with the Black Lives Matter movement? How is this solidarity reflecting a movement against anti-Black logics, practices, and policies throughout Europe? How can we understand the events of 2020 as part of an ongoing reckoning with Europe's colonial and imperial histories and legacies?

Black Lives Matter, as both a social movement and organizational network acknowledging Black humanity in the face of its continued neglect by the state, has been a crucial intervention against state violence against populations racialized as Black.[5] By state violence, I refer not only to the killings of such individuals by the police, but also to the myriad systemic ways that Black populations are devalued across various domains in society.

In what follows, I discuss how we might understand Black Lives Matter throughout Europe, not as a movement simply transferred from the United States to Europe, but rather as connected to ongoing antiracist struggles in Europe and part of a global conversation affirming the humanity of Black people across Europe, and the rest of the world. Such a framing requires us to understand the long presence of and struggle for Black people throughout continental Europe and its former colonies. Throughout this article, I frame Black Lives Matter in Europe less in terms of specific activist asserted affiliations and identifications, and more in terms framing anti-racist activism that is implicitly or explicitly in conversation with Black Lives Matter. I consider Black Lives Matter in Europe beyond specific protests to a consideration of broader anti-racist mobilization throughout Europe. I stress how Black Lives Matter in Europe builds upon and connects to past and present anti-racist mobilizations across Europe. I further explore key issues of Black Lives Matter in Europe, including challenging the denial of race and racism, fighting police violence, forcing Europe to grapple with its history of slavery and colonialism through decolonizing efforts, and asserting and affirming blackness across Europe. I conclude by discussing how considering Black Lives Matter in Europe is crucial.

Ultimately, Black Lives Matter in Europe challenges a European exceptionalism with regards to race and racism, and challenges Black Europeans' frequent designation as permanent outsiders within Europe.

[4]Moreover, European Commission vice president Margaritis Schinas decried the presence of 'US-style policing' in Europe (https://euobserver.com/social/148590).
[5]Alicia Garza, Patrisse Cullors, and Opal Tometti are often credited with starting the social movement BlackLives Matter, however the first use of the Black Lives Matter hashtag was by sociologist Marcus Anthony Hunter (Jones, 2019). Throughout this article, I use the term Black Lives Matter to refer to the broader social movement, versus individual BLM chapters and include a hashtag # to refer to the social media hashtag BlackLivesMatter.

I. 'We're Here because You Were There!': Black Europeans and Fighting Racial Denial in Europe

I use the term 'Black European' throughout this article to refer to Black individuals residing in Europe, regardless of their specific citizenship or immigrant status. Here, I also reference DeGenova's (De Genova, 2018) conceptualization of blackness in the European context beyond a synonym for African ancestry, to 'the pronouncedly heterogeneous spectrum of all those categories of humanity that European imperialism unrelentingly produced as its colonized natives' and 'positing a more expansive, if provisional, understanding of blackness as a racialized sociopolitical category that can be understood to encompass the full spectrum of social identities produced as specifically non-white' (1771).[6] Grappling with the conditions and struggle of Black Europeans across the continent includes considering what 'Black' and 'blackness' mean in the context of Europe, and moreover, the ways that the construction of Europe has historically centred whiteness to the exclusion of what is seen as non-white, including blackness, Black individuals, and Muslims.

In order to contextualize Black Lives Matter in Europe, we need to reckon with the long history and presence of Black populations throughout Europe. Longstanding anti-racist struggles are forcing Europe to grapple with how Black individuals have always been a part of Europe, rather than framing these populations as new and unwelcome arrivals. This presence is directly related to the European imperial and colonial project. In other words, how we presently understand and define Europe, its identity and borders relies on the labour and colonial rule of Black populations around the world, primarily in parts of Africa, the Caribbean, and Asia.

Stephen Small (2017) provides an overview of Black Europe, estimating that approximately seven million Black individuals reside in Europe today.[7] He writes:

> Black Europe is not just Black people in Europe. It did not begin in the second half of the twentieth century, when Europe actively recruited more Black people than ever before to fight and work and live here. It began with the invasion of Africa by Europeans; it continued with the kidnap, transportation, and enslavement of millions of Africans; and with the encompassing grasp of colonialism and imperialism across Africa, the Americas, and elsewhere (Small, 2017, p. 217).

Small (2017) reminds us that Black presence in Europe is consequential of a European invasion of and presence in Africa. As such, our understanding of the realities and challenges facing Black Europeans must begin with reckoning with Europe's imperial and colonial histories. Such scholarship on Black Europe has been generative for illustrating the complexities facing Black individuals in Europe today, especially those who are not immigrants (Perry and Thurman, 2016). Relatedly, historian Olivette Otele (2021) details how the history of Black populations in Europe has been continually erased, how they have been simultaneously feared and marginalized, as well as how Black Europeans have resisted this marginalization throughout history.

---

[6]In this way we can also understand similarly marginalized groups such as Maghrebin or North African-origin individuals or Roma individuals as both subject and resistant to similar structures of racism and police violence.
[7]Small (2017) includes in his definition people who are defined and defined themselves as Black.

In asserting that Black lives do matter, and have mattered, in Europe, Black Europeans also challenge the denial of race and racism throughout Europe (Boulila, 2019a; Boulila, 2019b; Dankertsen and Kristiansen, 2021; Ghorashi, 2020; Lentin, 2008; McEachrane, 2014; Michel, 2015). This denial is entrenched in language and data collection, or the lack thereof, related to racial and ethnic groups. For example, in the Netherlands, there are no specific terms for racial and ethnic groups, but rather 'Allochthone' is used to refer to foreigners or immigrants (in contrast with 'Autochtoon' to refer to native Dutch).[8] This is despite how that is often applied to non-white people in the Netherlands regardless of their place of birth (the Netherlands has *jus sanguis* citizenship). Even the more recent usage of the replacement term 'person with a migrant background' poses a similar problem – that is, why are people being identified by their ancestral origins, however distant they may be, versus their societal or national membership? And why is an 'immigrant background' euphemistic for non-white?

This dilemma about appropriate terminology persists (which is partly why I explained my usage of the term 'Black European'). Debates persist about terms as varied as 'African Europeans', 'Afro-Europeans', or 'Afroeuropeans'. And this is similarly contested with different country-specific terms, such as BAME (Black Asian Minority Ethnic, in the UK), 'Black British', 'Afro-German', or 'Afro-French' (El-Tayeb, 2003). There is also the persistent usage of euphemisms to refer to non-white populations through Europe, such as foreigner, immigrant, Muslim, or *banlieusard* (suburban resident, in the case of France) (Beaman, 2017; Germain and Larcher, 2018).

There exists both a social invisibility and statistical invisibility of Black Europeans, as, with the notable exception of the United Kingdom, state-level data on racial and ethnic minorities is not collected. Therefore data on the systemic nature of racism and discrimination is lacking. Discrimination is instead understood as individual-level phenomena, versus structural or systemic. And everyone is either Italian or not, or Dutch or not, or French or not, and so on. This lack of state-level categorization (and therefore ethnic statistics) serves to minimize specific race-related harms, be they related to employment and unemployment, educational attainment, or police violence, and complicate efforts to mobilize against these harms (Keaton, 2013; Boulila, 2019a).

This distancing vis-à-vis language and official terms reflects a separating out of Black and other non-white individuals from the construction of Europe, while simultaneously framing full societal membership and belonging as white (Lindsey and Wilson, 2019). Black Europeans are therefore asserting and affirming their place within Europe. They are also challenging race-blind or colourblind frameworks by asserting how race matters to Europe, has always mattered to Europe and still matters to Europe.[9] Race and racism are framed as US conceptions with no relevance to Europe, historically or presently. Scholars have long challenged the efficacy of colourblind/race-blind frameworks (Keaton, 2010; Salem and Thompson, 2016; Beaman and Petts, 2020). Anti-racist struggle in Europe, therefore, is fighting to even name and speak of race and racism (and get governments to acknowledge institutional and systemic racism). As I discuss later, part of Black Lives Matter in Europe, moreover, is forcing Europe to recognize and grapple

[8] https://www.dutchnews.nl/news/2016/11/government-agencies-to-ditch-allochtoon-to-describe-immigrants/
[9] This point perhaps becomes even clearer when we trace the genealogies of racial difference back to Europe (Goldberg, 2006). David Theo Goldberg's framework of racial Europeanization is instructive here for articulating how race and racial difference are situated as outside of Europe, versus within it or constitutive of it.

with its histories of colonialism, imperialism, and slavery. In doing so, anti-racist activists make visible the invisibility of Black Europeans, thereby challenging their frequent regard as 'permanent strangers' or outsiders (Merrill, 2013; Perry and Thurman, 2016; Small, 2017; Degele, 2020; Muvumbi, 2021).

II. Protesting Police Violence in Europe

Different modalities of colourblindness and race-blindness means that Black Lives Matter can manifest differently across Europe, yet the problems of racism spurring Black Lives Matter in the United States are also present and pervasive across Europe (and indeed, predate the Black Lives Matter movement itself). One of these problems is police violence. Despite colourblind and race-blind ideologies, it is still clear that that policing practices disproportionately target Black Europeans (Sollund, 2006; Jobard *et al.*, 2012; ENAR, 2014; Bonnet and Caillault, 2015).[10] The European Network against Racism (ENAR) defines police brutality as 'the physical and excessive use of force by law enforcement officials on a person' and notes that such 'violence can be both direct and structural – inflicted by the police as an institution as well as by individuals acting on behalf of or with the sanction of the state'. The European Court of Human Rights has identified excessive and unjustified use of force by police as 'chronic' throughout Europe.[11] Beyond specific deaths by the police, there is also the problem of racial and ethnic profiling through police stops (including identity checks by the police), harassment by the police (some of which leads to deaths), and the ongoing suspicion to which Black Europeans are forever subject (Body-Gendrot and Wihtol de Wenden, 2014; Jobard *et al.*, 2012; Terrasse, 2019).[12,13] Across Europe, lockdown measures due to the COVID-19 pandemic often led to increased discriminatory police stops (ENAR, 2020; see also Freedman, 2021 in this issue).

Therefore, Black Lives Matter protests and demonstrations in Europe are not just responding to incidents of Black American being killed by the police, but also to the patterns and practices of Black Europeans being brutalized by the police. And these demonstrations and protests are occurring in societies that continually minimize police violence as an example of systemic racism and frame such racism as exterior to Europe. For example, in a demonstration in June 2020 in Berlin, protestors held signs reading 'Black Lives Matter' and 'Germany, you have a racism problem too' (Hassan, 2016). Similarly, in demonstrations in the UK signs read 'the UK is not innocent', indicating that the UK should not frame racism as solely a US phenomenon, ignoring many Black British victims of state violence (Joseph-Salisbury *et al.*, 2021). As Milman *et al.* (2021) demonstrate in their analysis of Black Lives Matter in Germany, Italy, Denmark, and Poland, 'Globally relevant anti-racist frames interacted with national cultures of protest and domestic debates, including issues such as post-colonialism, antifascism, protest against police

---

[10]For more on experiences of racism and discrimination, including mistreatment by the police, see the European Union Agency for Fundamental Rights report: https://fra.europa.eu/sites/default/files/fra_uploads/fra-2018-being-black-in-the-eu_en.pdf.
[11]https://www.echr.coe.int/Documents/Handbook_European_Convention_Police_ENG.pdf
[12]For more on racial and ethnic profiling throughout Europe see: https://www.coe.int/en/web/commissioner/-/ethnic-profiling-a-persisting-practice-in-europe
[13]Part of the problem addressing ethnic profiling by the police is the lack of data, as police departments are reluctant to release data on racial and ethnic disparities in policing, in addition to the lack of ethnic statistics in many European societies.

brutality, and solidarity with ethnic and racialized minorities, leading to varying forms of protest events and framing' (p. 3).

Such protests illustrate that we should understand state violence as a global phenomenon affecting populations racialized as Black and that manifestations of Black Lives Matter in Europe connect Black Lives Matter in the United States with the local specificities of police violence in different European societies. So demonstrations will invoke the deaths of Freddie Gray, Michael Brown, Sandra Bland, and George Floyd, while also invoking Lamine Dieng (killed in France in 2007), Adama Traore (killed in France in 2016), Stephen Lawrence (killed in the UK in 1993), Mark Duggan (killed in the UK in 2011), Sheku Bayoh (killed in Scotland in 2015), Mame Mbaye (who died after being chased by the police in Spain in 2018), Oury Jalloh (who died under police custody in Germany in 2005), and many other victims.

Anthropologist Christen A. Smith (2016) uses the term 'sequelae' to refer to the lingering effects of police violence, long after specific incidents, and the trauma this enacts on particular communities. In other words, state violence is not to be solely identified or quantified based on specific incidents, but rather needs to be conceptualized through a broader understanding of what it means to be racialized as Black throughout Europe. State violence as a social problem extends beyond specific incidents to broader systemic and institutional racism throughout Europe, which among other things, explains the presence of the police in particular communities. Activists in Europe identify both hypersurveillance by the police and the threat and practice of police violence in particular communities as part of anti-racist struggle.

This resistance to police violence or state violence takes many forms besides 'traditional' mass demonstrations and protests. Much activism against police violence is also present online and in social media, through different Facebook pages and Twitter and Instagram accounts documenting incidents of state violence against Black individuals, including those often not covered by traditional media outlets. This is one of the ways anti-racist activists actively resist state violence and connect Black Lives Matter as a global movement to local struggles. This is in addition to protest actions aligned with BLM protests in the United States, including taking a knee (a protest act which began with American football player Colin Kaepernick kneeing during the national anthem before a game in 2016), marching with raised clenched fists, silent protests (for the length of time as Floyd's killing), or repeating slogans such as 'No Justice, No Peace' or 'Black Lives Matter' (Milman et al., 2021). One example is Afro-Swedish anti-racist activist Maria Teresa Asplund, whose photo of her with a raised fist in opposition to a neo-Nazi protest spread widely on social and traditional media, giving broader visibility to anti-racist struggles in Scandinavia (Osei-Kofi et al., 2018). This example also illustrates the long history – again, predating Black Lives Matter as a movement – of Black women leading anti-racist struggles throughout Europe (Elliott-Cooper, 2018; Bryan et al., 2018; Florvil, 2020; Otele, 2021).

III. Reckoning with Slavery and Colonialism

On 7 June 2020, protestors toppled Edward Colston's statue from its perch and threw it into the same harbour that once trafficked Africans in Bristol, England (Gayle, 2021). Colston, a slave trader, is known for his involvement with the Royal African Company, which dominated slave trading on the west coast of Africa. His statue was briefly replaced with another statue of a Black woman with a clenched raised fist (which was then subsequently removed by the city). A commission was formed to determine what to do next. Colston's statue has since been removed and installed in an exhibit about Black Lives Matter in Bristol's Shed Museum. The toppling of Colston's statue is just one example of how anti-racist activists across Europe are forcing their societies to grapple with histories and legacies of slavery and colonialism. In toppling or defacing statues, anti-racists seek to centre this history as integral to contemporary racism and state violence across the continent. In doing so, they challenge Europe's postcolonial amnesia and narratives of Black, immigrant, and refugee 'invasion', and employ a decolonial approach to centring the histories and experiences of Black Europeans.

Moreover, a crucial distinction between Black Lives Matter in Europe versus in the United States is the former's emphasis on grappling with Europe's colonial project and slave trade. In this way, BLM in Europe needs to be understood as a recent manifestation of longstanding anti-racist struggles for full recognition of Black Europeans. This matters not just for understanding how Europe's colonial empire structured and continues to structure Europe, but also for how colonialism enacted racial differentiation and defined Blackness as antithetical to Europe and its values. Therefore, for example, present-day policing practices can be understood as manifestations of colonial policing practices (Elliott-Cooper, 2019; Go, 2020; Elliott-Cooper, 2021).

The toppling of Colston's statue and other statues of colonial leaders across Europe represents a spatial practice forcing Europe to confront its racial and postcolonial amnesia (El-Tayeb, 2020). This should lead us to a broader consideration of what history gets remembered and what history is suppressed, particularly in the construction of national narratives in the post-colonial era (Trouillot, 1995). Ann Stoler (2011) writes of France's 'colonial asphasia' as an alternative to the terms 'forgotten history' or 'colonial amnesia' in that it emphasizes the occlusion of knowledge, a framework which can be applied to Europe more broadly. This erasure of the colonial leads to a 'panic' of the postcolonial.

Yet anti-racist activists, and the lifeworlds of Black Europeans more generally, remind the rest of Europe of what cannot be suppressed. Defacing or toppling statues has been linked to debates about removing statues of Confederate soldiers in the US. Yet, by defacing the statue of Jean-Baptiste Colbert, the author of the Code Noir which governed slavery in France's colonies, in front of Paris's National Assembly with red paint, or removing the statue of King Leopold II, known for atrocities during the colonial rule of the Congo, Black Europeans challenge conventional narratives for how European history has typically been framed and told, rather than merely parroting the actions of US activists. Black Europeans are explaining racism – including but not limited to state violence – through the prism of specific histories of colonialism and slavery. The present crises facing Black Europeans cannot be divorced from these histories, and anti-racist activists have long brought attention to these crucial connections. This is especially important as particular European societies do not just disregard the legacy of their colonial histories, as in the case of the UK or France, but also minimize it relative to other European societies who are therefore framed as worst colonizers than they, such as in Denmark, Italy, or Sweden (Muvumbi, 2021). This has been particularly central in anti-racism activism in these countries, which also seeks to situate all of Europe as a colonial project, versus just particular countries.

And Black Lives Matter in Europe is not just about removing statues or changing street names,[14] but also about articulating what comes next, such as the commission in Bristol I mentioned earlier. Beyond reckoning with history, there is the question of repair, redress, and reparation, including calls for economic reparations and to decolonize Europe, its educational institutions and curricula (Bhambra et al., 2018; Schütz, 2020). For example, anti-racist activists in France have mobilized for commemoration and reparations for French colonial slavery for decades, including the 2001 Taubira law which acknowledged slavery as a crime against humanity (Fleming, 2017; Laplanche-Servigne, 2017). More recently, the German government has acknowledged its colonial occupation and genocide of Herero and Nama populations in Namibia (BBC, 2021). Yet, anti-racist activists have criticized this move as merely a gesture without substantive repair to Herero and Nama peoples. Moreover, anti-racist activists have pushed for the restitution of colonial art and other artifacts from former European colonizers to the former colonies from where they were stolen (Garen et al., 2019).

IV. Movement Towards What?: Why Black Lives Matter in Europe Matters

Through anti-racist activism, including, but not limited to, Black Lives Matter protests and demonstrations, Black Europeans affirm and assert their Blackness both within and beyond Europe, and claiming a right to be both Black and European. We therefore need to understand Black Lives Matter in Europe as addressing a broader set of anti-Black logics and concerns beyond specific incidents of police brutality. As Milman et al. (2021) find, Black Lives Matter protests and demonstrations since the death of George Floyd in 2020 have given new visibility to anti-racist activism throughout Europe, especially for Black activists and new activists (who had not previously participated in mass demonstrations and protests). As such, this 'wave' of anti-racism is a new iteration of long-standing Black consciousness building and community formation.

As I discussed earlier, in affirming and asserting Blackness in Europe, Black Europeans also reject traditional conceptions of Europe and European as white (Skinner, 2019) and Black individuals in Europe as a recent or new presence. Through protests as well as social media campaigns, activists counter stereotypes and negative representations of Black Europeans. One example is the "Zwarte Piet is Racism" ("Black Pete is Racism") campaign started in the Netherlands in 2011 to counter the iconography of Black Pete, Santa Claus's 'helper' who is portrayed with Black face paint and described as dumb and silly (Garen et al., 2019). Anti-racist activists have long countered this Dutch tradition based on its anti-Black logic which serves to minimize its colonial history and marginalize the Black population in a 'colourblind' Dutch society. Another example is 'Black Speaks Back', an initiative created by activists in 2016 to represent the diversity of the Black population in Belgium and the Netherlands.[15]

The current wave of BLM protests and broader anti-racist mobilization is also a response to the limitations of legal frameworks, including anti-discrimination measures like the UK Race Relations Act of 1965 or the 2000 European Union Race Equality Directive, to address or even name systemic racism in the European Union and across Europe, as

[14]For example, in France: https://www.bbc.com/news/world-europe-53261948
[15]http://www.blackspeaksback.com/

political scientist Ilke Adams (2021) has noted. In March 2021, the EU held its first Anti-Racism Summit to address the implementation of its 2020–25 EU Action Plan to Combat Racism. Activists have argued that racism should be targeted as a structural or systemic problem, versus an individual phenomena, as it is often characterized.

Black Lives Matter in Europe both addresses the local specifies of anti-Black racism in different European societies, and travels beyond the boundaries of the nation-state to emphasize the global connections regarding what it means to be racialized as Black around the world. This is not new, but is crucial to pay attention to in order to better understand the realities of Black populations, not just in Europe, but around the world. A framing of how BLM has been translated in Europe that also takes into account the long history of anti-racist activism in Europe also reveals how anti-racist struggle, in particular struggles for Black liberation, is also global.

References

Adams, I. (2021) 'The EU's Fight Against Racism isn't Working'. *Politico*, 19 March 2021. https://www.politico.eu/article/eus-fight-against-racism-isnt-working/

Beaman, J. (2017) *Citizen Outsider: Children of North African Immigrants in France* (Oakland, CA: University of California Press).

Beaman, J. and Petts, A. (2020) 'Towards a Global Theory of Colorblindness: Comparing Colorblind Racial Ideology in France and the United States'. *Sociology Compass*, Vol. 14, No. 4, e12774.

Bhambra, G.K., Gebrial, D. and Nişancıoğlu, K. (2018) *DECOLONISING THE UNIVERSITY* (Pluto Press).

Body-Gendrot, S. and Wihtol de Wenden, C. (2014) *Policing the Inner City in France, Britain, and the US* (Springer).

Bonnet, F. and Caillault, C. (2015) 'The invader, the Enemy within and They-who-must-not-be-Named: How Police Talk about Minorities in Italy, the Netherlands and France'. *Ethnic and Racial Studies*, Vol. 38, No. 7, pp. 1185–201.

Boulila, S.C. (2019a) 'Race and Racial Denial in Switzerland'. *Ethnic and Racial Studies*, Vol. 42, No. 9, pp. 1401–18.

Boulila, S.C. (2019b) *Race in Post-Racial Europe: An Intersectional Analysis* (Rowman & Littlefield International).

British Broadcasting Corporation. (2021) 'Germany Officially Recognises Colonial-Era Namibia Genocide'. 28 May 2021. https://www.bbc.co.uk/news/world-europe-57279008

Bryan, B., Dadzie, S. and Scafe, S. (2018) *The Heart of the Race: Black Women's Lives in Britain* (London: Verso).

Collins, L. (2020) 'Assa Traoré and the Fight Black Lives in France'. *The New Yorker*, 18 June 2020, https://www.newyorker.com/news/letter-from-europe/assa-traore-and-the-fight-for-black-lives-in-france

Dankertsen, A. and Kristiansen, T.G.S. (2021) ''Whiteness isn't about Skin Color': Challenges to Analyzing Racial Practices in a Norwegian Context'. *Societies*, Vol. 11, p. 46.

De Genova, N. (2018) 'The 'Migrant Crisis' as Racial Crisis: Do Black Lives Mattter in Europe?' *Ethnic and Racial Studies*, Vol. 41, No. 10, pp. 1765–82.

Degele, N. (2020) 'Naming matters: Black lives matter in Germany'. *European Journal of Women's Studies*, pp. 135050682097889. https://doi.org/10.1177/1350506820978895

Elliott-Cooper, A. (2018) 'The Struggle that cannot be Named: Violence, Space and the Re-articulation of Anti-Racism in Post-Duggan Britain'. *Ethnic and Racial Studies*, Vol. 41, No. 14, pp. 2445–63.

Elliott-Cooper, A. (2019) '"Our Life is a Struggle": Respectable Gender Norms and Black Resistance to Policing'. *Antipode*, Vol. 51, No. 2, pp. 539–57.

Elliott-Cooper, A. (2021) *Black Resistance to British Policing* (Manchester: Manchester University Press).

El-Tayeb, F. (2003) '"If You Can't Pronounce My Name, You Can Just Call Me Pride': Afro-German Activism, Gender and Hip Hop'. *Gender & History*, Vol. 15, No. 3, pp. 460–86.

El-Tayeb, F. (2020) 'The Universal Museum: How the New Germany Built its Future on Colonial Amnesia'. *Nka: Journal of Contemporary African Art*, Vol. 2020, No. 46, pp. 72–82.

ENAR (2014) *Invisible Visible Minority: Confronting Afrophobia and Advancing Equality for People of African Descent and Black Europeans in Europe* (Brussels: European Network Against Racism).

ENAR (2020) *#RACIALJUSTICE: Policing Racialised Groups – Briefing*. https://www.enar-eu.org/IMG/pdf/policing_racialised_groups_-_briefing_ojeaku_without_cover_10_revised_22062020.pdf

Fleming, C.M. (2017) *Resurrecting Slavery: Racial Legacies and White Supremacy in France* (Philadelphia: Temple University Press).

Florvil, T.N. (2020) *Mobilizing Black Germany: Afro-German Women and the Making of a Transnational Movement* (Champaign-Urbana, IL, University of Illinois Press).

Freedman, J. (2021) 'Immigration, Refugees and Responses'. *Journal of Common Market Studies*, pp. 1–11. https://doi.org/10.1111/jcms.13258

Garen, M., Carleton, M.-H. and Swaab, J. (2019) 'Zwarte Piet: Black Pete is "Dutch racism in full display"' 27 November 2019. *Aljazeera*. https://www.aljazeera.com/features/2019/11/27/zwarte-piet-black-pete-is-dutch-racism-in-full-display

Gayle, D. (2021) 'Toppled Edward Colston Statue Goes on Display in Bristol'. *The Guardian*, 4 June 2021. https://www.theguardian.com/uk-news/2021/jun/04/toppled-edward-colston-statue-display-bristol-blm-protests-exhibition

Germain, F. and Larcher, S. (2018) *Black French Women and the Struggle for Equality, 1848–2016* (Lincoln: University of Nebraska Press).

Ghorashi, H. (2020) 'Taking racism beyond Dutch innocence'. *European Journal of Women's Studies*, pp. 135050682097889. https://doi.org/10.1177/1350506820978897

Go, J. (2020) 'The Imperial Origins of American Policing: Militarization and Imperial Feedback in the Early 20th Century'. *American Journal of Sociology*, Vol. 125, No. 5, pp. 1193–254.

Goldberg, D.T. (2006) 'Racial Europeanization'. *Ethnic and Racial Studies*, Vol. 29, No. 2, pp. 331–64.

Hassan, J. (2016) '"How the Black Lives Matter Movement is Sweeping the Globe". *The Washington Post*. 11 July 2016. https://www.washingtonpost.com/news/worldviews/wp/2016/07/11/how-the-black-lives-matter-movement-is-sweeping-the-globe/

Jobard, F., Lévy, R., Lamberth, J., Névanen, S. and Wiles-Portier, E. (2012) 'Measuring Appearance-Based Discrimination: an Analysis of Identity Checks in Paris'. *Population*, Vol. 67, No. 3, pp. 349–75.

Jones, F. (2019) *Reclaiming our Space: How Black Feminists are Changing the World from the Tweets to the Streets* (Boston: Beacon Press).

Joseph-Salisbury, R., Connelly, L. and Wangari-Jones, P. (2021) '"The UK is not Innocent": Black Lives Matter, Policing, and Abolition in the UK'. *Equality, Diversity, and Inclusion*, Vol. 40, No. 1, pp. 21–8.

Keaton, T.D. (2010) 'The Politics of Race-Blindness: (Anti) Blackness and Category-Blindness in Contemporary France'. *Du Bois Review: Social Science Research on Race*, Vol. 7, No. 1, pp. 103–31.

Keaton, T.D. (2013) 'Racial Profiling and the 'French Exception''. *French Cultural Studies*, Vol. 24, No. 2, pp. 231–42.

Laplanche-Servigne, S. (2017) 'A 'Black Parisian' March in Remembrance of Slavery: Challenging the French Collective Imagination'. *African and Black Diaspora: An International Journal*, Vol. 10, No. 1, pp. 25–34.

Lentin, A. (2008) 'Europe and the Silence about Race'. *European Journal of Social Theory*, Vol. 11, No. 1, pp. 487–503.

Lindsey, L. and Wilson, C.E. (2019) 'Reinventing European History to show that Black Lives do Matter'. *EuropeNow Journal*, 4 April 2019 (https://www.europenowjournal.org/2019/04/04/reinventing-european-history-to-show-that-black-lives-do-matter/#_edn1).

McEachrane, M. (2014) 'There's a White Elephant in the Room: Equality and Race in (Northern) Europe'. In McEachrane, M. (ed.) *Afro-Nordic Landscapes: Equality and Race in Northern Europe* (Routledge Press), pp. 87–119.

Merrill, H. (2013) 'Who Gets to be Italian?: Black Life Worlds and White Spatial Imaginaries'. In Twine, F.W. and Gardener, B. (eds) *Geographies of Privilege* (Routledge), pp. 135–59.

Michel, N.V. (2015) 'Sheepology: The Postcolonial Politics of Raceless Racism in Switzerland'. *Postcolonial Studies*, Vol. 18, No. 4, pp. 410–26.

Milman, N., Ajayi, F., della Porta, D., Doerr, N., Kocyba, P., Lavizzari, A., Płuecenniczak, P., Reiter, H., Sommer, M., Steinhilper, E. and Zajak, S. (2021) 'Black Lives Matter in Europe. Transnational Diffusion, Local Translation and Resonance of Anti-Racist Protest in Germany, Italy, Denmark and Poland'. DeZIM Research Notes #06/21. Berlin: German Center for Integration and Migration Research (DeZIM).

Muvumbi, A.K. (2021) 'Black lives matter in Italy'. *European Journal of Women's Studies*, pp. 135050682097890. https://doi.org/10.1177/1350506820978900

Neuman, S. (2020) 'Medical Examiners Autopsy Reveals George Floyd Had Positive Test for Coronavirus'. https://www.npr.org/sections/live-updates-protests-for-racial-justice/2020/06/04/869278494/medical-examiners-autopsy-reveals-george-floyd-had-positive-test-for-coronavirus

Osei-Kofi, N., Licona, A.C. and Chávez, K.R. (2018) 'From Afro-Sweden with Defiance: The Clenched Fist as Coalitional Gesture?' *New Political Science*, Vol. 40, No. 1, pp. 137–50.

Otele, O. (2021) *African Europeans: An Untold History* (New York: Basic Books).

Perry, K. H. and Thurman, K. (2016) 'Black Europe: A Useful Category of Historical Analysis'. *Black Perspectives*, 20 December 2016.

Rhrissi, L. (2020) 'Assa Traoré: "Je Donne del lEspoir à la Nouvelle Génération"'. *Antidote*, 8 October 2020. https://magazineantidote.com/mode/enzo-lefort-escrime/

Salem, S. and Thompson, V. (2016) 'Old Racisms, New Masks: On the Continuing Discontinuities of Racism and the Erasure of Race in European Contexts'. *Nineteen Sixty Nine: An Ethnic Studies Journal*, Vol. 3, No. 1.

Schütz, M. (2020) 'Rewriting Colonial Heritage in Bristol and Marseille: Contemporary Artworks as Decolonial Interventions'. *Heritage & Society*, Vol. 13, No. 1–2, pp. 53–74.

Skinner, R.T. (2019) 'Walking, Talking, Remembering: An Afro-Swedish critique of being-in-the-world'. *African and Black Diaspora: An International Journal*, Vol. 12, No. 1, pp. 1–19.

Small, S. (2017) *20 Questions and Answers on Black Europe* (The Hague, The Netherlands: Amrit Publishers).

Smith, C.A. (2016) 'Facing the Dragon: Black Mothering, Sequelae, and Gendered Necropolitics in the Americas'. *Transforming Anthropology*, Vol. 24, pp. 31–48.

Sollund, R. (2006) 'Racialisation in Police Stop and Search Practice – the Norwegian case'. *Critical Criminology*, Vol. 14, pp. 265–92.

Stoler, A.L. (2011) 'Colonial Aphasia: Race and Disabled Histories in France'. *Public Culture*, Vol. 23, No. 1, pp. 121–56.

Terrasse, M. (2019) 'Dimensions of Belonging: Relationships between Police Identity Checks and National Identity in France'. *Journal of Ethnic and Migration Studies*.

Trouillot, M.-R. (1995) *Silencing the Past: Power and the Production of History* (Beacon Press).

JCMS 2021 Volume 59. Annual Review. pp. 115–123   DOI: 10.1111/jcms.13238

'Our European Friends and Partners'? Negotiating the Trade and Cooperation Agreement

SIMON USHERWOOD
Open University, Milton Keynes

Introduction

One of the main straplines of the Conservative Party's December 2019 general election campaign was 'get Brexit done'. This contained the double notions of completing the highly-tortured process of ratifying the Withdrawal Agreement between the EU and the UK that had been the central political challenge of the past year and of the much more prosaic idea that with this completed, the country could get back to the simple and quiet life. In short, it was a gamble that most of the British voting public were essentially tired of hearing about meaningful votes and backstops and wanted to feel they could move on: a gamble that paid off handsomely for Boris Johnson.

But as subsequent events have demonstrated, even the rapid conclusion of the Withdrawal Agreement ratification for the UK's formal exit from the European Union on 31 January 2020 could not produce a situation that might be reasonably described as 'done': while public opinion undoubtedly drifted from the high salience of preceding years, the two contracting parties almost immediately plunged into a new round of negotiations, to map out more properly their future relationship. Whereas the Withdrawal Agreement had been concerned solely with the resolution of the UK's departure from the EU, this new treaty would establish a system for ongoing cooperation.

This article focuses on those negotiations and their ultimate production of a Trade and Cooperation Agreement (TCA) for the end of 2020, a feat that looked to be much less than likely even prior to the arrival of Covid-19 on European shores. In particular, it asks the question of whether it was simply the Withdrawal Agreement, part 2, in the sense of a replication of underlying interests and positions, or rather a fundamentally new stage in the relationship. It argues firstly that while there was a lot of continuity on the British side, this was a function of ongoing uncertainty about the position of EU (and European) relations within the broad context of the UK's foreign and domestic policy: the drivers of negotiations were very largely negative ones of avoiding entanglements and commitments. By contrast, the EU displayed a more significant change in its approach – notwithstanding the continuities of negotiating personnel – that reflected the UK's switch from being a member state to a becoming a third country. This resulted in an attitudinal change on the part of both negotiators and the EU27 in their willingness to accommodate British demands, such as they were.

The result was an Agreement that reflected the progressive normalization of the UK by the EU as an external partner, albeit one with various significant on-going challenges, and also the UK's persistent inability to determine a clear and broadly-accepted logic for

Brexit: the basic conundrum of the 2016 referendum – leaving, but for what purpose? – remained as unclear at the start of 2021 as it had a year earlier.

The process of negotiation was fixed in part by the terms of the Political Declaration (DExEU, 2019) that accompanied the 2020 Withdrawal Agreement (OJEU, 2019), which specified an end date of 31 December 2020 to a transition period during which the UK would continue to follow all obligations and processes of EU membership, but without voting or representation rights (Eeckhout and Patel, 2017). This date had been fixed in the original version of the Withdrawal Agreement in late 2018 but was not amended following the various extensions to the Article 50 process. Even with the rapid turnaround of negotiating mandates a month after the entry into force of the Withdrawal Agreement at the end of January 2020, there were less than 10 months left for discussions. These were held within the framework of negotiating rounds – four between March and June; five between late July and September, after calls to 'intensify' the process – before a rolling set of daily meetings from mid-October until Christmas Eve tried to unblock progress. Much of this occurred remotely in the spring and autumn, due to Covid restrictions, leaving minimal opportunities for either principals or technical-level negotiators to interact. In parallel, both sides were also continuing their implementation work on the Withdrawal Agreement – and notably its Northern Ireland Protocol that would come into effect at the end of the transition period – and contingency work to prepare citizens and businesses in the event of no deal, something that looked increasingly pressing in the latter half of the year.

The article considers the TCA firstly from the perspective of the legacies of the Article 50 process that produced the Withdrawal Agreement, to consider how each party arrived at the start of the future relationship negotiations in March 2020. It then switches to an analysis of the final Agreement to reflect on the extent to which the EU and the UK achieved their objectives, before concluding with a discussion on the likely implications for the future of the relationship.

I. The Legacy of the Article 50 Process

The sharp proximity of the Withdrawal Agreement to the future relationship negotiations is a key factor in understanding the latter's unfolding. Indeed, it should be recalled that the division and sequencing of these elements was the subject of one of the very first disagreements after the UK submitted its notification to withdraw under Article 50 TEU in March 2017. The UK considered that matters of ending membership were intrinsically linked to any future cooperation and so should be treated together (Allen Green, 2017). The EU's position was that this would be an infringement of the remit of Article 50 (since it does not mention post-membership relations, covered elsewhere in the treaties) and so impossible. More politically, the very early identification and entrenchment of a set of EU negotiating objectives also pointed towards splitting up the steps: the declaration by EU leaders immediately after the 2016 referendum result (Council, 2016) highlighted the centrality of preserving the value of membership for the EU27, ahead of forging any new links with the UK. In practical terms this meant a tight focus within Article 50 negotiations on addressing the key liabilities of ending membership – citizens' rights, finances and the Irish dimension – so that these could be ring-fenced from what already appeared an unclear set of British preferences about what might follow. The difference between the two sides, billed by UK lead negotiator David Davis as 'the row of the summer', was resolved very quickly in the EU's favour in June 2017, laying the groundwork for the segmentation found in 2020.

The division mattered not only in the substantive remit of the negotiations but also in establishing a set of practices and understandings. The lessons learnt by each side during the Article 50 process are worth exploring here, given their impact on the unfolding of the future relationship stage. In both cases, the experience was one that incentivized continuation over starting afresh.

On the EU side, the decision to convert the Article 50 Task Force into the Task Force for Relations with the UK, under the leadership Michel Barnier, avoided the need to engage in securing a new set of personnel and carried over the preliminary work under the banner of the Political Declaration. The Task Force's success in concluding the Withdrawal Agreement was matched by member states' close proximity to the negotiation and the repeated accommodation of their views (see Laffan, 2019; Barnier, 2021). But the continuity also spoke to more general concerns about the reliability of the British as an interlocutor: from the surprise 2017 general election immediately after notification to the Democratic Unionist Party's blockage of the Joint Report later that year, from the collapse of the Chequers plan in 2018 and the protracted ratification crises in 2019 to Boris Johnson's reversal on the Northern Ireland Protocol, the pattern encountered by the EU was of a UK that needed to be handled with extreme caution. This was also evident in the negotiating mandate's language on 'good faith' negotiations and implementation (European Council, 2020a). The experience of the Article 50 negotiations had been that British rhetoric was rather different from British action – most obviously around the Protocol – so that clarity of text and commitment was essential.

By contrast, the British government and the Conservative party appeared willing to accept the rhetorical presentation by Johnson as an accurate reflection of how the negotiations had gone: tough talking and being firm, not least through doing everything possible to avoid further time extensions, had resulted in the EU making important concessions. In his own words, 'they said that we couldn't re-open the Withdrawal Agreement, Mr Speaker, they said we couldn't change a comma of the Withdrawal Agreement, they said we couldn't abolish the backstop, Mr Speaker, we've done both.' (Johnson, 2019). The brevity of Parliamentary consideration of the final version of the Withdrawal Agreement was both a function of the 'get Brexit done' message from Number 10 and of the minimal interest of Tory MPs to unpack the implications of what had been agreed. Seen in this light, the antagonistic discourse towards the EU not only had value for domestic audiences in reassuring them of the step-change from the May period, but also as a more general approach towards the future relationship negotiations. As with the EU, the UK maintained many of the same people around the continuing chief negotiator, David Frost. The success of Frost in communicating that he had the ear of Johnson – in a way that previous UK negotiators had not necessarily done (Kassim, 2021) – made him the obvious choice for the UK, just as it also reaffirmed the EU's priorities to pin the UK down on any text.

This combination of tight timings, issue segmentation, roll-over of key personnel and the differing lessons about what had worked drove both sides to enter the future relationship process very much in the mindset of a continuation of what had come before. This was to be reflected in the pattern of the negotiations through 2020, especially in the persistent question about whether the Covid pandemic required more time to be given to talks; a question that the UK never gave any ground on, even at the point where full ratification had to be pushed back by the EU because of the need for European Parliament debate and approval. Each round of negotiation came with a barrage of media briefings, with periodic (if largely unproductive) nudges from principals on both sides.

At the same time, the shift of legal basis from Article 50 to Article 218 TFEU, and the concomitant change in status of the UK from member state to third country, must be noted. Not only did the UK lose its access to EU decision-making bodies of all kinds, but the EU had now secured its fundamental priorities in the Withdrawal Agreement. This would become progressively more consequential as talks continued.

II. Did the TCA Meet the Needs of all Sides?

That an agreement was reached at all – let alone one reached under such extreme time constraints and with much remote interaction – is certainly something of an achievement. In early 2020, as Covid's effects were becoming ever clearer, the view was largely that modern trade agreements are complex and time-consuming to negotiate, so full use of the two-year extension to the transition period would be in order (see Zuleeg *et al*., 2020 for a typical example). The maintenance of the timeline highlights the absolute priority given to it by the UK side – driven by the need to keep moving through the Brexit process at pace – but also the related decision by the UK to ask for a relatively modest free trade agreement. A short wish list was seen variously as a way of underlining the UK's departure from the Union and as a tool to reduce the cross-leverage that the EU might try to exert, quite beyond the obvious reduction in matters to be resolved (Connelly, 2020). The focus on removing tariffs on trade in goods was only enlarged to meet some basic needs in transport, energy, police and judicial cooperation, and possible participation in EU programmes, with fisheries added in at the EU's insistence: the effective absence of services, security and many other areas stood in contrast to the much more ambitious agendas of other EU deals in train at the time. As so ably predicted by Hix (2018), a basic free trade agreement might not have been all that either side wanted, but it represented the most that they would be able to agree on together.

Of course, the timely conclusion of an agreement has no bearing on whether that agreement is suitable for its purpose: the growing swell of domestic UK discontent about the parallel implementation of the Withdrawal Agreement was only the most obvious example of this. While there had been clear and consistent signals throughout the negotiations about areas of agreement – zero tariffs and zero quotas on goods, the small opening on services, social security cooperation, the framework for participation in EU programmes, much of energy and transport – a number of disagreements were equally clear and consistent throughout the process.

The most symbolic of these – in economic terms – was fisheries. The UK's desire to remove itself entirely from the Common Fisheries Policy (CFP) ran up against the EU's insistence on continuing access under international law. Further complication came from most British fish being sold to EU member states and most fish eaten in the UK coming from the EU, thus connecting it to the trade stream of negotiations (UK in a Changing Europe, 2020). The final compromise of a phased downwards adjustment of the EU's percentage of permitted catch over five and a half years somewhat obscured the continuation of the EU's involvement in management, albeit not directly under the CFP. In particular, the provisions allow for the EU to take retaliatory action if their share of quotas is reduced any further after the transition, much to the dismay of UK fishing bodies (NFFO, 2020).

Much more substantive was the question of 'level playing field' provisions. The removal of tariffs and quotas on goods had raised concerns for the EU that the UK might be able to take advantage of this by cutting standards in areas such as the protection of labour or environment or by cutting taxes and/or providing state aid, which would both undercut EU producers and compromise these areas. Therefore it pushed for 'sufficient guarantees ... so as to uphold corresponding high levels of protection' (European Council, 2020a), including dynamic alignment that would tie the UK to EU standards over time and the continuing use of EU state aid rules by the UK. The UK's concern was that this was effectively a continuation of the obligations of membership, and that a commitment to not abuse such policy areas would suffice; something that the experience of the Withdrawal Agreement had made equally unacceptable to the EU. Here the outcome ended up closer to the EU's preferences, even if the demand on state aid was dropped: both parties signed up to domestic enforcement and dispute settlement mechanisms, with a right to take unilateral action should the other party engage in unfair competition.

The complexity of this settlement stemmed in part from another pinch point in the negotiations: the role of the Court of Justice of the EU (CJEU). As another symbol of the failings of membership, giving the Court any say in dispute settlement or interpretation of the TCA was ruled out by British negotiators, even against the EU's rejoinder that where matters of EU law might be concerned there was a clear obligation on the EU to use the CJEU for definitive rulings. Despite having accepted the EU's line for the Withdrawal Agreement, the UK was not willing to move on this, ultimately securing a system of dispute settlement that dispensed with it. At the same time, the UK did have to give ground on the EU's desire to create a single framework of governance for the post-membership relationship, rather than separated, narrow subjects, akin to the Swiss model.

The overall pattern of these flashpoints is one of the UK being driven to secure symbolically significant concessions, even at the price of economic efficiency. The TCA avoided the worst-case effects of a non-agreement, without obviously compromising the 'performative divergence' of the rhetoric of 'Brexit means Brexit': it is at least as important that leaving the EU is seen to mean change as it is for any changes to actually occur.[1] The political value of removing the CJEU from the treaty, extracting the UK from the CFP and avoiding a system of dynamic alignment on level playing field was significant in allowing the government to push through ratification in the brief period before the end of 2020, not least in forestalling some of the more obvious objections that Conservative MPs might have had. As examples of being able to move the EU off its starting positions, they also let the government argue that they had succeeded where observers had said they had no good chance: the multiplicity of exit clauses (both for sub-elements and the entire treaty) also left them with much more accessible ways out down the line than were available in the Withdrawal Agreement (the TCA contains 13 such clauses).

---

[1] Credit to Sam Lowe and the rest of Trade Twitter for the use of the term 'performative divergence'.

© 2021 The Authors. JCMS: Journal of Common Market Studies published by University Association for Contemporary European Studies and John Wiley & Sons Ltd.

However, the success in moving the EU should not be confused with a securing of original British positions. At most, the final treaty took the harder edges off the EU's preferences, while still tying the UK into a system of governance and dispute settlement that could have major effects; a reflection of that initial EU concern about the UK's 'good faith'. In contrast to the unified dispute settlement mechanism of the Withdrawal Agreement, the TCA provides for various procedures for different sections, notably Article 411 with its rebalancing mechanism for 'material impacts on trade or investment' resulting from a party's non-compliance with the level playing field areas. This is a very fast system, allowing for almost immediate implementation of proportionate countermeasures and a tribunal ruling within two months. Moreover, persistent problems under this can result in a more systematic review of the heading, up to and including its termination.

Moreover, the initial decision to go for a small deal has left much on the table between the UK and EU. While there was a small side agreement on citizens' security, this is very limited in scope. Perhaps the biggest gap remains any cooperation on foreign policy or external security and defence, a decision that has already resulted in uncoordinated action on sanctions towards Myanmar and statements on the treatment of Uyghur Muslims in China (Guardian, 2021). The UK has talked more about using NATO as a conduit to maintaining links with most EU member states, as well as making more of the United Nations, but there appears to be no interest of the Johnson government to consider a specific bilateral instrument, primarily because of the antipathy to anything that is labelled as formal cooperation with the EU.

This divergence-for-the-sake-of-divergence remains the EU's biggest challenge from the experience of the TCA negotiation. As much as the Commission was able to protect all of the key interests of member states and the Union as a whole in the talks, including a robust dispute settlement mechanism, the process did not provide any improvement in the politics of the relationship with the UK. At no point was this clearer than in the events surrounding the Internal Market Bill in the autumn of 2020. The Bill was introduced in early September with the aim of addressing a number of areas of regulation of UK internal trade following withdrawal from the EU, but with the addition of provisions that specifically and explicitly disapplied parts of the Withdrawal Agreement in relation to Northern Ireland. These provisions had not been included in the earlier White Paper, suggesting that the 'break[ing of] international law in a very specific and limited way' (in the words of the Northern Ireland Secretary Brandon Lewis (BBC, 2020)) was motivated not only by a desire to weaken the UK's obligations to fulfil the Withdrawal Agreement itself, but also to apply pressure in the TCA negotiations.

This clear and unambiguous contravention of obligations under international law presented the EU with a very fundamental problem, not least since the EU itself is based in such obligations. For the UK even to suggest that treaties cannot bind signatories if they so choose – rather than for any usually accepted reason of *force majeur* or fundamental change of circumstance – was to call into question the entire exercise then in train. The strength of the EU's response may be marked by the extraordinary meeting of the Withdrawal Agreement's Joint Committee (Commission, 2020) and discussion at the European Council (2020b), both of which strongly pushed back on the UK's move, while also strengthening work on EU preparedness for all outcomes of the TCA negotiations, including no agreement. The removal of the offending clauses to the Bill only occurred in mid-December, when the government conceded the matter as part of the final days of those negotiations, but still after the House of Commons had finished its approval: while the House of Lords had rebelled several times over the wording, that would not have been enough to halt passage if the government had not given way. This demonstration of the capacity and willingness of the UK government to renege on its commitments marks as much of a failure for the EU in securing a stable and constructive relationship with the UK as any substantive aspect of the TCA.

III. Beyond the Trade & Cooperation Agreement, but beyond to What?

The Trade & Cooperation Agreement was supposed to mark and institutionalize the start of a new phase of the relationship between the EU and the UK following the end of membership. At the level of a legal instrument, this was successful, with the completion of ratification in April 2021. But at the political level, the impression is much less positive. In particular, there appears to be no clear trajectory for future relations, either in the implementation of the Withdrawal Agreement and the TCA, or in the use of these or any other means to conduct a stable set of interactions.

The process of negotiation was one that did nothing to improve relations between the two sides, and indeed likely worsened them as trust was undermined and the willingness to make accommodations reduced. The EU's concern about British adherence to the norms of international law have already been covered, but an equivalent dynamic was also evident on the UK side, as the traditional representation of the EU as an opponent of British interests fitted better the new realities of non-membership. The perceived otherness of the UK now had a material basis, coupled to a political imperative of performative divergence.

In addition, the increasingly problematic implementation of the Withdrawal Agreement – not aided by the Commission's brief mistaken mention of the Article 16 procedure in relation to vaccines in January 2021 (BBC, 2021) – laid the groundwork for questions about whether the same would be true for the TCA. Even with the various adjustment periods contained within the latter, the EU has repeatedly noted that the UK has not appeared to be undertaking the necessary work on infrastructure or policies to ensure that provisions are fully operational in time (Šefčovič, 2021).

Ironically, despite these concerns over implementation, the conclusion of the TCA potentially draws a line under any active efforts on either side to move things along: Hix's (2018) constraints still apply on what might be possible or even desirable. The EU has now secured both its fundamental interests in the Withdrawal Agreement and protected itself in the TCA, and appears to have minimal interest in pushing for any more cooperation. Brexit was certainly an important part of the EU's work since 2015, but it always had to share attention with other priorities: the very success of the model used for Article 50 in containing and managing the UK meant that European Councils spent minimal time on the matter after the Salzburg meeting of September 2018. Even with all of the issues raised, the UK remains one of the less actively difficult neighbours of the EU.

For the UK, the persistent issue (Usherwood, 2017, 2019) remains one of a lack of a strategic purpose to leaving the EU. The 2016 referendum served up a decision without a rationale and the only person ever in a position to back up a plan with a robust Parliamentary majority, Boris Johnson, has yet to map out how withdrawal fits into a coherent vision of the UK's role in the world. The trope of 'Global Britain' sits very uneasily with the wilful refusal to consider any explicit cooperation with the EU on political matters, or to pursue a comprehensive economic integration. The EU appears now in British discourse as a more fully externalized 'other', to blame for problems and to position as a competitor. That this has continued beyond the TCA negotiations suggests that this was not a tactic, but a default setting, and one that will carry on for the life of this government.

This means that as imperfect and challenging as the new architecture of the relationship might be, it is going to be the one that will have to be used for the foreseeable future: neither side has an acceptable alternative, even if they were ready to endure yet more negotiations. Therefore, the real test is going to be the extent to which the UK is prepared to push the limits of the treaties and the extent to which the EU will tolerate this. With little sign in the first months of 2021 that trust-building is a priority, it must be expected that the relationship is one that will worsen before it improves.

References

Allen Green, D. (2017) 'The Significance of the Brexit Sequencing U-turn'. *Financial Times*, 20 June 2017.

Barnier, M. (2021) *La Grande Illusion* (Paris: Gallimard).

BBC (2020) https://www.bbc.co.uk/news/uk-politics-54073836

BBC (2021) 'Gove: EU "Made a Mistake" in Triggering Article 16'. 30 January 2021. Available at https://www.bbc.co.uk/news/av/uk-55873899. Accessed 17 June 2021.

Commission. (2020) Statement by the European Commission following the extraordinary meeting of the EU–UK Joint Committee. Press release,10 September 2020, available at: https://ec.europa.eu/commission/presscorner/detail/en/statement_20_1607. Accessed 17 June 2021.

Connelly, T. (2020) 'Brexit is Done: Now for the Hard Part'. RTÉ News, 1 February 2020, available at: https://www.rte.ie/news/analysis-and-comment/2020/0201/1112309-brexit/. Accessed 17 June 2021.

Council. (2016) 'Statement by the EU Leaders and the Netherlands Presidency on the Outcome of the UK Referendum'. 24 June 2016. Available at https://www.consilium.europa.eu/en/press/press-releases/2016/06/24/joint-statement-uk-referendum/, accessed 17 June 2021.

DExEU. (2019) 'New Withdrawal Agreement and Political Declaration'. 19 October 2019, Department for Exiting the European Union. Available at https://www.gov.uk/government/publications/new-withdrawal-agreement-and-political-declaration, accessed 17 June 2021.

Eeckhout, P. and Patel, O. (2017) 'Brexit Transitional Arrangements: Legal and Political Considerations'. UCL European Institute Brexit Insights, 17 November 2017. Available at https://doi.org/10.2139/ssrn.3073310, accessed 17 June 2021.

European Council (2020a) 'EU–UK relations: Council Gives Go-Ahead for Talks to Start and Adopts Negotiating Directives'. Press release, 25 February 2020. Available at https://www.consilium.europa.eu/en/press/press-releases/2020/02/25/eu-uk-relations-council-gives-go-ahead-for-talks-to-start-and-adopts-negotiating-directives/. Accessed 17 June 2021.

European Council (2020b) 'European Council conclusions, 15–16 October 2020'. Available at https://www.consilium.europa.eu/en/press/press-releases/2020/10/16/european-council-conclusions-15-16-october-2020/. Accessed 17 June 2021.

Guardian (2021) 'US and Canada Follow EU and UK in Sanctioning Chinese official over Xinjiang'. *The Guardian*, 22 March 2021.

Hix, S. (2018) 'Brexit: Where is the EU–UK Relationship Heading?' *Journal of Common Market Studies*, Vol. 56-S1, pp. 11–27.

Johnson, B. (2019). PM Statement in the House of Commons: 19 October 2019. Available at https://www.gov.uk/government/speeches/pm-statement-in-the-house-of-commons-19-october-2019. Accessed 17 June 2021.

Kassim, H. (2021) 'The European Council, the European Commission, and the Article 50 Negotiations: Entrepreneurial Institutions and the EU27'. Paper presented to European Consortium on Political Research Standing Group on the European Union 10th Conference, 10–12 June 2021.

Laffan, B. (2019) 'How the EU27 Came to Be'. *Journal of Common Market Studies*, Vol. 57-S1, pp. 13–27.

NFFO (2020) 'Miniscule, Marginal, Paltry, Pathetic'. National Federation of Fishermen Organisation press release, 26 December 2020. Available at https://www.nffo.org.uk/miniscule-marginal-paltry-pathetic/. Accessed 17 June 2021.

OJEU (2019) Agreement on the Withdrawal of the United Kingdom of Great Britain and Northern Ireland from the European Union and the European Atomic Energy Community, Official Journal of the European Union, CI 384/1, 12 November 2019. Available at https://eur-lex.europa.eu/legal-content/EN/TXT/?uri=CELEX:12019W/TXT(02). Accessed 17 June 2021.

Šefčovič, M. (2021) 'Press Statement by Vice-President Maroš Šefčovič Following Today's Joint Committee and Partnership Council Meetings'. Press release, 9 June 2021. Available at https://ec.europa.eu/commission/presscorner/detail/en/SPEECH_21_2927. Accessed 17 June 2021.

UK in a Changing Europe (2020) 'Fisheries and Brexit'. Research paper, 11 June 2020. Available at https://ukandeu.ac.uk/research-papers/fisheries-and-brexit-3/. Accessed 17 June 2021.

Usherwood, S. (2017) 'Brexit as a Cause and a Consequence of Political Change in the UK'. *Foreign Affairs*, Vol. 96, p. 122.

Usherwood, S. (2019) 'Getting Brexit Done, or Getting Brexit Done Right?' *Political Insight*, Vol. 10, No. 4, pp. 32–4.

Zuleeg, F., Lock, T. and Wachowiak, J. (2020) 'The Brexit Transition Extension 2.0'. European Policy Centre discussion paper, 11 June 2020. Available at https://www.epc.eu/en/publications/The-Brexit-transition-extension-20~344ab8. Accessed 17 June 2021.

JCMS 2021 Volume 59. Annual Review pp. 124–136

DOI: 10.1111/jcms.13248

Community Resilience in Belarus and the EU response

ELENA KOROSTELEVA[1] and IRINA PETROVA[1,2]
[1]University of Kent, Canterbury [2]School of Slavonic and East European Studies (SSEES) UCL, London

> The search for a 'better lens' is exactly what is needed anywhere where polities … and societies are democratically challenged (Sadiki, 2015, p. 709).

Introduction

The presidential election held on 9 August 2020 and the subsequent popular mobilization marked the end of an era in the history of post-Soviet Belarus. Cautious and apolitical for three decades, Belarusian society seems to have awakened (Petrova and Korosteleva, 2021), in a short space of time observing a profound transformation of state-society relations taking them to a qualitatively new level of self-awareness and self-organization.

The 2020 presidential election, following fraudulent practices of the past (Potocki, 2011; Ash, 2015; Bedford, 2017; OSCE, 2020a), aimed to suppress opposition at all stages. Popular opposition figures, Viktor Babariko, Sergey Tikhanovskiy, Pavel Severinets and Nikolai Statkevich were arrested during canvassing, while Valeriy Tsepkalo was forced to flee the country. In their stead three female leaders emerged, led by Svetlana Tikhanovskaya as a newly registered candidate to replace her husband (Korosteleva, 2020a). On the election day, massive administrative resources were mobilized to provide a high level of support for the incumbent president (Ioffe, 2020; Shraibman, 2020). The official results accounted for 80.1 per cent (4,661,075 votes) for Alexander Lukashenko and 10.1 per cent (588,622 votes) for Svetlana Tikhanovskaya (Venkina, 2020). The sheer discrepancy between the official and alternative figures registered by digital platforms Golos, Zubr and Chestnye Lyudi[1] was so stark that it caused massive backlash throughout the country with the hundreds of thousands of Belarusians gathering for peaceful protests in Minsk and other major cities.

The authorities responded with the unprecedented levels of violence which shocked the nation (Auseyushkin and Roth, 2020; Walker, 2020). Numerous videos shared on social and independent media recorded OMON's (state security forces) appalling brutality beating up thousands of people, including children and elderly (Chernyshova, 2020). Six months on, around 45,000 people have been detained, fined and sentenced for up to several years in prison; while some key opposition figures are facing trial and death sentence (Viasna, 2021).

[Correction added on 8 October 2021, after first online publication: 'Societal' has been changed to 'Community' in the article title.]
[1]Golos: https://belarus2020.org/homeZubr: https://zubr.in/elections/aboutChestnye lyudi: https://honest-people.by/

Belarusian society, however, responded with a remarkable feat of tenacity and creativity. Next to the regular Sunday protest marches, attracting hundreds of thousands of people in Minsk,[2] the pensioner protests on Mondays with Nina Baginskaya as their figurehead became an instructive phenomenon on its own as the elderly were always seen as a safe base of Lukashenko's electorate. Separately, women's chains of solidarity dressed in white-red-white colours of the Belarusian historic flag carrying flowers, aimed to convey a peaceful "stop the violence" message. Memorials emerging on the site of protesters' murder (for example A. Taraikovsky, R. Bondarenko), spontaneous flash mobs, festivities with music, chants and flags, graffiti art, tea-drinking meetups in apartment blocks' public spaces (*dvory*) and many other forms of solidarity and protest emerged in the first months of the election. While some observers argued that these protests would dry out in the space of a few months, they instead transformed into less visible, yet still powerful local forms of resistance and self-help, united by a shared feeling that 'we will never be the same' (BBC, 2020). Previously unseen degrees of solidarity, activism and mobilization among the Belarusians, despite the OMON brutality and fears over job losses signal the emergence of the new and unprecedented *spirit of societal ownership*. Observing this development, the article asks how to understand these new social dynamics in Belarus. Relatedly, given the European Union's (EU) commitment to democracy support in its neighbourhood, we analyse what the implications of these developments for the EU are, and what the EU's response should be.

These new dynamics have been often referred to in the mainstream literature, as the processes of Belarusian nation-building and/or as delayed democratization (Kulakevich, 2020; Kazharski, 2021; Moshes and Nizhnikau, 2021). While this categorization may explain some aspects of the occurring change, we argue that there is more to this process. A detailed understanding of what is currently unfolding requires 'a better lens' (Sadiki, 2015, p. 709) to understand the role of societal relations and resilience, in the context of complex life. Hence, we believe that applying Complex IR (Kavalski, 2007, 2016), may be more suitable here. This approach covers aspects of identity, nation-building and democratization, but also allows us to make sense of the key processes of emergence, self-organization and relationality, which are at the heart of the new social dynamics in Belarus. In addition, by looking through 'the local lens' on the process of change, it helps us avoid the Western-centric bias normally associated with the transition paradigm and democracy promotion agenda (Kukri and Hobson, 2009). Complex IR explicitly highlights the need for the full decentring of external democracy support to the level of the local communities and their self-governing initiatives as is demonstrated below. Furthermore, this approach also accommodates uncertainty and impossibility to plan and control the developments in a complex world, which the above theories struggle to explain.

We argue elsewhere (Korosteleva and Petrova, 2021) that unlike the mainstream IR or social identity and transition theories, Complex IR shifts away from the Newtonian principles of linearity and causality, whereby it seems possible to expect that, for example, certain levels of economic well-being, education or external investment may inevitably result in some form of democratic progress and anticipated institutional settings necessary for the endurance of democracy. Instead, Complex IR argues that the world should be seen as an open system, unpredictable and uncontrollable, made of entanglements in

---

[2]For additional information see: https://www.euronews.com/2020/09/27/belarus-protests-how-did-we-get-here

constant dynamics, which alter the very nature of objects depending on their positionality,
relations and changes in the system. This perspective on the world, also described as a
'mesh' (Morton, 2010, 2013; Kurki, 2020), is characterised by nonlinearity, meaning that
an input is not directly or causally-related to an output. The famous butterfly effect is
perhaps the best illustration of nonlinearity, which essentially signifies the principle of
unknowability, taking root in natural sciences and Heisenberg's uncertainty principle
(1927) in particular. Unpredictability and hence uncontrollability are therefore inherent
in a complex world, to which current dynamics observed in Belarus, fully testify: for
example despite massive and persistent protests that had united almost every strata of
the population, the Lukashenko regime still stands, and yet, at the same time, there is a
clear sense of its finality which could not be forecast, or controlled, but change is clearly
underway.

The mesh/entanglement view of the world emphasises that ongoing processes are
essentially *processual* and *relational* (Bousquet and Curtis, 2011). Relations here are
not just '"interactions" of individuals or things...they are not to be thought of as existing
against an 'empty background'. Instead, relations precede things and relations are "the
mesh" from which, in which and of which "things" are made' (Kurki, 2020, p.107). This
perspective repositions our understanding of relations as being equally intra- and inter-
active processes simultaneously constituting political actors and the world, inside-out
and around us (Kavalski, 2016). Such understanding of relationality is directly linked
to another principal feature of a complex world – *emergence*. As the term of natural
sciences, it means self-organization when individual actions with no central control
respond to a changing environment at a macro-level. Emergence can be understood as a
formation of the whole, where the whole is qualitatively more than just a sum of its parts
(Kauffman, 1995). In the context of Complex IR, it would also imply self-reference and
self-reliance which through feedback loops may lead to the emergence of a new order,
building on a shared vision, inherent strength, capacities and resources of a system, thus
making it resilient (Korosteleva and Petrova, 2021). These tenets of complexity-thinking
naturally lead us to the principal conceptual frame of this article – *societal resilience as a
process of self-organization* – which encapsulates and explains the gist of the recent
developments in Belarus, and helps us understand why *the rise of peoplehood* as a
process of emergence in the country may result in irreversible change.

I. Peoplehood in Belarus as a Process of Emergence and Resilience

Resilience entered the EU policy discourse in the 2010s, being defined as 'the inherent
strength of an entity – an individual, a household, a community or a larger structure –
to better resist stress and shock, and the capacity of this entity to bounce back rapidly
from the impact' (European Commission, 2012, p. 5). The principle is further articulated
in various policies and EU official documents (European Commission, 2017; European
External Action Service, 2018). It nevertheless carried the same principal limitations:
while 'the local' communities indeed were seen as critical beneficiaries and 'keepers' of
resilience, their development was conceived as externally rendered, for example via EU
risk-management and definition of 'vulnerabilities'; top-down implemented via 'nation-
ally embedded programmes' and 'capacity-building' plans to prepare for adversity; and

narrowly conceived as 'bouncing back' and simply adapting to, rather than *transforming with change* (Korosteleva, 2018; Anholt and Sinatti, 2020; Petrova and Delcour, 2020).

In this article, and elsewhere (Korosteleva and Flockhart, 2020; Petrova and Korosteleva, 2021), we argue that not only must resilience be 'home-grown', inside-out and relational, it is also 'always more' (Bargués-Pedreny, 2020) – a way of thinking, living and governing – which in the context of complex life posited above, should be seen both as *a quality of a system* (for example the human community in Belarus impressing the world with its incredible tenacity, creativity, stamina and perseverance). Additionally, it is also *a process of self-organization* demonstrating a system's ability not just to adapt and survive, but most crucially, to transform with, and *learn from change*, which a prominent democracy scholar Larbi Sadiki (2015, 2021) refers to as 'democratic knowing' by doing when examining the Arab Spring. One of the reasons why external templates and top-down preparedness may not work in the face of adversity, and why what is emerging as a societal response to change, may be seen as irreversible, is because societal resilience works in different ways, via bottom-up and horizontal relations. These relations are premised on the intergenerational knowledge system imbued in public memory and traditions (which Sadiki described as *makhzun* in Arabic), and socio-cultural imaginary of the future (*al-mikhyal*) helping people to 'make sense of the world in the quest for self-conception' (Taylor, 2004, p. 23, in Sadiki, 2015, p. 704). This means that *resilience is all about people*, and how they think, intra- and inter-act with their community of relations, which, once mobilized, can demonstrate remarkable tenacity and commitment to their shared vision of 'the good life', that glues and makes them stronger *together* in the face of adversity or crisis. This cross-fertilization of *makhzun* and *mikhyal*, or intergenerational knowledge and visions of the future, as Sadiki argues, is 'closely tied to a society's biggest project of creation of all: "self-creation"' (Castoriadis, 1994, p. 149 in Sadiki, 2015, p. 704). Once 'activated', it takes societal resilience to a new level, triggering a chain reaction towards 'self-creation', sweeping and irreversible, even if seemingly slow or temporarily impeded by authorities, as is presently the case in Belarus.

Societal resilience, in the context of a complex life, therefore, embodies an *emergent, relational* and very much *local*, mesh/entanglement of *identity* 'as manifested through the future [vision]' (Berenskoetter, 2011, p.652) in the pursuit of the *'good life'* – for example through the imaginaries of dignity and freedom; symbols of belonging and suffering; as well as cultural poetics against injustice. This is further supplemented by *communal support and resource infrastructures* (from immediate neighbourhoods or *supol'nasts* in Belarusian, to the social movement or *hramada* in Belarusian), and even, in some cases, involving the rise of *peoplehood* (*lyudzmi zvatstsa*) as a 'bottom-up ground swell of activism accompanied by openings for potential cultural, political and social transformation. Or, in the absence of transformation, a novel revolutionary or rebellious impulse, taking peaceful or violent forms, to exert pressure for change bottom-up' (Sadiki, 2015, p. 703). We can see here many parallels with the Arab Spring again, which is a still ongoing process of learning democracy, by doing and trying. Belarus' year-long protests embody just that, a commingling of an emergent community's vision for a just and dignified future. Additionally, it is also characterised by 'unruliness' forged in public squares, *dvory*, universities, factories, hospitals, media platforms and even prisons as a shared space for spontaneous *civic apprenticeship*. This movement signals to Lukashenko's regime of its inevitable demise. Just like in the Arab Spring, it may not result in immediate change, but democratic learning has already endued, triggering long but inevitable transformation, as a bottom-up relational process of self(−re)organization:

> 'In the quest for dignity and freedom, unruliness is society's agential deployment against the 'occupiers' of the authoritarian state. Central to this unruliness, apart from informally engendering bottom-up notions of sovereign identities and participatory citizenship in the public squares of protest, is *the people's coming together* to ephemerally substitute the authoritarian regimes' practice.., with their own conceptions of political practice, thought and terminology (Sadiki, 2015, p. 715).

This 'people's coming together' to even ephemerally challenge the *status quo* is very powerful and instructive: it symbolises a rare and palpable moment of *becoming with*, and is deeply political. It is both spontaneous and long-coming, building on a dream of the 'good life', free and fair, and identity as representation of *otherness to the regime* reinforced via protest symbols (for example white-red-white flag in Belarus – see Scollon, 2020), music, language (Belsat TV Channel in Belarusian with half-a-million subscribers), humour (see for example Komissarenko, 2021; Luxta Telegram channel), and imageries of art (Norris, 2021) and poetry (PEN/opp, 2020), fuelled by an acute sense of injustice and pain. It is also more than a society: it turns into a transformative political entity, encapsulating the pain of crisis, and the fragility of life – of Alexander Taraikovskiy, Roman Bondarenko and many more, martyred for freedom in Belarus. It is exactly this '*al-hirak*' or *swell of indignation* (Sadiki, 2015) that is currently happening a year on, past the August 2020 election in the country, in a variety of forms, including student protests; women's marches; doctors, artists, journalists, workers, pensioners' remonstrations; mass rallies for dignity and solidarity; astounding creativity and the mushrooming of neighbourhood enclaves of resistance in response to the brutality, and lies of Lukashenko's regime, that have turned people's resilience into a transformational force.

The moment of *becoming with*, a *Belarusian peoplehood* has not emerged overnight. It has been brewing for years, if not centuries, premised on the past imaginaries of intense suffering (especially during World War II), subjugation, abuse and the suppressed identity of the future, powerfully expressed by a Belarusian poet Yanka Kupala in 'We, the People' [*Lyudzmi zvatstsa*], 1905–07:

> And, say, who goes there? And, say, who goes there? In such a mighty throng assembled, O declare? Belarusians! And what is it, then, for which so long they pined, Scorned throughout the years, they, the deaf, the blind? To be called PEOPLE!

This seemingly sudden mobilization *en-masse* was not at all unexpected: while long-coming, it was a public response to 'the viciousness with which their vision [for better life] was attacked... break[ing] the Belarusian camel's back' (Chernyshova, 2020, p. 2). With over 45,000 arrested, and 'the sickening torture of detainees in custody [where] many, including minors, were forced to kneel for hours, beaten, deprived of water and food, verbally abused, and raped' that galvanized even those Belarusians 'who had previously kept away from politics' (Chernyshova, 2020, p. 2). The vision of the future, mundanely associated with leading 'your own quiet little life' (female, 51 years old, Vitebsk), 'avoiding any change on a daily basis' (Male, 65 years old, Gomel); 'feeling safe, stable and protected' (student, 23 years old, Minsk) and having 'a sense of moral satisfaction with life' (female, 45 years old, Grodno)[3] in the country previously decimated by war, unquestionably gave way to the powerful ground swell of indignation which mobilized everyone, in their fight to be called 'people' – '*lyudzmi zvatstsa*'. This sense of 'the good life' suddenly became crystal clear and unifying no matter what age, nationality or profession: to be justly treated as 'people', rather than '*narodets*' (derogatory notion of people), '*bydlo*' (animals), '*ovtsy*' (sheep), '*narkomany i prostitutki*' (drug-addicts and whores), which Lukashenko's administration repetitively used towards Belarusians (see for example Kryzhanovskaya, 2020). The emergence of this acute sense of injustice meant the realisation of the single truth which seems to matter to everyone representing a moment of unity – *the dignity to be human*. This single moment, however, meant moving well beyond adaptation and endurance, to a new transformative force of becoming 'peoplehood' (*al-hirak*), with no turning back.

This moment of becoming was also facilitated by communal *support infrastructures* which seemingly emerged from out of nowhere, in a society thought to be fully atomized and devoid of community networks. Yet, these support infrastructures resurfaced, being first triggered by the COVID-19 pandemic, which the state failed to recognise and respond to. These hitherto dormant structures range from *supol'nasts, talaka* (togetherness), to *hramada* and a sense of *tuteishyya* ('the people who live here'). When the force of the regime was unleashed on the peaceful protesters in August 2020, these communal networks literally metamorphozed into a ground swell of *self-organization* across the entire country (Astapenia and Marin, 2020; Chernyshova, 2020; Douglas, 2020; Shraibman, 2020). These protests were physically leaderless, and yet they seemed well-concerted; they were sporadic and dotted, yet powerful and undermining of authorities; they were creative and peaceful, yet confronted by rubber bullets and stun grenades; and *they were fearless*, united by people's shared experience of grief and pain which 'cannot be undone in Belarus' (Minchenia and Husakouskaya, 2020) reaching a moment of 'actioned resilience' – *becoming a 'peoplehood'*. It was simply mesmerising to watch hundreds of thousand-strong crowds every Sunday coming from different corners of a city to merge into a unifying *hramada;* demonstrations of the disabled, sportsmen, medics, students, and the elderly; the memorials and festivities organized to raise the spirits up – with music, food banks and cheering; unstoppable graffiti art, and thematic resistance on a daily basis fuelled by the intoxicating sense of the lost lives of Roman Bondarenko and his last words: 'I am coming out!'.

These essentialized *makhzun* of the past and the new memories of repression and injustice, have now become interwoven with *mikhyal,* powerful and mobilizing socio-cultural imaginaries of what the Belarusians want to be – *to be called people* – thus turning them into a permanent (even when clandestine) feature of the changing political landscape. Imaginaries of Belarusian *vyshyvanka* (traditional clothes), giant hand-made models of a cockroach (aka Lukashenko), coffin and death, murals and signs of heart, fist and victory made famous by now imprisoned Maria Kolesnikova, fled Svetlana Tikhanovskaya and Veronica Tsepkalo – they all became enduring symbols of Belarusian resistance and resilience (Kazharski, 2021; Petrova and Korosteleva, 2021). The songs of

---

[3]These are some excerpts of the six focus groups conducted in Belarus during May–June 2019 as part of the GCRF COMPASS project (ES/P010849/1). They were conducted in all regional centres of Belarus, including Brest, Gomel, Grodno, Minsk, Mogilev and Vitebsk. Each focus group involved up to 11 participants, totalling 54 respondents representing all the socio-demographic groups (by gender, age and level of education) in equal proportions.

Victor Tsoi 'Peremen' (Changes), Belarusian songs 'Mury' (Walls) and 'Three Tortoises', and even a Russian song 'They beat us up, but we are flying' by Alla Pugacheva became like an anthem to the Belarusians, every Sunday continuingly drawing bigger crowds until the regime's repression hardened eight months into the protests (Abdurasulov, 2020).

It is worth noting a particular role of digital means of communication and resistance including platforms such as telegram, facebook, twitter, instagram, whatsapp, viber and more. The telegram communities Golos, Chestnye Lyudi, Byson, Nexta, Lukhta, etc. – grew from a few thousand subscribers to over several millions by the end of August 2020, whose influence for a country of 9,5 million is hard to underestimate (VOA, 2020). Furthermore, beside large online communities listed above, self-organization was also facilitated by micro-chats arranged by many apartment blocks (for example Borovaya; Kamennaya Gorka; Serebryanka; Novinki), allowing for the communities of neighbours to form, keep together and coordinate their activities (Herasimenka *et al.*, 2020).

This new sense of *togetherness*, accelerated by digital means and solidarity of the Belarusian diaspora around the world, as well as an enduring feeling of pain and injustice that have snowballed into an enormous burden that only a peoplehood could carry - all of these not only made the Belarusians instantaneously more resilient and mobilized. It turned them into a truly transformational and transformative force, which will be difficult to contain even with ever-hardening measures of repression by Lukashenko's regime.

II. The EU's Response and how to Rethink Resilience

How did the EU respond to these inconceivable levels of state brutality and unprecedented popular mobilization in this neighbouring state, geographically situated in the heart of Europe? The EU's engagement has been slow and timid, failing to promptly engage with the unfolding crisis in Belarus, which by then, saw many lives threatened, disappeared, beaten, intimidated and abused. Perhaps cautious not to repeat the mistakes of Ukraine's crisis (2013–14), and eager to maintain balance between its support for civil society and official dialogue with Lukashenko, being aware of the need to take Russia's position into account, who pledged its support to Lukashenko's regime, the EU has truly struggled to develop a coordinated response, manifest in the delayed actions and indeterminate statements. The Baltic officials, led by Lithuania (Rettman, 2020), had to issue their own measures by early September, together with Poland (Pempel and Plucinska, 2020), urgently calling on the EU to offer a unified response. The EU adoption of sanctions was further delayed by Cyprus using the Belarusian crisis for their internal bargaining vis-à-vis the EU to introduce restrictive measures against Turkey. As a result, the UK and Canada were the first Western powers to adopt sanctions (including travel bans and asset freezes) against eight Belarusian officials in late September 2020, in a Magnitsky Act style (Foreign, Commonwealth, and Development Office, 2020). On 2 October, the EU agreed to impose a travel ban and an asset freeze on 44 Belarusian officials failing to include Lukashenko (European Union, 2020). The latter together with another 14 Belarusian officials was added by mid-November, and in December, the EU imposed a third round (European Council, 2021) of sanctions targeting economic actors, and prominent businessmen and companies which directly benefited Lukashenko's regime.

The effect of sanctions however has been widely debated, and was openly derogated by the Belarusian officials (Lukashenko, 2021). In response, two months into the crisis, the EU outlined a 'four lines of action' – a semblance of strategy promising, in addition to the list of restrictive measures, to support the Organization for Security and Cooperation in Europe (OSCE) in facilitating the national dialogue; to organize a full review of EU–Belarus relations by scaling them down; and to continue supporting the Belarusian population (Borrell, 2020). Notably, support included a special measure 'The EU4Belarus: Solidarity with the People of Belarus' (European Commission, 2020a), which put forward a €24 million assistance package to support civil society, small and medium-sized enterprises (SME), youth and health sectors in Belarus. Additional €1 million and €6 million were allocated respectively to support independent media and SMEs outside of the 'EU4Belarus' measure. Around €2.7 million were also targeted to support victims of repression (European Commission, 2020b). This came as part of the overall €53 million support announced by the European Commission in August, and in addition to the COVID-19 tailor-made measures worth €980 million for the Eastern Partnership and €60 for Belarus in particular (Council of the EU, 2020), mobilized earlier to tackle the immediate needs of the pandemic crisis, including support for Belarus' medical staff with PPE, training and equipment; support for vulnerable citizens, the elderly and children; and national and local administrations to cope with negative effects of the pandemic and provide support for economic recovery.[4]

All the above measures were also supplemented[5] by the Lithuanian prosecutors' initiative to launch the first pre-trial investigation into crimes against humanity by Lukashenko's regime under the universal jurisdiction (European External Action Service, 2020); the US Treasury sanctions against nine state-owned entities (US Department of Treasury, 2020) and later a Belarus Democracy Act signed by the US President Biden in December 2020 (US Congress, 2020), as well as the OSCE invocation of the 'Moscow Mechanism' (OSCE, 2020b) to trigger expert mission to report on the human rights situation in the country, which due to the rejection by the Belarusian authorities to participate, was conducted online and published in November 2020, outlining a pathway towards a possible dialogue for mediation, to resolve the gridlock. In the meantime, Russia put its own pressure on the incumbent, forcing him to start drafting a new Constitution, and to complete negotiations on the Russia-Belarus Union State Integration roadmap, in return for its financial and military support to ensure the country's stability.

The EU's protracted engagement with Belarus in the time of crisis has been instructive in many different ways. On the one hand, its actions failed to support its own declaration of becoming more geopolitical under the von der Leyen Commission, which aimed to revive 'the EU's role as a relevant international actor, and to shape a better global order through reinforcing multilateralism' (Bassot, 2020). Not only has this intention fallen short of real action in Belarus to stand up to Russia as another geopolitical player there; it was also further undermined by its limited presence in resolving the escalation in Nagorno-Karabakh, where Turkey and Russia's influences once more explicitly prevailed. On the other hand, the EU also demonstrated its limitations in putting to practice its 'resilience agenda' initiated as part of the Global Security Strategy (2016)

---

[4]It is worth noting that €30 million of this support given to the national authorities were recalled to be reprofiled by the Commission for the civil society, but this was never fully recovered under the new sanction measures - from private conversations of the authors with EU officials.
[5]For account of other measures see https://www.robert-schuman.eu/en/doc/divers/Chronology_of_revolution_in_Belarus.pdf

(Tocci, 2020). The resilience strategy aimed to increase preparedness for potential challenges by diversifying resources and strengthening local ownership, this way trying to enhance societal capacities of developing countries to withstand the pressure of auto-cratic regimes. The traditional instruments offered by the EU to support the societal fight against repression to increase resilience were not only rigid in their accessibility especially in the time of crisis; they were also inadequate and unable to respond to the im-mediate needs of societal resilience having premeditated thematic priorities, pre-planned objectives, and benchmarks for assessing the outcomes.[6] This shows that the EU's under-standing of resilience remains superficial, deeply rooted in positivist epistemology, which, as argued above, does not work in a world of nonlinearity and complexity. The analysis of the EU's handling of the Belarusian crisis calls for a profound revision of the EU's conceptualization of resilience to account for the mesh ontology premised on relations.

Resilience as an analytic of (self-)governance focusing on unlocking local resources and communal capacities for transformation in the face of crisis or adversity, has an enor-mous potential for people who wish to build a life they have reason to value. Notably, by enhancing local ownership and changing the top-down patterns of governance and outside-in democracy promotion tools, this could unlock self-organization and self-reliance, or what we call resilience elsewhere (Korosteleva and Petrova, 2021). For example, whereas some initiatives, such as the complementary support measures 'in favour of civil society' (European Commission, 2017) aiming to enable local communi-ties to be creative about tackling their respective needs and priorities, as part of the European Neighbourhood Instrument (ENI) programming (Korosteleva, 2020b), are more in line with complexity-thinking and supporting the local emergence, the EU still struggles to understand how resilience as self-governance, especially in crisis, could work in practice, to give an empowering sense of ownership and freedom to communities to fend for themselves. Current programmes carrying a sizeable monetary value do not yet form a 'democratic/learning loop' (Sadiki, 2015, 2021) required for forging democratic knowledge (*makhzun*) by communities themselves, to fully connect with the socio-cultural imaginaries of the future (*mikhyal*), in order to activate people's resilience proper, in their own project of self-creation.

Conclusion

The Belarusian crisis of 2020–21, echoing the Arab Spring and the Revolution of Dignity in Ukraine, we argue, is more than just a process of identity- and nation-building, or indeed that of transition and democratization. It is a moment of '*becoming with*' - emergence and self-organization of local communities - which, while drawing on their identity and collective sense of the good life, local support infrastructures, resources and networks, make them more resilient in the face of adversity turning them into people-hood to transform with change. Premised on Complex IR, we argue that rather than seeing this process as a top-down or bottom-up, outside-in or inside-out, it is more instructive to think of it as a mesh made of the totality of all relations. Resilience as the ability to transform with change, comes from intra- and interactions within that mesh, it is therefore

---

[6]See, for instance, the recent EUROPAID emergency calls to support civil society in Belarus: https://webgate.ec.europa.eu/ europeaid/online-services/index.cfm?ADSSChck=1619012759472&do=publi.detPUB&aoref=171256&nbPubliList= 15&orderbyad=Desc&page=1&searchtype=QS&orderby=upd&userlanguage=en

local, emergent and *relational,* which cannot be built on external templates or financial injections. Suffering the unprecedented state pressure, Belarusian society has risen anew, hardly resembling its feeble self only three decades ago: its new quality was forged due to the spirits of ownership and solidarity, being connected by pain and indignation, to bring about the moment of peoplehood thus forming a new and tangible order of tomorrow.

In order to effectively support this locally-grown and outward dynamic, external actors, and the EU in particular, need to rethink their strategies to co-creatively engage in the mesh of relations and the 'environment around' (Kavalski, 2016). This is where Sadiki's concept of a democratic learning loop gives an important insight into how cooperation could work in practice. An important task is sensing (Chandler, 2018) the local dynamic and engaging in continuous inter- and intra-actions in order to understand what the local visions, strengths, capacities, and needs are to support the initiatives of self-organization, rather than trying to categorize and benchmark them the pre-set objectives and straightjacket them into the known evaluation criteria. Such approach envisages genuinely flexible mechanisms of interaction - not the EU's usual understanding of flexibility as giving partners an opportunity to choose from a list of predefined options, but rather following the local dynamics and building agile partnerships.

Acknowledgments

Herewith we would like to acknowledge the financial support of GCRF UKRI for our COMPASS project (ES/P010849/1) and the editorial support of the JCMS Annual Review [Correction added on 6 October 2021, after first online publication: Acknowledgements section has been added.].

References

Abdurasulov, A. (2020) 'Belarus Protesters Battered, Bruised but Defiant after 100 Days'. *BBC News.* https://www.bbc.co.uk/news/world-europe-54961111

Anholt, R. and Sinatti, G. (2020) 'Under the Guise of Resilience: The EU Approach to Migration and Forced Displacement in Jordan and Lebanon'. *Contemporary Security Policy,* Vol. 41, No. 2, pp. 311–35. https://doi.org/10.1080/13523260.2019.1698182

Ash, K. (2015) 'The Election Trap: The Cycle of Post-Electoral Repression and Opposition Fragmentation in Lukashenko's Belarus'. *Democratization: The Journal of Post-Soviet Democratization,* Vol. 22, No. 6, pp. 1030–53. https://doi.org/10.1080/13510347.2014.899585

Astapenia, R., and Marin, A. (2020) Belarusians Left Facing COVID-19 Alone. *Chatham House,* 16 April. https://www.chathamhouse.org/2020/04/belarusians-left-facing-covid-19-alone

Auseyushkin, Y. and Roth, D. (2020) Belarus Election: Lukashenko's Claim of Landslide Victory Sparks Widespread Protests. *The Guardian,* 10 August. https://www.theguardian.com/world/2020/aug/09/belarus-election-lukashenko-landslide-victory-fixing-claims

Bargués-Pedreny, P. (2020) 'Resilience is "Always More" than our Practices: Limits, Critiques, and Skepticism about International Intervention'. *Contemporary Security Policy,* Vol. 41, No. 2, pp. 263–86. https://doi.org/10.1080/13523260.2019.1678856

Bassot, E. (2020) 'The von der Leyen Commission's priorities for 2019–2024'. European Parliament Briefing, PE 646.148. https://www.europarl.europa.eu/RegData/etudes/BRIE/2020/646148/EPRS_BRI(2020)646148_EN.pdf

BBC (2020, December 25) 'Just Dressed White Dresses and Took Flowers. Why Women Became the Main Protest Power'. https://www.bbc.com/russian/features-55400540

Bedford, S. (2017) '"The Election Game:" Authoritarian Consolidation Processes in Belarus'. *Demokratizatsiya: The Journal of Post-Soviet Democratization*, Vol. 17, No. 4, pp. 381–405.

Berenskoetter, F. (2011) 'Reclaiming the Vision Thing: Constructivists as Students of the Future'. *International Studies Quarterly*, Vol. 55, No. 3, pp. 647–68. https://doi.org/10.1111/j.1468-2478.2011.00669.x

Borrell, J. (2020) Belarusians Courageously Demand Democratic Change. European External Action Service. https://eeas.europa.eu/headquarters/headquarters-homepage/85548/belarusians-courageously-demand-democratic-change-eu-must-stand-them_en

Bousquet, A. and Curtis, S. (2011) 'Beyond Models and Metaphors: Complexity Theory, Systems Thinking and International Relations'. *Cambridge Review of International Affairs*, Vol. 24, No. 1, pp. 43–62. https://doi.org/10.1080/09557571.2011.558054

Chandler, D. (2018) *Ontopolitics in the Anthropocene: An Introduction to Mapping, Sensing and Hacking* (Routledge).

Chernyshova, N. (2020) 'A Very Belarusian Affair: What Sets the Current Anti-Lukashenka Protests Apart'. PONARS Eurasia Policy Memo.

Council of the EU (2020). 'Facts and Figures about EU–Belarus Relations'. https://www.consilium.europa.eu/media/44399/685-annex-5-c-belarus-factsheet.pdf

Douglas, N. (2020) Belarus: From the Old Social Contract to New Social Identity (Issue 6). https://en.zois-berlin.de/fileadmin/media/Dateien/3-Publikationen/ZOiS_Reports/2020/ZOiS_Report_6_2020.pdf

European Commission (2012). *The EU Approach to Resilience: Learning from Food Security Crises. Communication from the Commission to the European Parliament and the Council. COM 586 Final*. http://ec.europa.eu/echo/files/policies/resilience/com_2012_586_resilience_en.pdf

European Commission (2017) Strategic Approach to Resilience in the EU's External Action. Joint Communication to the European Parliament and the Council. JOIN 21final. https://eeas.europa.eu/sites/default/files/join_2017_21_f1_communication_from_commission_to_inst_en_v7_p1_916039.pdf

European Commission (2020a). Commission Implementing Decision of 11.12.2020 On the Special Measure in Favour of the Republic of Belarus for 2020. C(2020) 8954 Final. https://ec.europa.eu/neighbourhood-enlargement/sites/default/files/c_2020_8954_f1_commission_implementing_decision_en_v2_p1_1110385.pdf

European Commission (2020b) 'EU–Belarus Relations'. https://ec.europa.eu/neighbourhood-enlargement/neighbourhood/countries/belarus_en

European Council (2021) 'Timeline – EU Restrictive Measures against Belarus'. https://www.consilium.europa.eu/en/policies/sanctions/restrictive-measures-following-the-2020-belarus-presidential-elections/belarus-timeline/

European External Action Service (2018). 'From Shared Vision to Common Action: Implementing the EU Global Strategy. Year 2'. http://www.ieee.es/Galerias/fichero/OtrasPublicaciones/Internacional/2018/EU_Global_Strategy_Jun2018.pdf

European External Action Service (2020). 'The EU Continues to Stand with the People of Belarus'. https://eeas.europa.eu/headquarters/headquarters-homepage_en/90975/TheEUcontinuestostandwiththepeopleofBelarus

European Union (2020) 'Council Implementing Decision (CFSP) 2020/1388 of 2 October 2020 Implementing Decision 2012/642/CFSP Concerning Restrictive Measures against Belarus'. *Official Journal of the EU*, Vol. 63. https://eur-lex.europa.eu/legal-content/en/TXT/PDF/?uri=OJ:L:2020:319I:FULL&from=EN

Foreign, Commonwealth & Development Office (2020). 'Belarus: UK Sanctions 8 Members of Regime, Including Alexander Lukashenko'. FCDO Press Release. https://www.gov.uk/government/news/belarus-uk-sanctions-eight-members-of-regime-including-alexander-lukashenko

Herasimenka, A., Lokot, T., Onuch, O. and Wijermars, M. (2020) 'There's More to Belarus's "Telegram Revolution" than a Cellphone App'. *Washington Post*, 11 September.

Ioffe, G. (2020) 'Belarus: Elections and Sovereignty'. *Eurasia Daily Monitor*, Vol. 111, No. 17. https://jamestown.org/program/belarus-elections-and-sovereignty/

Kauffman, S. (1995) *At Home in the Universe: The Search for Laws of Complexity* (Penguin Books).

Kavalski, E. (2007) 'The Fifth Debate and the Emergence of Complex International Relations Theory: Notes on the Application of Complexity Theory to the Study of International Life'. *Cambridge Review of International Affairs*, Vol. 20, No. 3, pp. 435–54. https://doi.org/10.1080/09557570701574154

Kavalski, E. (2016) *World Politics at the Edge of Chaos: Reflections on Complexity and Global Life* (SUNY Press).

Kazharski, A. (2021) 'Belarus' New Political Nation? 2020 Anti-Authoritarian Protests as Identity-Building'. *New Perspectives*, Vol. 29, No. 1, pp. 69–79. https://doi.org/10.1177/2336825X20984340

Komissarenko, S. (2021) 'New about Chyk-Chyryk'. https://www.youtube.com/watch?v=8vrfK95HnjA

Korosteleva, E.A. (2018) 'Paradigmatic or Critical? Resilience as a New Turn in EU Governance for the Neighbourhood'. *Journal of International Relations and Development*, pp. 1–15. https://doi.org/10.1057/s41268-018-0155-z

Korosteleva, E. A. (2020a). 'A Changing Belarus? The Country in the Eye of the Storm'. *Dahrendorf Forum*. https://www.dahrendorf-forum.eu/a-changing-belarus-the-country-in-the-eye-of-the-storm/

Korosteleva, E.A. (2020b) 'Reclaiming Resilience Back: A Local Turn in EU External Governance'. *Contemporary Security Policy*, Vol. 41, No. 2, pp. 241–62. https://doi.org/10.1080/13523260.2019.1685316

Korosteleva, E.A. and Flockhart, T. (2020) 'Resilience in EU and International Institutions: Redefining Local Ownership in a New Global Governance Agenda'. *Contemporary Security Policy*, Vol. 41, No. 2, pp. 153–75. https://doi.org/10.1080/13523260.2020.1723973

Korosteleva, E.A. and Petrova, I. (2021) 'From "the Local" to "the Global": What Makes Communities Resilient in Times of Complexity and Change?' *Cambridge Review of International Affairs*, Vol. 35, No. 3 forthcoming.

Kryzhanovskaya, E. (2020) Europe should Talk about Belarus with Putin, not Lukashenko. https://www.dw.com/ru/o-belarusi-evropa-dolzhna-govorit-ne-s-lukashenko-a-s-putinym/a-54612819

Kukri, M. and Hobson, C. (2009) 'Democracy and Democracy Support: A New Era', *OpenDemocracy*, https://www.opendemocracy.net/en/democracy-and-democracy-support-a-new-era/

Kulakevich, T. (2020) 'National Awakening in Belarus: Elite Ideology to "Nation" Practice'. *SAIS Review of International Affairs*, Vol. 40, No. 2, pp. 97–110. https://doi.org/10.1353/sais.2020.0027

Kurki, M. (2020) *International Relations in a Relational Universe* (Oxford University Press).

Lukashenko, A. (2021) 'Consultation on Counteraction to Sanctions. President of the Republic of Belarus'. https://president.gov.by/ru/events/soveshchanie-o-protivodeystvii-sankcionnym-meram

Minchenia, A., & Husakouskaya, N. (2020) 'For Many People in Belarus, Change Has Already Happened'. *OpenDemocracy*. https://www.opendemocracy.net/en/odr/many-people-belarus-change-has-already-happened/

Morton, T. (2010) *The Ecological Thought* (Harvard University Press).

Morton, T. (2013) *Hyperobjects: Philosophy and Ecology after the End of the World* (University of Minnesota Press).

Moshes, A. and Nizhnikau, R. (2021) 'The Belarusian Revolution: Sources, Interim To Be Learned'. *Democratization, Demokratizatsiya: The Journal of Post-Soviet*, Vol. 29, No. 2, pp. 159–82.

Norris, S. (2021) 'History, Memory, and the Art of Protest in Belarus'. *Interzine*. https://interzine.org/2021/06/01/history-memory-and-the-art-of-protest-in-belarus/

OSCE (2020a) OSCE/ODIHR Alarmed by Increasing Threats to Human Rights in Belarus Following Presidential Election. https://www.osce.org/odihr/460693

OSCE (2020b) Note Verbale No 358/2020. https://www.osce.org/files/f/documents/2/b/469539.pdf

Pempel, K. and Plucinska, J. (2020) 'Poland Offers New Support for Belarus Civil Society, Media'. Reuters, 14 August. https://www.reuters.com/article/instant-article/idUKL8N2FG52Z

PEN/opp (2020) Protest Poems. https://www.penopp.org/articles/protest-poems?language_content_entity=en

Petrova, I. and Delcour, L. (2020) 'From Principle to Practice? The Resilience–Local Ownership Nexus in the EU Eastern Partnership Policy'. *Contemporary Security Policy*, Vol. 41, No. 2, pp. 336–60. https://doi.org/10.1080/13523260.2019.1678280

Petrova, I. and Korosteleva, E. (2021) 'Fragility and Resilience Community Strategies in Belarus'. *Journal of Eurasian Studies*. https://doi.org/10.1177/18793665211037835

Potocki, R. (2011) 'Belarus: A Tale of Two Elections'. *Journal of Democracy*, Vol. 22, No. 3, pp. 49–63. https://doi.org/10.1353/jod.2011.0050

Rettman, A. (2020) 'Lithuania Seeks EU Reaction to Belarus Killing'. *EUObserver*, 13 November. https://euobserver.com/foreign/150059

Sadiki, L. (2015) 'Discoursing 'Democratic Knowledge' & Knowledge Production in North Africa'. *Journal of North African Studies*, Vol. 20, No. 5, pp. 688–90. https://doi.org/10.1080/13629387.2015.1081455

Sadiki, L. (2021) 'On EU–Arab Democratisation: Towards a Democratic 'Learning Loop''. In Pace, M., Huber, D. and Bouris, D. (eds) *Routledge Handbook on EU–Middle East Relations* (Routledge).

Scollon, M. (2020) 'Flying The Flag: Belarusians Show Their True Colors In Solidarity With Protests'. *RadioFreeEurope*, 9 September. https://www.rferl.org/a/belarusians-red--white-flag-protests-solidarity/30829635.html

Shraibman, A. (2020) 'Stress-Test for Lukashenko'. In *Analytics. Discussions. Opinions 2020*. Friedrich Ebert Stiftung. http://library.fes.de/pdf-files/bueros/kiew/17379.pdf

Tocci, N. (2020) 'Resilience and the Role of the European Union in the World'. *Contemporary Security Policy*, Vol. 41, No. 2, pp. 176–94. https://doi.org/10.1080/13523260.2019.1640342

US Congress (2020) Belarus Democracy, Human Rights, and Sovereignty Act of 2020. https://www.congress.gov/bill/116th-congress/house-bill/8438

US Department of Treasury (2020) *Belarus Sanctions*. https://home.treasury.gov/policy-issues/financial-sanctions/sanctions-programs-and-country-information/belarus-sanctions

Venkina, E. (2020) 'Belarusian Central Election Commission Confirmed Official Election Results'. *Deutsche Welle*, 14 August. https://www.dw.com/ru/cik-belarusi-utverdil-itogi-vyborov/a-54572693

Viasna (2021) 'Human Rights Situation in Belarus: March 2021'. http://spring96.org/en/news/102738

VOA (2020) 'Telegram App Helps Drive Belarus Protests'. *Voice of America*, 21 August. https://www.voanews.com/silicon-valley-technology/telegram-app-helps-drive-belarus-protests

Walker, S. (2020) 'Protesters Clash with Police in Belarus after Lukashenko Sworn in Again'. *The Guardian*, 24 September. https://www.theguardian.com/world/2020/sep/23/lukashenko-sworn-in-belarus-president-secretive-ceremony

JCMS 2021 Volume 59. Annual Review. pp. 137–149   DOI: 10.1111/jcms.13255

Territorial Conflict, Domestic Crisis, and the Covid-19 Pandemic in the South Caucasus. Explaining Variegated EU Responses

TOBIAS SCHUMACHER[1] and CENGIZ GÜNAY[2]
[1] NTNU – Norwegian University of Science and Technology, Trondheim, Norway & College of Europe, Natolin campus, Warsaw
[2] Austrian Institute for International Affairs (OIIP), Vienna

Introduction

For the three countries of the South Caucasus region, Armenia, Azerbaijan, and Georgia, linked to the EU through its European Neighbourhood Policy (ENP), the Eastern Partnership (EaP) and a diverse set of Association, Cooperation and Partnership Agreements (Simão, 2018; van Gils, 2020), 2020 brought about three developments of supposedly seismic magnitude. The most significant event, affecting the region's geopolitical order, was the outbreak of the 44-day war between Armenia and Armenia-supported forces of the breakaway region of Nagorny Karabakh and Azerbaijan, aided by its brotherly ally Turkey. Preceded by skirmishes and small-scale military confrontations that had erupted intermittently since 1994 when Armenia and Azerbaijan had signed the Bishkek Protocol (Freizer, 2014, p. 110) that terminated the first war (1991–94), the 2020 war broke out on 27 September and ended on 9 November, following a Russia-mediated ceasefire agreement.[1] Throughout the six weeks of armed conflict, 5,970 combatants were killed[2] and thousands of Armenian settlers displaced. As de Waal (2021) noted, the military conflict and the ensuing agreement resulted in 'reversed roles of victor and defeated' as Azerbaijan regained approximately one third of Armenia-occupied Nagorny Karabakh and the seven territories adjacent to it, held by Armenia since 1994.

The second major development in 2020 was the outbreak of domestic political crises in Armenia and Georgia. Their origins differed but effectively revolved around questions of legitimacy of, and alleged abuse of power by, the incumbent governments. In Armenia, in response to military defeat and the loss of territory, two multi-party alliances stoked nationalist sentiments and mobilized thousands of Armenians to engage in weeks-long protests against Prime Minister Pashinyan's war management, calling for his resignation.[3] In contrast, Georgia's crisis centered around contentious electoral reforms. Allegations of voting fraud in the parliamentary elections, held on 31 October, incited mass protests in Tbilisi against the ruling Georgian Dream Party, and on 8 November, leaders of the united opposition declared to boycott the second round of elections on 21 November and participation in future parliamentary sessions.[4]

---

[1] https://www.economist.com/europe/2020/11/12/a-peace-deal-ends-a-bloody-war-over-nagorno-karabakh
[2] https://www.crisisgroup.org/content/nagorno-karabakh-conflict-visual-explainer#1
[3] https://www.rferl.org/a/armenian-opposition-names-joint-candidate-in-bid-to-pressure-pm/30982610.html
[4] https://jam-news.net/georgian-opposition-calls-on-public-to-boycott-the-second-round-of-elections/

The third development that compounded events on the local and regional level was the outbreak and spread of the Covid-19 pandemic. While the first wave could be contained by authorities in the three countries rather quickly, the number of new daily infections and deaths peaked in late 2020.[5] Regimes resorted to different measures such as limiting public life intermittently and forcing economies into temporary shutdowns. These, in conjunction with the global fallouts of the pandemic, have led to steep economic contractions of 5 per cent (Azerbaijan), 6 per cent (Georgia) and 8 per cent (Armenia)[6] and, according to the UNDP (2021), a deterioration of already strained public finances and exchange-rate instabilities. Also, unemployment has soared in all three countries,[7] reinforcing endemic poverty, inequality, and poor micro-economic development.

How has the EU responded to these developments and how have they impacted EU-South Caucasus relations? After all, the ENP Review of 2015 had promised active involvement in the region. It pledged to 'offer a tailor-made approach to cooperating on security-related matters' [and to] 'actively ensure that our overall engagement is conflict-sensitive' (European Commission and HR/VP, 2015, p. 4). It declared that 'all means available will be used [...] to support the management of crises and the settlement of protracted conflicts in the neighbourhood' (ibid., p. 13). The EU also committed itself to continue 'to work with partner governments, civil society and citizens on human rights and democracy related issues, including electoral processes' (ibid., p. 6). Lastly, the ENP heralded to 'put stronger emphasis on health security aspects by strengthening country capacities to respond effectively to health threats including communicable diseases.' (ibid., p. 14).

As will be discussed by this article, EU relations with the three countries of the South Caucasus remained largely unaffected by domestic crises and regional conflict, whereas EU responses variegated considerably. It is argued that variance is due to a mix of factors. On one hand, local and regional scope conditions and the role of other extra-regional actors provided differentiated opportunity structures for EU engagement. On the other hand, variegated responses are the result of intra-EU dynamics that oscillated between passivity, disinterest, go-alone attitudes of individual Member States, and consensus when action seemed needed and possible.

The article is divided into three main sections. The first section discusses the relevance of the Armenia–Azerbaijan war for EU relations with the two countries and examines EU (in)action. The subsequent section analyses and explains EU engagement in the domestic political crises in Armenia and Georgia, whereas the last section explains the reasons for, and nature of, EU responses to the Covid-19 pandemic in the three countries. The article will conclude by offering reflections on the future of EU policies towards the South Caucasus in a post-pandemic setting.

I. The EU and the Armenia–Azerbaijan War

Almost one and a half decades ago, German (2007) argued that the EU was 'visibly invisible' in what regards conflict resolution in the South Caucasus. Some 15 years later, and

[5]Johns Hopkins University & Medicine Coronavirus Resource Center, 7 May 2021.
[6]https://reliefweb.int/report/armenia/poverty-and-welfare-impacts-covid-19-and-mitigation-policies-armenia
[7]https://jam-news.net/50-of-working-age-adults-are-unemployed-in-georgia/; https://tradingeconomics.com/azerbaijan/un-employment-rate; https://tradingeconomics.com/armenia/unemployment-rate

after 44 days of military conflict in and around Nagorny Karabakh, this sobering assessment remains largely valid. Virtually all observers who commented on the EU's role in the 2020 war share the view that the EU acted as a mere 'bystander' (de Waal, 2020), that it was 'sidelined' (Broers, 2021) or even 'paralyzed'.[8] When judged against the European Commission's much-noticed communication of December 2006, which claimed that the EU needs to proactively address protracted conflicts in the Southern Caucasus to prevent the further undermining of regional stability (European Commission, 2006, p. 9), one observer even went so far as to argue that the EU 'failed, yet again, and in a spectacular fashion, to be a relevant player and a peace broker on its eastern periphery' (Grgic, 2020).

The EU's inability to adopt a proactive role, exert power and act as a conflict mediator can be explained through regional power shifts and intra-EU-related factors. After years of strategic large-scale investment in its military capabilities (Schumacher, 2016), and growing public dissatisfaction with the status quo (Schumacher, 2020), Azerbaijan was increasingly determined to seek a military solution to the conflict and re-conquer territory. Resorting to high-tech, precision-guided drone systems of Israeli and Turkish origin, and the deployment of foreign mercenaries,[9] Azerbaijan quickly advanced into, and rapidly recaptured, Armenia-occupied territories, sensing military victory from the outset. These territorial gains, accompanied by inflammatory regime propaganda and domestic 'war euphoria', decreased Azerbaijan's interest in peace negotiations or potential mediation efforts by the EU which is not even part of the OSCE Minsk Group, established in 1994 and co-chaired by Russia, France, and the United States with the task of finding a peaceful solution to the conflict.

Similarly, also Armenia's post-revolutionary government of Prime Minister Pashinyan had adopted a more confrontational course. Over the course of time, it abandoned the OSCE Minsk Group's 'Basic Principles' for the phased and peaceful settlement of the conflict (agreed upon in November 2007),[10] and embraced 'an agenda of territorial aggrandizement far beyond the original goal of self-determination and security for Upper Karabakh' (Socor, 2021). Moreover, the government made highly confrontational statements that 'Artsakh [Nagorny Karabakh] is Armenia',[11] or that even 'new territories would [be seized]' in the 'event of a new war' (cited in Socor, 2021). De facto, the Armenian government seemed no longer willing to consider previously discussed land-for-peace options or make these subjects of any deliberations with the EU.

Changes in the two parties' approach to the conflict were not the only developments on the regional level that hampered EU engagement. Most importantly, Russia had no interest in involving other international actors in the resolution of the conflict. Although, in its capacity as co-chair of the OSCE Minsk Group, it had called in October and November repeatedly upon the conflict parties to cease hostilities and agree on a ceasefire, it did nothing to empower the Minsk Group and let it play any mediation role. Instead, Russia viewed the conflict as an opportunity to pursue its own geopolitical objectives to strengthen its role in the region by playing the two conflict parties off against one

[8] https://www.tert.am/en/news/2021/03/19/amanda-paul/3556167
[9] https://www.wsj.com/articles/turkish-backed-syrian-fighters-join-armenian-azeri-conflict-11602625885;   https://www.ohchr.org/EN/NewsEvents/Pages/DisplayNews.aspx?NewsID=26494
[10] https://www.osce.org/mg/51152
[11] https://oc-media.org/pashinyan-calls-for-unification-between-nagorno-karabakh-and-armenia/

another further than it had already done in the past. From this perspective, the conflict allowed Russia to make itself an indispensable and dominant party of any future post-war arrangement, to expand its military footprint in the region through the deployment of Russian peacekeepers to Nagorny Karabakh,[12] to increase Armenia's security dependency, and to weaken the pro-democratic government of Prime Minister Pashinyan, which it had eyed with suspicion ever since it came to power in the Velvet Revolution of 2018.[13] This predominant role was facilitated by the strategic retreat of the United States from the South Caucasus.

By the same token, Turkey's provision of military hardware, intelligence support and military advisors to Azerbaijan[14] tipped the military balance in favour of the latter and expanded its political and military presence in the region, thereby challenging Russia's quest for regional hegemony. Turkish President Erdoğan questioned the legitimacy of established international conflict resolution mechanisms and claimed Turkey's active involvement in the reshaping of the post-war regional order.[15] This demand was reinforced by Russia's and Turkey's decision to establish a 'Joint Russian-Turkish Centre for Monitoring the Ceasefire in Karabakh' in the Aghdam district of Azerbaijan and the decision to create a land corridor connecting mainland Azerbaijan with its exclave Nakhchivan. Such a corridor, to be controlled by the Russian Federal Security Service, is in Turkey's interest as it will help facilitating Turkish trade with Azerbaijan and Central Asia. All in all, these developments serve as powerful examples of how altered regional scope conditions have further diminished the already limited opportunity structures for the EU in 2020.

As far as intra-EU factors hampering EU action in the conflict are concerned, it is noteworthy that the Nagorny Karabakh war was in the periphery of EU interests. On one hand, this can be explained by the absence of influential policy entrepreneurship on the part of EU Member States and the limited salience of both the region and the conflict on their respective foreign policy agendas. While the German EU Council Presidency and various Member States' governments condemned the hostilities and called for an immediate ceasefire, they did not become active.[16] Only France pursued a more active role, though outside the EU framework. Already shortly after the outbreak of the war, French President Macron attacked President Erdoğan, arguing that his war-related statements were 'reckless and dangerous'[17] and that France would not accept the violent acquisition of territory by Azerbaijan. Also, by remarking 'I say to Armenia and to the Armenians, France will play its role',[18] Macron did not just signal France's support for Armenia –

---

[12]Russia has two military bases in Armenia. According to the ceasefire agreement, Russia deploys for a period of at least five years in Nagorny Karabakh and along the so-called Lachin corridor, linking the former with mainland Armenia, 1.960 Russian peacekeepers, 90 armoured personnel carriers and 380 military vehicles.
[13]https://www.euractiv.com/section/global-europe/opinion/the-velvet-revolution-is-affecting-armenias-ties-with-russia/
[14]https://studies.aljazeera.net/en/policy-briefs/nagorno-karabakh-war-new-balance-power-southern-caucasus
[15]https://www.hurriyetdailynews.com/us-russia-france-involvement-for-ceasefire-in-karabakh-unacceptable-erdogan-158761
[16]https://www.osce.org/files/f/documents/6/2/469719.pdf; https://www.osce.org/permanent-council/471552; https://www.dw.com/en/germany-under-pressure-to-take-sides-in-nagorno-karabakh-conflict/a-55364432; https://www.riksdagen.se/sv/dokument-lagar/dokument/skriftlig-fraga/konflikten-i-nagorno-karabach_H811154
[17]https://www.france24.com/en/20200930-macron-condemns-turkey-s-bellicose-statements-on-nagorno-karabakh-fighting
[18]ttps://www.france24.com/en/20200930-macron-condemns-turkey-s-bellicose-statements-on-nagorno-karabakh-fighting

which eventually materialized in the form of humanitarian flights and the establishment of a 'mechanism to assist Armenians affected by the conflict in Nagorno-Karabakh'.[19] He also put France in opposition to other Member States that favoured a more balanced approach. France's pro-Armenian bias – the French Senate had even called for the recognition of Nagorny Karabakh[20] – not only undermined the Minsk Group's legitimacy and eliminated its chances of becoming active as a mediator, but also harmed the EU's image as a potentially neutral power broker in the eyes of Azerbaijan.

On the other hand, following the fraudulent presidential elections of 9 August 2020 in Belarus and the subsequent use of state-sponsored violence by the regime of Alexander Lukashenko, and considering energy disputes in the Eastern Mediterranean, EU Member States' governments in the second half of the year were predominantly occupied by other crises. This was further accentuated by the ongoing negotiations over a Brexit agreement, negotiations on the Multi-Annual Financial Framework with the European Parliament, and the management of the Covid-19 pandemic. European Council President Michel, determined to carve out a role for himself as regards representing the EU globally, repeatedly spoke on the phone with the Azerbaijani President and the Armenian Prime Minister, hosted Armenian President Sarkissian, and resorted to his personal Twitter account to express his condemnation of the violence and support for renewed negotiations. Uncoordinated with Member States, these efforts, though, blatantly underestimated conflict developments in and around Nagorny Karabakh and the fact that the conflict parties – and their respective societies – were neither interested in finding compromise solutions nor requesting EU mediation.

The EU's little interest in the conflict and its holding on to an outdated 'negotiations-for-peace' narrative was also demonstrated by the few occasions the 27 Heads of States and Governments addressed the issue. Of the three European Council summits that took place between October and December 2020, only the Special European Council, held on 1–2 October, touched upon the war. The relevant paragraph in the Summit Conclusions – seven lines long – was a repetition of past uninspiring EU discourses, calling for a 'cessation of hostilities', '[urging] the parties to recommit to a lasting ceasefire and the peaceful settlement', arguing that there 'can be no military solution', '[expressing continuous] support for the OSCE Minsk Group', and requesting the High Representative for Foreign Affairs and Security Policy, Josep Borrell, 'to examine further EU support' (European Council, 2020, p. 11).

This call for peace and negotiations equally dominated the ensuing discourse of the two Foreign Affairs Council meetings on 12 October and 19 November and formed the cornerstone of subsequent declarations by Borrell (Council of the EU, 2020a; Council of the EU, 2020b). Concrete EU support did materialize, though in the form of announced humanitarian aid packages, totaling 3.9 million EUR for conflict-affected civilians in and around Nagorny Karabakh.[21] On the occasion of the EU-Armenia Partnership Council and the subsequent EU-Azerbaijan Cooperation Council, held on 17 and 18 December, Commissioner for Neighbourhood and Enlargement Várhelyi made a commitment to 'contribute €10 million to further humanitarian assistance and to work towards more

---

[19]https://www.diplomatie.gouv.fr/en/country-files/armenia/news/article/armenia-france-establishing-a-mechanism-to-assist-armenians-affected-by-the

[20]https://jam-news.net/french-senate-adopted-a-resolution-on-the-recognition-of-nagorno-karabakh/

[21]https://ec.europa.eu/commission/presscorner/detail/en/IP_20_2161

comprehensive conflict transformation and longer-term socio-economic development'.[22] However, the European Commission, tasked with the provision of emergency aid, failed to specify how it aimed to disburse aid in Russia-controlled areas in Nagorny Karabakh, and Várhelyi's two announcements regarding DGNEAR's financial assistance were particularly striking as their wording was identical, even though 'comprehensive conflict transformation' has distinctively different connotations and de facto implications for Armenia and Azerbaijan in the new regional post-war configuration.

Finally, these developments occurred after EU Special Representative for the South Caucasus and the crisis in Georgia (EUSR), Toivo Klaar, was received by Azerbaijani President Aliyev in Baku just two days before the start of the hostilities.[23] During the meeting, Aliyev – in a humiliating show of force – kept Klaar in the dark regarding Azerbaijan's true intentions of waging full-scale war, thus giving the EU's presumptive 'conflict sensitivity' and ambition to develop a 'tailor-made approach to cooperating on security-related matters' (European Commission and HR/VP, 2015, p. 4), which the 2015 ENP Review had ambitiously spoken of, a rather cynical touch.

II. The EU and Domestic Political Crisis in Armenia and Georgia

EU responses to the domestic political crises in Armenia and Georgia variegated, and, in both cases, it was a set of extra- and intra-EU-related factors that explain variance. Whereas these precluded the EU from adopting an active and tangible role in Armenia, they enabled the EU to actively involve itself in Georgia and contribute to a partial defusing of a crisis that overshadowed much of Georgian domestic politics in 2020.

In Armenia, the signing of the ceasefire accord by Prime Minister Pashinyan, entailing de facto recognition of Armenia's defeat and Azerbaijan's reconquest of Armenia-held territories, plunged the country into serious domestic political turmoil. Shortly after news broke that Pashinyan had signed the agreement, which he referred to as 'unfavourable',[24] protesters seized government buildings in Yerevan, stormed the parliament, assaulted the Speaker of the National Assembly, and accused Pashinyan of high treason for single-handedly accepting the terms of the armistice agreement and surrendering supposedly Armenian lands to Azerbaijan. Fueled by the aggressive rhetoric of two multiple party alliances, composed of former ruling and marginalized opposition parties, protests and nationalist sentiments grew until late December 2020. Pashinyan's pre-war popularity decreased dramatically, and his legitimacy was put even more in question when President Sarkissian, leaders of the Armenian Apostolic Church and former presidents called on him to resign, hand over to a government of national accord, and call for early legislative elections.[25] Opposition forces nominated in early December Vazgen Manukian, a former Prime Minister and ex-Defense Minister, as head of an interim government. But Pashinyan refused to step down and also rejected the idea of early elections, putting on public display the deep polarization between his pro-democratic movement and old regime forces that has been predating the 2020 crisis.

---

[22]Council of the EU, Meeting Information, 17 December 2020, and Council of the EU, Meeting Information, 18 December 2020.
[23]https://www.commonspace.eu/index.php/news/eu-special-envoy-meets-azerbaijani-president-0
[24]https://www.primeminister.am/en/statements-and-messages/item/2020/11/12/Nikol-Pashinyan-Speech/
[25]https://oc-media.org/live-updates-armenian-president-calls-on-pashinyan-to-resign/

Although the EU had committed itself 'to contribute to the strengthening of democracy and of political, economic and institutional stability in the Republic of Armenia' (Comprehensive and Enhanced Partnership Agreement, 2018), it did nothing to safeguard Armenia's endangered democratization process. The EU–Armenia Partnership Council of December and the preceding meeting between HR/VP Borrell and Armenian Foreign Minister Ayvazyan touched upon Armenia's crisis in passing. However, neither the European Council and the Foreign Affairs Council nor the HR/VP issued a single declaration on the issue or offered their services to mediate between opposition forces and the government. Only Commissioner for Neighbourhood and Enlargement Negotiations Varhelyi tweeted on 17 December that 'we stand ready to explore how to further support Armenia under the current challenging circumstances'.[26] This tweet, though, left much room for interpretation as to whether he referred to Armenia and the Nagorny Karabakh conflict, Armenia's exposure to the Covid-19 pandemic, or in fact the country's domestic crisis. The EU's passive attitude towards Armenia's domestic crisis was due to the widespread notion among the EU-27 that Armenia needed to be regarded as a country that is highly exposed to Russian influence and viewed through the lens of its territorial conflict and thus concerns that hostilities may resume. Therefore, it was no surprise that also the Partnership Implementation Report on Armenia (European Commission and HR/VP, 2020), published one day before the Partnership Council for the purposes of internal use, entirely ignored the domestic crisis. On the other hand, passivity was also a function of a deliberate decision on the part of the Council to exercise self-restraint. It refrained from openly supporting the democratically elected pro-democracy government out of fear that such expressions may offer Russia a pretext to interfere in Armenia's domestic affairs and re-enact the illegal and interventionist practices it has been pursuing in Ukraine since 2013. Undoubtedly, this 'strategic silence' has undermined the EU's image as a credible normative power in the eyes of Armenia's considerably large pro-democracy supporters[27] and demonstrated, once more, the EU's limited geopolitical agency.

In contrast, and with regards to Georgia, local and regional scope conditions, as well as intra-EU dynamics differed significantly, offering the EU a conducive opportunity structure to involve itself and contribute to defusing the domestic crisis that had erupted already in mid-2019. At the time, the Georgian Dream-led government, primarily in an attempt to end mass protests and meet public demands for electoral system reform, had pledged to hold legislative elections in 2020 based on a fully proportional electoral system. However, on 14 November 2019 it reneged and stopped the constitutional amendments in parliament. In response and concerned about the continuous application of the mixed electoral system that had benefited the ruling Georgian Dream party, opposition parties and civil rights activists orchestrated new protests in the capital of Tbilisi which culminated in violent clashes between riot police and protesters and countless arrests some two weeks later.[28] The EU, and outgoing HR/VP Mogherini, left it to the EU Delegation in Tbilisi to respond. Already on 17 November, in a joint statement with the US Embassy to Georgia, the Delegation recognized 'the deep disappointment of a wide segment of Georgian society at the failure of Parliament to pass the constitutional

[26]Twitter Oliver Varhelyi, 17 December 2020.
[27]https://euobserver.com/foreign/150051
[28]https://eurasianet.org/georgia-protests-resume-election-reforms-firewood-and-beans

amendments'. It pointed to the 'increased mistrust and heightened tensions between the ruling party and other political parties and civil society' and called on them 'to restore trust through a calm and respectful dialogue'.[29] The EU's Head of Delegation and the US Ambassador to Georgia then jointly initiated and mediated a multi-party dialogue which started on 30 November 2019. After five rounds of deliberations, the process was finalized on 8 March 2020 with the adoption of a memorandum of understanding, defining electoral reform-related constitutional amendments that were signed by Georgian Dream and opposition party representatives (Memorandum of Understanding, 2020).[30]

These mediation efforts proved decisive for the passing of a new law, amending the Georgian constitution to change the electoral system, which entered into force on 29 June. While the new law was welcomed by the EU's Head of Delegation,[31] it did not, however, and in spite of the release of three straightforward statements the Delegation had jointly issued with the other facilitators of the political dialogue,[32] preclude Georgian Dream from diluting the law regarding aspects such as voter intimidation, electoral commission compositions, and dispute resolutions.[33] Likewise, the EU could neither guarantee a smooth conduct of the first round of legislative elections, held on 31 October,[34] nor could it convince the defeated opposition parties which claimed systematic election fraud, to refrain from boycotting the second round of elections on 21 November and organizing new mass protests. Yet, mirroring the previous multi-party talks, the EU succeeded in facilitating in November/December a new dialogue between opposition forces and Georgian Dream, during which a general understanding was reached that further electoral reforms were needed.

What made EU action in Georgia possible? Firstly, as far as extra-EU factors are concerned, Georgia has been one of the few ENP partner countries where local support for the EU and European integration has been continuously high (Lejava, 2021). This applies to societal actors as well as political parties, all of which share Georgia's aspiration to integrate with Euro-Atlantic structures. Against the backdrop of Russia's territorial occupation of Abkhazia and South Ossetia and the absence of a potentially popular alternative norms provider, the EU, like the United States, enjoys high degrees of external legitimacy which has bestowed upon it significant leverage. Over the years, these factors have provided the EU with a favourable opportunity structure to increase its physical and ideational presence across the country – a process that has been aided by a pro-active EU Delegation which closely follows and regularly contributes to the national public discourse. Secondly, against the backdrop of the nationwide consensus that European integration is the country's ultimate foreign policy priority, both Georgian Dream and the opposition parties, despite their profound aversion for one another, understood that a rejection of EU mediation efforts and continuous discord over electoral reform and the conduct of elections could seriously damage Georgia's prospect of being provided with further EU integration offers. Thirdly, and as regards intra-EU factors,

[29]https://eeas.europa.eu/delegations/georgia/70557/statement-eu-delegation-and-us-embassy-georgia-regarding-going-events-tbilisi_en
[30]https://civil.ge/archives/341385
[31]https://agenda.ge/en/news/2020/2108
[32]EEAS, 11 May, 15 May, and 19 June 2020.
[33]Constitutional Law, No. 6500-RS, On the Amendments to the Constitution of Georgia.
[34]https://www.osce.org/odihr/elections/georgia/480494

Georgia, ever since it had signed its Association Agreement in June 2014, has been viewed by the EU as a frontrunner as far as legal approximation with, and adoption of, the internal market acquis is concerned. Therefore, and motivated by concerns that passivity on the part of the EU or openly voiced critique of the Georgian authorities may undermine the country's status as a presumptive 'success story' and negatively affect the EaP, Georgia's political crisis offered an opportunity to demonstrate agency and score a foreign policy success that was within easy reach.

III. The EU and the Covid-19 Pandemic in the South Caucasus

In contrast to the EU's handling of the war between Armenia and Azerbaijan and the political crisis in Armenia, the EU's response to the outbreak of the Covid-19 pandemic in the region was characterized by determination and responsiveness. This was facilitated by intra-EU developments, most notably the launch of Team Europe, which represents a multilateral effort to pool contributions of EU Member States, EU institutions, implementing agencies, the European Investment Bank, the European Bank for Reconstruction and Development, and development finance institutions. Externally, local scope conditions in the region, such as weak healthcare systems and local elites' recognition that external support was urgently needed, in conjunction with the absence of local and regional veto-players, potentially hampering politically insensitive EU aid provision, enabled the EU to support Armenia, Azerbaijan and Georgia soon after the outbreak of the pandemic.

Covid-19 reached the region relatively early. The first confirmed case was reported on 26 February in Georgia,[35] to be followed by Azerbaijan on 28 February[36] and Armenia on 1 March.[37] While the immediate closure of borders, the imposition of partial lockdowns and restrictions on movement contained the first wave of the pandemic, infections and deaths peaked in all three countries towards the end of 2020, leading to some of the world's worst Covid-19 outbreaks in Armenia and Georgia.[38]

Pandemic management has brought about an extensive growth in executive powers, newly imposed restrictions for the media and opposition forces, and violations of citizen rights. For example, the Armenian government tried to monitor media coverage and pushed through parliament a law that allowed the tracing of citizens' contacts and whereabouts through cellular phones (Stronski, 2020).[39] In Azerbaijan, the regime used the pandemic as a pretext to crack down on activists and journalists, leading to the arrest of dozens of civil activists on the grounds of alleged violations of quarantine rules (Samadov, 2020).

The pandemic has not only exposed authoritarian practices and deepened polarization, but it also laid open the socio-economic weaknesses of the three countries of the South Caucasus, as their economies are heavily dependent on external income sources. Whereas Azerbaijan, whose oil and gas sector account for 45 per cent of the economy,[40] was

[35]https://www.reuters.com/article/china-health-georgia-idUSL5N2AQ7LC
[36]Tass-Russian News Agency, 30 June 2020.
[37]Tass- Russian News Agency, 1 March 2020.
[38]https://eurasianet.org/georgias-covid-outbreak-grows-from-molehill-to-everest
[39]https://eurasianet.org/armenia-seeks-to-stem-coronavirus-spread-by-tracking-phones
[40]https://www.reuters.com/article/health-coronavirus-azerbaijan-economy-idUSL8N2BV2PI

suddenly faced with sharp oil price drops and declining international demand for its hydrocarbon goods, Armenia and Georgia have both suffered from the disruption of remittances of migrant workers and the collapse of tourism and corresponding revenues.[41] Moreover, as more than a quarter of workers in the region are employed in sectors that are most affected by the pandemic, such as retail, construction and tourism, the closure of borders and lockdowns have induced a significant rise in unemployment rates.[42]

Team Europe, which had originated in DG DEVCO, was established rather unbureaucratically and with the support of Member States and operated in defiance of comitology practices. Since early April 2020, it has been focusing on three main areas: (a) responding to the Covid-19 crisis and humanitarian needs; (b) strengthening health, water and sanitation systems, and (c) mitigating the socio-economic consequences of the pandemic. As argued elsewhere (Jones and Teevan, 2021), mainly due to the absence of established intra-EU rules and the urgency of a rapidly deteriorating public health situation, EU support in the three priority areas was conducted in an ad-hoc, flexible and even bottom-up fashion and – in the South Caucasus and beyond – differed according to the country and local scope conditions in question. Within the EU, the Commission, and in particular DG DEVCO, has harnessed the pandemic and strengthened its position vis-à-vis other Directorates and the European External Action Service by taking the lead and deepening its work with the Delegations in Armenia, Azerbaijan, and Georgia as far as delivery and communication were concerned. This swiftness and readiness on the part of both the Commission and the Member States led to the mobilization of more than 1 billion EUR in emergency aid for health systems in the Eastern neighbourhood and countries' short and medium-term socio-economic recovery, as well as 58 million EUR for immediate aid (European Commission, 2021). Of the latter, 11.3 million EUR were earmarked for grants and sub-grants for the most vulnerable groups in society, while the former entailed over 700 million EUR in the form of grants and credit lines through the EU4Business initiative and the European Fund for Sustainable Development (European Commission, 2021). Out of these, Team Europe mobilized 96 million EUR for Armenia, 31 million EUR for Azerbaijan and 183 million EUR for Georgia (ibid.). It is noteworthy, though, that the aid-per capita ratio was the highest for Georgia, even though Armenia was arguably in even greater need of EU assistance. Also, as was discussed elsewhere,[43] most of the mobilized financial aid was reshuffled and redirected from existing funds and financing instruments, putting the EU's self-portrayed generosity into question.

Conclusions

If crisis is the best test of friendship, developments in the countries of the South Caucasus in 2020 seem to demonstrate that the EU – when seen from a larger perspective – is indeed a friend mainly the political elites in Armenia, Azerbaijan and Georgia rely on. EU responses were characterized by mainly four behavioural features, all of which reinforced friendly relations: (a) The EU did not interfere in regional and domestic affairs

[41]Remittances account for 12 percent of Georgia's and 11 percent of Armenia's GDP, according to the UNDP (21 March 2021).
[42]OECD Policy Responses to Coronavirus 13 October 2020.
[43]ecdpm, 26 June 2020.

© 2021 The Authors. JCMS: Journal of Common Market Studies published by University Association for Contemporary European Studies and John Wiley & Sons Ltd.

(unless this was requested and deemed possible); (b) it did not hold regimes accountable for potential violations of international (humanitarian) law; (c) it invested political leverage (to the extent it exists) only when asked, and (d) provided quick and unconditional aid in an emergency situation such as the Covid-19 pandemic. Positive as such an assessment may appear from the angle of local elites, though, it cannot conceal that EU foreign policy towards the region – throughout 2020 and in fact already before – is primarily dependent on external scope conditions and the opportunity structures regional and local stakeholders offer. This finding calls for greater consideration of outside-in perspectives and is grist to the mills of those who have long been calling for a decentred approach to EU foreign policy analysis (Fisher Onar and Nicolaïdis, 2013; Keuleers et al., 2016). At the same time, this dependency, in conjunction with the lack of geopolitical clout, the continuous absence of hard power resources, and most Member States' ongoing tendency to turn a blind eye to the EU's neighbourhood, bereaves the EU of agency. It renders many of the ENP's core objectives null and void and is a major blow to peace- and reform-minded actors in the region who have been looking towards 'EUrope' for support.

Against this backdrop, it is rather likely that EU agency vis-à-vis the South Caucasus countries will continue to remain tangible in areas and contexts where capabilities, resources and willingness to act exist and where conducive local and regional scope conditions, allowing for such agency to come to the fore, are in place. This surely applies to healthcare, as well as to the EU's role as a facilitator of domestic political dialogue in a highly pro-EU setting such as Georgia. However, as far as the conflict between Armenia and Azerbaijan is concerned, and in what regards reconciliation, opportunity structures continue to be unfavourable. While the fate of the entire region has fallen prey to the geopolitical and hegemonic ambitions of Russia and Turkey, societies in Armenia and Azerbaijan – after decades of socialization into nationalist thinking and the emergence of new grievances after the 2020 war – remain stuck in unforgiving narratives of enmity and hatred. For the EU, all these limitations may be difficult to accept. But sooner or later they might serve as powerful lessons for it to eventually embark on a transformative path towards becoming what could be called a capable power – if it intends to maintain some relevance in the eyes of others in the South Caucasus and beyond.

References

Broers, L. (2021) 'The EU and Karabakh: Picking up the Pieces, Looking for a Role', *Eurasianet*, 20 January. Available online at: https://eurasianet.org/perspectives-the-eu-and-karabakh-picking-up-the-pieces-looking-for-a-role. Last accessed: 8 May 2021.

Comprehensive and Enhanced Partnership Agreement between the European Union and the European Atomic Energy Community and their Member States, of the one part, and the Republic of Armenia, of the other part (2018) Official Journal of the European Union, L 23/4, 26 January.

Council of the EU (2020a) Nagorno-Karabakh: Declaration by the High Representative on behalf of the European Union, press release, 11 October. Available online at: https://www.consilium. europa.eu/en/press/press-releases/2020/10/11/nagorno-karabakh-declaration-by-the-high-representative-on-behalf-of-the-european-union/. Last accessed: 12 May 2021.

Council of the EU (2020b) Nagorno-Karabakh: Declaration by the High Representative on behalf of the European Union, press release, 19 November. Available online at: https://www. consilium.europa.eu/en/press/press-releases/2020/11/19/nagorno-karabakh-declaration-by-the-high-representative-on-behalf-of-the-european-union/. Last accessed: 12 May 2021.

De Waal, T. (2020) 'What Role for Europe in the New Post-War Caucasus?' *Carnegie Europe*, 19 November. Available online at: https://carnegieeurope.eu/strategiceurope/83267. Last accessed: 8 May 2021.

De Waal, T. (2021) 'Unfinished Business in the Armenia-Azerbaijan Conflict'. *Carnegie Europe*, 11 February. Available online at: https://carnegieeurope.eu/2021/02/11/unfinished-business-in-armenia-azerbaijan-conflict-pub-83844. Last accessed: 7 May 2021.

European Commission (2006) Communication from the Commission to the Council and the European Parliament on strengthening the European Neighbourhood Policy. COM (2006) 726 final, 4 December. Available online at: https://eur-lex.europa.eu/LexUriServ/LexUriServ.do?uri= COM:2006:0726:FIN:EN:PDF. Last accessed: 8 May 2021.

European Commission (2021) 'The EU's Response to the Coronavirus Pandemic in the Eastern Partnership'. Available online at: https://ec.europa.eu/neighbourhood-enlargement/sites/near/files/coronavirus_support_eap.pdf. Last accessed: 18 May 2021.

European Commission and HR/VP (2015) Joint Communication to the European Parliament, the Council, the European Economic and Social Committee and the Committee of the Regions. Review of the European Neighbourhood Policy. JOIN (2015) 50 final, 18 November. Available online at: https://eeas.europa.eu/archives/docs/enp/documents/2015/151118_joint-communication_review-of-the-enp_en.pdf. Last accessed: 15 May 2021.

European Commission and HR/VP (2020) Joint staff working document. Partnership Implementation Report on Armenia. SWD (2020) 366 final, 16 December. Available online at: https://eeas.europa.eu/sites/default/files/armenia_partnership_implementation_report_2020.pdf.   Last accessed on: 15 May 2021.

European Council (2020) Special meeting of the European Council (1 and 2 October 2020) – conclusions. EUCO 13/20. Available online at: https://www.consilium.europa.eu/media/45910/021020-euco-final-conclusions.pdf. Last accessed: 12 May 2021.

Freizer, S. (2014) 'Twenty Years after the Nagorny Karabakh Ceasefire: An Opportunity to Move Towards More Inclusive Conflict Resolution'. *Caucasus Survey*, Vol. 1-2, pp. 109–22.

German, T. (2007) 'Visibly Invisible: EU Engagement in Conflict Resolution in the South Caucasus'. *European Security*, Vol. 16, No. 3–4, pp. 357–74.

Grgic, B. (2020) 'The EU Suffered a Major Loss in Nagorno-Karabakh'. *Aljazeera Opinions*, 23 November. Available online at: https://www.aljazeera.com/opinions/2020/11/23/the-biggest-loser-in-nagorno-karabkh-is-not-armenia. Last accessed: 8 May 2021.

Jones, A. and Teevan, C. (2021) 'Team Europe: Up to the Challenge?'. ECDPM Briefing Note No. 128, January. Available online at: https://ecdpm.org/wp-content/uploads/Team-Europe-Up-To-Challenge-ECDPM-Briefing-Note-128-January-2021.pdf. Last accessed: 18 May 2021.

Keuleers, F., Fonck, D. and Keukeleire, S. (2016) 'Beyond EU Navel-Gazing: Taking Stock of EU-Centrism in the Analysis of EU Foreign Policy'. *Cooperation and Conflict*, Vol. 51, No. 3, pp. 345–64.

Lejava, N. (2021) 'Georgia's Unfinished Search for its Place in Europe', *Carnegie Europe*, 6 April. Available online at: https://carnegieeurope.eu/2021/04/06/georgia-s-unfinished-search-for-its-place-in-europe-pub-84253. Last accessed: 17 May 2021.

Memorandum of Understanding (2020). Available online at: https://ge.usembassy.gov/wp-content/uploads/sites/165/Memorandum-of-Understanding.pdf. Last accessed: 15 May 2021.

Fisher Onar, N. and Nicolaïdis, K. (2013) 'The Decentring Agenda: Europe as a Post-colonial Power'. *Cooperation and Conflict*, Vol. 48, No. 2, pp. 283–303.

Samadov, B. (2020) 'Azerbaijan – COVID-19 and a Divided Opposition'. Caucasus Analytical Digest No. 115, Heinrich Böll Stiftung, May. Available at: https://ge.boell.org/sites/default/files/2020-05/CAD115_0.pdf. Last accessed: 13 May 2021.

Schumacher, T. (2016) 'Armenia, Azerbaijan and the Nagorno-Karabakh Conflict: Why the Black Garden will not Blossom any Time Soon'. Egmont Security Policy Brief No. 71, 16 April. Available online at: https://www.egmontinstitute.be/content/uploads/2016/04/PB71.pdf?type=pdf. Last accessed: 10 May 2021.

Schumacher, T. (2020) 'War in Nagorno Karabakh. Why This Time is Different', *New Eastern Europe*, 9 October. Available online at: https://neweasterneurope.eu/2020/10/09/war-in-nagorno-karabakh-why-this-time-is-different/. Last accessed: 10 May 2021.

Simão, L. (2018) *The EU's Neighbourhood Policy towards the South Caucasus. Expanding the European Security Community* (Houndmills, Basingstoke: Palgrave).

Socor, V. (2021) 'Armenia's 44-Day War: A Self-inflicted Trauma', *Eurasia Daily Monitor*, 6 January. Available online at: https://jamestown.org/program/armenias-44-day-war-a-self-inflicted-trauma-part-one/. Last accessed: 10 May 2021.

Stronski, P. (2020) 'Coronavirus in the Caucasus and Central Asia', *Carnegie Endowment for International Peace*, 8 July. Available at: https://carnegieendowment.org/2020/07/08/coronavirus-in-caucasus-and-central-asia-pub-81898. Last accessed: 13 May 2021.

UNDP (2021) *Covid-19 and the countries of South Caucasus, Western CIS and Ukraine. Implications for Business Support, Employment and Social Protection Policies and Programming for Sustainability* (UNDP Press).

Van Gils, E. (2020) *Azerbaijan and the European Union* (London: Routledge).

JCMS 2021 Volume 59. Annual Review. pp. 150–161   DOI: 10.1111/jcms.13245

Elastic Relations: Looking to both Sides of the Atlantic in the 2020 US Presidential Election Year

STEPHANIE C. HOFMANN
Graduate Institute of International and Development Studies, Geneva

Introduction

Regardless of how we define the so-called liberal order, its global reach and actor-composition (Eilstrup-Sangiovanni and Hofmann, 2020), most if not all pundits and scholars alike agree that the transatlantic relationship lies at the heart of this order (Ikenberry, 2000). At the core of the transatlantic relationship is a security commitment tying the US to the European continent and *vice versa*. This commitment is not only encapsulated in an international treaty, the North Atlantic Treaty of 1949, but also in a formal intergovernmental organization (IGO), the North Atlantic Treaty Organization (NATO). Some even argue that the liberal order has never extended much beyond the transatlantic relationship, as US alliance-building in Europe has greatly differed from alliance-building in the Middle East and East Asia (Staniland, 2018).

Although the US, Canada, and European countries have formalized their security relationships and opened up communication channels – not only across capitals, but also through regular (daily) meetings in NATO – crises and cooperation are both common to the relationship (Hofmann and Yeo, 2015). Strong disagreements over military interventions, such as in Vietnam or Iraq, or whether and where to station nuclear missiles, were stress tests. The Trump administration's policy towards NATO was the most recent reminder that political cohesion is not a given among allies. In President Trump, many saw a challenge or even danger to the transatlantic relationship (Barnes and Cooper, 2019).

In the run-up to the 2020 presidential elections in the US, the transatlantic relationship was under enormous pressure. The Trump administration flexed its political muscles to demonstrate its 'America First' approach towards Europe. Many in Europe feared that a second Trump administration could mean the end of NATO. How do formalized interstate relations accommodate grave political tensions? In other words, what holds the core of the liberal order together despite many crises?

By introducing a concept recently used in sociology, namely institutional elasticity, I argue that the transatlantic relationship is able to withstand many crises because it is elastic. Its elasticity does not absorb political shocks, but helps restore the relationship after major crises. I argue that in international institutions, two properties, which can mutually reinforce or weaken each other, are essential to understanding elasticity: generalized trust and diffuse reciprocity. The Trump administration's threat to withdraw from NATO (reduced trust) and its transactional approach (no diffuse reciprocity) severely stretched and deformed the transatlantic relationship. Especially the run-up to the 2020 US presidential elections provided Trump with a platform to accentuate his 'America First' agenda. However, the relationship has not been overstretched to the breaking point. Instead, other trust-inducing actors (for example the US Congress) pulled in the other direction by insisting on shared values and experiences (diffuse reciprocity). Trump's electoral loss has reduced the pressure on the transatlantic relationship as not only the US Congress but also President Biden have reemphasized trust and diffuse reciprocity. However, the transatlantic relationship is not perfectly elastic; that is, it does not return to its original state intact but remains marked by the deformations caused by prior experiences (Fioretos, 2017). The Trump presidency made its mark on the transatlantic relationship by making European allies aware that the elastic can break.

This argument focuses on factors endogenous to institutions to better grasp the social fabric that sustains them (Henke, 2019). This is not to say that exogenous factors such as geopolitical changes and tensions (for example the rise of China and Russia's assertiveness) do not also impact an institution's elasticity. Rather, the argument here suggests that exogenous and endogenous pressures on an institutional relationship both test the trust and diffuse reciprocity relationships that sustain institutions.

Introducing elasticity to the study of transatlantic relations and institutionalized interstate relations more generally provides us with a better understanding that institutional change is not always unidirectional or enduring. Through the lens of elasticity, we can theoretically and conceptually grasp under what conditions certain changes may revert back to a state resembling the previous status quo, while other changes are here to stay.

I. Institutional Elasticity and Political Relationships

Nothing about interstate relations is inevitable or immutable. Relations between states can exist and change in form, frequency, and size (for example formal, informal, regular, occasional, equal, asymmetric). A focus on formalized intergovernmental relations reveals that many are stable for an extended period of time, but IGOs can also die (Eilstrup-Sangiovanni, 2020) or resemble zombies (Gray, 2018). They can go through extended periods of crisis (Kreuder-Sonnen, 2019; Haftel *et al.*, 2020) or become more robust over time (Gocaj and Meunier, 2013). In addition, individual governments can change their appreciation for interstate relations over time (Hofmann, 2013). This has implications for where countries invest their time, expertise, and resources. In the following section, I will briefly explore what a focus on elasticity helps us understand about institutional relationships by discussing some key theoretical questions: What enables IGOs to stay together in crises and major shocks? What brings elasticity about and how can it be sustained? What makes elastic relations break apart slowly? What makes them break apart abruptly?

What enables IGOs to hold together while experiencing crises and major shocks? I introduce the concept of institutional elasticity to better understand this phenomenon. While elasticity has been employed (anecdotally by some) in management, sociology, and economics (Watanabe *et al.*, 2004; Hijzen and Swaim, 2010; Awasthi *et al.*, 2020; Knoblach and Stöckl, 2020), few have applied it to institutionalized interstate relations (Hofmann and Mérand, 2012). Elasticity is commonly understood as 'the tendency of a body to return to its original shape after stretching, stress, or compression' (Hofmann and Mérand, 2012). Through the lens of elasticity, a researcher can draw attention to changes that occur in the properties of relationships, as well as to whether some of these changes are not durable but can instead bounce back. Hofmann and Mérand (2012) have looked at strong versus weak institutional elasticity to determine what kind of changes are possible in intergovernmental settings. However, they did not pay much attention to elasticity over time. When looking across time, Awasthi *et al.* (2020) assume that institutional relations revert back to their initial state. This malleability is just one side of the coin, however. No rubber band continues to exist forever; it can become brittle and, with each small stretch, the danger of it breaking increases. Or it can overextend under too much pressure and rip.

What brings elasticity about and how can it be sustained? Elastic interstate relations have at least two properties: they are based on generalized trust (Rathbun, 2011) and on at least some degree of diffuse reciprocity (Keohane, 1986). Both of these properties stress social aspects of institutionalized relationships, a glue that can keep counterparts in conversation with one another even in times of major shocks and crises. 'Generalized trust must be moralistic, based not on an assessment of others' interests but on their character and honesty ... It helps sustain cooperation when the exchange of benefits is not consistent or frequent over time' (Rathbun, 2011, p. 3). Generalized trust enables reliance on others and political concessions – as does diffuse reciprocity. Diffuse reciprocity means 'to contribute one's share, or behave well toward others, not because of ensuing rewards from specific actors, but in the interests of continuing satisfactory overall results for the group of which one is a part' (Keohane, 1986, p. 20). These properties set the parameters for political contestation and non-detrimental disagreements regardless of individual state characteristics and preferences (Hofmann and Yeo, 2015). Diplomatic embeddedness (Henke, 2019) facilitates mutual trust and diffuse reciprocity. The more diplomatic ties actors have with one another, the more likely it is that at least some counterparts can communicate trust and diffuse reciprocity to one another. However, the communication between political leaders remains essential. Security communities, for example, are elastic, while alliances are not necessarily so. This is not to say that institutionalized relationships are perfectly elastic – that is, that they automatically return to their original shape after the pressure is removed. Instead, shared experiences and memories can have lasting effects (Hofmann and Mérand, 2020); hence, some changes or at least fears are likely to stay.

What makes elastic relations break apart slowly or abruptly? If actors start questioning generalized trust and/or diffuse reciprocity, they stress the institutionalized relationship and test its elasticity. Every stretch leaves its mark and, over time, the rubber band can become brittle and break. In relationships of any kind, strong disagreements can be overcome but not necessarily forgotten. They can leave partners in a state of worry and fear that the stretch, stress or compression could occur again. And during the stretch, stress or compression period, some policy decisions might have been decided that are not easy to revert (Fioretos, 2017). As such, repeated crises and political shocks can lead to the hollowing out of international relations, with IGOs becoming zombies (Gray, 2018) or dying altogether. And if we overextend a rubber band, it can rip. When looking at interstate relations, unreasonable demands paired with too much pressure on the relationship can break it apart. These demands depart from the confines of broad political consensus and instead move into the realm of overt antagonism. One example of this could be Brexit (see Usherwood, 2021, in this issue).

II. Elastic Transatlanticism

NATO was stretched to its limits in 2020. Political tensions and frustrations on both sides of the Atlantic abounded. Trump was frustrated with European reluctance to invest more in their own security despite their increased pledges at the NATO Wales Summit during the Obama administration, as well as with certain countries' (like Germany) relations with Russia. European governments understood Trump's political style and policies as threatening the principle of diffuse reciprocity; unilateral US policy decisions further diminished trust among political elites. In the run-up to the 2020 US presidential election, the Trump administration introduced a series of unilateral policy decisions that challenged and threatened European allies with withdrawal of support under the banner of 'America First'. European allies reacted to some of Trump's challenges with a reinvigorated discourse on 'strategic autonomy' or new European Union (EU) military capacity initiatives but, overall, they waited for the result of the US elections.

Overstretch? Trump's 'America First' Approach

Throughout Trump's presidency, NATO was sidelined in his 'America First' foreign and security policy approach. Like previous administrations before him, Trump was frustrated with European reliance on the US security umbrella. However, he translated this frustration into a political approach that differed from his predecessors. Interactions with NATO and NATO allies became primarily transactional, elevating the decade-old burden-sharing debate to the most pressing issue at hand (Becker, 2019). Prioritizing the transactional approach meant ignoring the principle of diffuse reciprocity and generalized trust between allies.

The signals coming out of the White House were arguably more mixed in Trump's first years in office. The Trump administration might have been oscillating between two positions. Some emphasized that 'President Donald Trump shook the foundations of NATO more than any of his predecessors' (Pothier and Vershbow, 2017, p. 1). Trump's 'America First' led many to question whether the US president would be willing to defend allies if they called for help (Borger, 2019), which hurt the credibility of NATO's Art. V mutual defense clause and reduced trust in the US commitment to NATO. Others argued that 'Trump has kept much of American foreign policy within familiar boundaries' (Sperling and Webber, 2019, p. 513) and 'personnel choices have signaled a lack of intent to overhaul foreign policy' (Sperling and Webber, 2019, p. 514).

In his last year in office and in the run-up to the November elections, Trump's 'America First' approach became more aggressive towards NATO and individual NATO allies, as well as towards the confidence-building treaties that surround the transatlantic relationship. Trump not only stretched the transatlantic relationship but also started overextending it. One *New York Times* headline from 3 September 2020 reads 'Allies and Former U.S. Officials Fear Trump Could Seek NATO Exit in a Second Term'; in the article, its author recounts 'Recent accounts by former senior national security officials in the Trump administration have ... len[t] credence to a scenario in which Mr. Trump, emboldened by re-election and potentially surrounded by an inexperienced second-term national security team, could finally move to undermine – or even end – the United States' NATO membership' (Crowley, 2020). Some of these accounts stemmed from Trump's former national security adviser John Bolton. Not only did Trump feel emboldened; in the many reconfigurations of his national foreign, security and defense policy staff, he also reconfigured his cabinet and advisors so that in 2020 most advisors and cabinet members were no longer 'seasoned officials with a strong loyalty to the alliance and the trans-Atlantic relationship ... Their successors are not thought to be acting as strong checks on Mr. Trump's instincts' (Crowley, 2020). This intentional diplomatic dis-embedding was yet another signal to European counterparts that a transactional approach was guiding this US administration.

Trump's unilateral policy decisions, taken with no prior consultation with allies, decreased European trust in the Trump administration (Wheeler, 2020, p. 637). It was in 2020 that the Trump administration announced a few policy changes that also began overextending the transatlantic security relationship. In May 2020, he announced that he wanted to withdraw from the Open Skies Treaty. NATO Secretary General Jens Stoltenberg responded by stating how important this agreement is for NATO and that all other allies remain committed to it (NATO, 2020).

> As for Open Skies, many have pointed out that European NATO states' capacity to track Russian military movements in the region would be diminished. The four multinational NATO battalion groups deployed to the Baltics and Poland as part of NATO's Enhanced Forward Presence would also suffer should they not be able to mobilize quickly in case of a Russian military incursion. This erosion of information-sharing and confidence-building exposes the vulnerabilities in NATO and, in turn, benefits Russia's strategic interests (McGee, 2020).

Regardless, the US government provided formal notification of withdrawal to the other treaty parties on 22 May and withdrew from the treaty on 22 November 2020.

In July 2020, Trump announced his decision to remove around 10,000 US soldiers from Germany, a decision at least partly motivated as a punishment for Germany not paying enough for its own security and defense (Williams, 2020). Nearly half of these troops were ordered back to the US, while the rest were redistributed to Italy and Belgium, "a move that sent shockwaves through NATO" (McGee, 2020). To many NATO analysts, US military bases in Germany are vital to the Alliance (Williams, 2020). For example, they host US Africa Command and its European Command, support US drone communications, and include a net of US military hospitals.[1]

One of his last unilateral decisions – which occurred during the period when Trump refused to concede the elections to Joe Biden – was further military withdrawals from Afghanistan and Iraq. While the Afghanistan withdrawal is in line with an agreement reached between the US and the Taliban in Qatar in February 2020, under which the US pledged to withdraw its forces by May 1, 2021, Trump accelerated the planned

---

[1] This is not to say that all European allies were suspicious of Trump's policies. Instead, 'There are some allies such as Poland's President Andrzej Duda who are embracing the Trump administration to advance their own short-term domestic interests, while undermining the long-term cohesion of NATO' (McGee, 2020).

withdrawal. Neither the initial agreement with the Taliban, nor the later decision to accelerate the withdrawal, occurred with prior consultation or coordination with NATO allies – some of which also have troops stationed in Afghanistan Instead, they happened against warnings from NATO Secretary General Stoltenberg 'in a rare rebuke of U.S. policy' (Taylor and Birnbaum, 2020), as well as against the warning of Trump's own Defense Secretary Mark T. Esper, who consequently got fired (Schmitt et al., 2020).

Resisting Overstretch and Bouncing Back: The US Congress and the Biden Administration

While Trump's announcements and decisions began overextending the transatlantic relationship, other parts of the US government tried to induce trust in their European allies and to move away from a transactional approach. The US legislature worked on the elasticity of the relationship by softening the disagreement on both sides of the Atlantic. Both the House of Representatives and the Senate repeatedly sent signals across the Atlantic to show that the US legislative branch still broadly supported NATO. 2019 ended with a bill in which the US Senate Foreign Relations Committee unanimously voted 'to stop Donald Trump from withdrawing the US from Nato ... amid uncertainty over the president's intentions towards the alliance' (Borger, 2019). This bill obliges the US president to get the consent of the US Senate should he want to withdraw from NATO.[2] In 2020, in reaction to Trump's announcement to reduce the US military presence in Germany, Republicans in the US House of Representatives' Armed Services Committee issued a letter urging Trump to reconsider. They declared:

> We believe that such steps would significantly damage U.S. national security as well as strengthen the position of Russia to our detriment ... In Europe, the threats posed by Russia have not lessened, and we believe that signs of a weakened U.S. commitment to NATO will encourage further Russian aggression and opportunism. In addition, the overall limit on troops would prevent us from conducting the exercises that are necessary for the training and readiness of our forces and those of our allies. The troop limit would also significantly reduce the number of U.S. forces that can flow through Germany for deployment to bases around the world, causing serious logistical challenges (House of Representatives, 2020).

After Trump's electoral loss, the change in government heralded a reduction of pressure on the transatlantic relationship. If one wanted to summarize the Trump administration's approach to NATO with a song, The Clash's 'Should I stay or should I go' comes to mind, while the incoming Biden administration instead resonates with Al Green's 'Let's stay together'. 'The U.S. election results were greeted with relief inside NATO's glassy new headquarters in Brussels' (Taylor and Birnbaum, 2020). Biden is a known Atlanticist since his time as a US Senator. He immediately signaled towards allies that he wants to change the tone towards NATO, re-establish trust, and move away from a purely transactional approach. However, to say that the relationship has bounced back to its pre-Trump

---

[2]By the time the Trump administration left office, the bill had not been picked up by the full Senate. Sen. Tim Kaine and Sen. Marco Rubio therefore reintroduced it in April 2021.

form would also exaggerate the Biden approach, which likely will insist on European allies taking on more of their security and defense expenditures in a volatile international/global security environment.

Carefully Testing Bounce Capacity: European Strategic Autonomy

Trump might have stretched the transatlantic security relationship as no other US president before him, but he was not the first US president to push European allies to invest more in their own security, and he will not be the last. So far, US presidents have favored increased European military spending (and purchases of American military hardware) over greater EU institution-building to coordinate policy-making and develop, or even consolidate, the European defense industry. In short, many US presidents like the idea of a strong Europe, but not an autonomous one.

Trump's particular stance toward NATO nurtured a lack of trust across the Atlantic and questioned the diffuse reciprocity principle underlying the Alliance. In the eyes of many European politicians, it made the US a less reliable ally: if Trump won the 2020 election, then the US might leave NATO and if Trump lost, then nothing would prevent 'another Trump' from winning in the future.[3] This realization gave political traction to a two-decade-old, half-hearted European debate that the French introduced to the EU political discourse with the catchphrase 'European strategic autonomy' (Borrell, 2020), and that European Council President Charles Michel called 'the aim for our generation' (Michel, 2020).

Trump was not the only factor enabling the sincerity with which this tired debate is now taking place across the EU; other factors include a changing security environment and Brexit, which was finalized at the end of 2020. Shortly after the Brexit vote, the EU revitalized the Permanent Structured Cooperation (PESCO) and created the European Defence Fund (EDF),[4] which help plan for and invest in EU defense capabilities, thereby addressing some capability gaps and increasing joint deployment capability/abilities. Previously, British governments had hindered the development of a more autonomous European security and defense policy because they feared fragmenting NATO. Brexit and Trump formed the momentum to potentially bring about greater strategic coherence within the EU, create new institutions such as a headquarters, bolster the European defence industry, and improve overall capabilities.

European strategic autonomy could redefine the transatlantic relationship. However, while the debate was thriving in 2020 and some decisions were taken towards more autonomy, it also has since become apparent that neither a US president with isolationist tendencies nor a changing security environment will entice EU politicians to act more decisively or make big investment decisions in a chain reaction. They were waiting for the US presidential election to see where and how to further invest in security. As the

---

[3] After the May 2017 NATO summit, when Trump refused to endorse NATO's Article V collective defense commitment, German Chancellor Angela Merkel reacted with 'the time in which we could rely fully on other – they are somewhat over' and Europe 'really take our fate in our own hands' (Merkel quoted in Smale and Erlanger, 2017) and in 2018 'Angela Merkel has said EU leaders should one day consider "a real, true European army" shortly after Donald Trump ramped up a Twitter attack on Emmanuel Macron over the same idea' (Rankin, 2018).
[4] While NATO facilitates European purchases of US military equipment, the EDF creates incentives to coordinate European industrial efforts.

2020 PESCO strategic review reveals, only 23 out of 47 projects will be delivered by 2025 (Council of the European Union, 2020) and the Coordinate Annual Review on Defence (CARD) showed that not all members meet the EU's High Impact Capability Goals (European Defence Agency, 2020). EU countries reacted to some of Trump's threats and challenges but otherwise moved slowly.

This stands in stark contrast to how 2020 started rhetorically. Just before the new year, French President Emmanuel Macron called NATO 'brain dead' after President Trump had decided to pull out US troops of north-eastern Syria without consulting with allies, which enabled Turkey to launch a military operation against Kurdish forces there. 'You have no coordination whatsoever of strategic decision-making between the United States and its Nato allies.' He went on, pointing out that 'Things that were unthinkable five years ago – to be wearing ourselves out over Brexit, to have Europe finding it so difficult to move forward, to have an American ally turning its back on us so quickly on strategic issues – nobody would have believed this possible' (Macron cited in The Economist, 2019). While many leaders in the EU, foremost among them Angela Merkel, did not appreciate the style and tone of the message, it led to an internal NATO reflection process and revived debate about European strategic autonomy.

One possible step towards greater strategic autonomy happened in June 2020 as the EU launched the Strategic Compass under the German EU Council presidency. The Strategic Compass is a tool for joint threat analysis across EU member states, as well as a tool for identification of common actions and means. It could serve as the appropriate tool to systematically define the EU's common level of ambition, instead of pursuing rhetoric that is not matched by political action, by enabling policymaking to deal with cross-cutting challenges while also addressing national defense planning processes. However, the Strategic Compass tool is only scheduled to become operational in 2022, well into Biden's presidency.

COVID-19 will most likely further contribute to a piecemeal European strategic autonomy. Due to the pandemic, the EU expects a drop in gross domestic product (GDP) across its member states and pandemic recovery initiatives will most likely take away from defense budgets. Hence, while some steps towards a more cohesive Europe have been taken, they do not make Europe more autonomous in the foreseeable future and enable the continuation of the transatlantic relationship, if current and future US governments are so inclined.

The jury is still out on how exactly the EU's strategic autonomy will look and how it will relate to the transatlantic relationship. But 2020 ended with a particular vision of how European strategic autonomy could relate to transatlantic burden-sharing, emphasizing generalized trust and diffuse reciprocity. In anticipation of a revitalized transatlantic relationship, the European Commission and the High Representative put forward a proposal for a new transatlantic agenda on 2 December. 'Unprecedentedly, European Union (EU) member states have not squabbled to get Washington's attention, nor have they waited for the new U.S. leadership to set the agenda to reinvigorate the transatlantic relationship. Rather, the Europeans have capitalized on the optimism of change to propose initiatives for collaboration and renew diplomatic efforts' (Balfour, 2021). In this new agenda, the EU warns that 'We should also not fall into the trap of false debates that seek to oppose a stronger Europe and a stronger transatlantic partnership. A united, capable and self-reliant EU is good for Europe, good for the transatlantic partnership and good for the multilateral system' and recognizes that 'Over the last years, the EU has made unprecedented progress in security and defence cooperation, with landmark initiatives tackling capability shortfalls while incentivising defence spending and burden-sharing.' It therefore proposes that 'The EU and the US should reaffirm our joint commitment to transatlantic and international security. A stronger EU role in defence, including through supporting investment in capability development, will benefit NATO and transatlantic cooperation' and promises that 'The EU is ready to fulfil its responsibilities, enhance its strategic autonomy and ensure better burden-sharing. The EU and NATO's capability priorities should be largely aligned. To frame our cooperation, a structured EU-US Security and Defence Dialogue should be established, taking a comprehensive approach to security and based on a shared strategic vision' (European Commission and High Representative, 2020).

III. Looking Ahead

While the year 2020 will go down in history as the year in which COVID-19 spread across the globe, it also is the year that saw President Donald Trump voted out of office and the conclusion of Brexit. All these developments impacted the transatlantic relationship and its elasticity. However, the transatlantic security relationship neither ended in 2020 nor did it create an autonomous EU. Instead, the transatlantic relationship almost got overstretched before bouncing back into a more tenable long-term position in which political disagreements, not only across the Atlantic but also within the US and the EU, will persist within the confines of established trust and political concessions that resemble diffuse reciprocity.

Right after taking office, President Biden reversed or changed the conduct of many of Trump's foreign policy decisions. While he continued with the decision to withdraw troops in Afghanistan, he does so in coordination with allies. He decided to prolong the departure beyond the May 1 deadline negotiated by the Trump administration, which leaves Germany, the country with the second largest contingent in Afghanistan after the US, time to coordinate an orderly departure (Ryan and DeYoung, 2021). Biden also halted the withdrawal of US troops from Germany and ordered a review of US force deployment. These examples show that transatlantic elasticity is not only about continued US involvement in Europe, but about a transatlantic coordinated approach that rests on trust and diffuse reciprocity.

Some things are harder to reverse than others. Fear of a future US administration resembling Trump's will remain with a generation of European political leaders. And subsequent US administrations will most likely continue to fear European evasion of further burden-sharing and therefore keep insisting that European governments pay more for their own security. Whether considering internal NATO reflection processes or the EU's strategic autonomy debate, these abstract discussions in both organizations leave open many possibilities for concrete developments.

Acknowledgements

I would like to thank Marina Henke, Catherine Hoeffler and Emanuele Massetti for insightful comments and suggestions.

References

Awasthi, K., Gopakumar, K. V. and Ojha, A. K. (2020) 'Why Do Institutions Revert? Institutional Elasticity and Petroleum Sector Reforms in India'. *Business & Society*. https://journals. sagepub.com/doi/pdf/10.1177/0007650320949829?casa_token= 8HUlxmjfeBsAAAAA:2Zthpms4X0NrJ_jkxmuOSXdnqlwooLCpdlv2uiOAZD_ZzZsbREIY_ 5g2WzOoGDmxX1in8R8 MFCycw.

Balfour, R. (2021) 'Working with the Biden Administration: Opportunities for the EU'. *Carnegie Europe*. https://carnegieeurope.eu/2021/01/26/working-with-biden-administration-opportuni- ties-for-eu-pub-83560.

Barnes, J. and Cooper, H. (2019) 'Trump Discussed Pulling U.S. from NATO, Aides Say Amid New Concerns over Russia', *New York Times* (January 14). https://www.nytimes.com/2019/ 01/14/us/politics/nato-president-trump.html.

Becker, J. (2019) 'Accidental Rivals? EU Fiscal Rules, NATO, and Transatlantic Burden-Sharing'. *Journal of Peace Research*, Vol. 56, No. 5, pp. 697–713.

Borger, J. (2019) 'Senate committee passes bipartisan bill to stop Trump withdrawing from Nato'. *The Guardian* (11 December). https://www.theguardian.com/world/2019/dec/11/senate-com- mittee-passes-bipartisan-bill-stop-trump-withdrawing-nato.

Borrell, J. (2020) 'Why European Strategic Autonomy Matters'. HR/VP blog. https://eeas.europa. eu/headquarters/headquarters-homepage/89865/why-european-strategic-autonomy-matters_ en.

Council of the European Union (2020) *Council Conclusions on the PESCO Strategic Review 2020* (13188/20), 20 November 2020. https://data.consilium.europa.eu/doc/document/ST-13188- 2020-INIT/en/pdf.

Crowley, M. (2020) 'Allies and Former U.S. Officials Fear Trump Could Seek NATO Exit in a Second Term'. *New York Times* (3 September). https://www.nytimes.com/2020/09/03/us/poli- tics/trump-nato-withdraw.html.

Eilstrup-Sangiovanni, M. (2020) 'Death of International Organizations. The Organizational Ecology of Intergovernmental Organizations, 1815–2015'. *Review of International Organizations*, Vol. 15, No. 2, pp. 339–70.

Eilstrup-Sangiovanni, M. and Hofmann, S.C. (2020) 'Of the Contemporary Global Order, Crisis, and Change'. *Journal of European Public Policy*, Vol. 27, No. 7, pp. 1077–89.

European Commission and High Representative (2020) 'Joint Communication to the European Parliament, the European Council and the Council. A New EU–US Agenda for Global Change'. JOIN(2020)22final. https://ec.europa.eu/info/sites/info/files/joint-communication- eu-us-agenda_en.pdf.

European Defence Agency (2020) CARD Report. Executive Summary, November 2020. https:// www.eda.europa.eu/docs/default-source/reports/card-2020-executive-summary-report.pdf.

Fioretos, O. (2017) *International Politics and Institutions in Time* (Oxford: Oxford University Press).

Gocaj, L. and Meunier, S. (2013) 'Time Will Tell: The EFSF, the ESM, and the Euro Crisis'. *Journal of European Integration*, Vol. 35, No. 3, pp. 239–53.

Gray, J. (2018) 'Life, Death, or Zombie? The Vitality of International Organizations'. *International Studies Quarterly*, Vol. 62, No. 1, pp. 1–13.

Haftel, Y.Z., Wajner, D.F. and Eran, D. (2020) 'The Short and Long (er) of It: The Effect of Hard Times on Regional Institutionalization'. *International Studies Quarterly*, Vol. 64, No. 4, pp. 808–20.

Henke, M.E. (2019) *Constructing Allied Cooperation. Diplomacy, Payments, and Power in Multilateral Military Coalitions* (Ithaca: Cornell University Press).

Hijzen, A. and Swaim, P. (2010) 'Offshoring, Labour Market Institutions and the Elasticity of Labour Demand'. *European Economic Review*, Vol. 54, No. 8, pp. 1016–34.

Hofmann, S.C. (2013) *European Security in NATO's Shadow. Party Ideologies and Institution Building* (Cambridge: Cambridge University Press).

Hofmann, S.C. and Mérand, F. (2012) 'Regional Organizations à la Carte: The Effects of Institutional Elasticity'. In Paul, T.V. (ed.) *International Relations Theory and Regional Transformation* (New York: Cambridge University Press), pp. 133–57.

Hofmann, S.C. and Mérand, F. (2020) 'In Search of Lost Time: Memory-Framing, Bilateral Identity-Making, and European Security'. *Journal of Common Market Studies*, Vol. 58, No. 1, pp. 155–71.

Hofmann, S.C. and Yeo, A.I. (2015) 'Business As Usual: The Role of Norms in Alliance Management'. *European Journal of International Relations*, Vol. 21, No. 2, pp. 377–401.

House of Representatives (Armed Services Committee, Ranking members) (2020) 'Letter to US President Donald Trump on June 9, 2020'. https://republicans-armedservices.house.gov/sites/republicans.armedservices.house.gov/files/USTroopsWithrdrawalfroGermany.pdf.

Ikenberry, J. (2000) *After Victory* (Princeton: Princeton University Press).

Keohane, R.O. (1986) 'Reciprocity in International Relations'. *International Organization*, Vol. 40, No. 1, pp. 1–27.

Knoblach, M. and Stöckl, F. (2020) 'What Determines the Elasticity of Substitution between Capital and Labor? A Literature Review'. *Journal of Economic Surveys*, Vol. 34, No. 4, pp. 847–75.

Kreuder-Sonnen, C. (2019) *Emergency Powers of International Organizations. Between Normalization and Containment* (Oxford: Oxford University Press).

McGee, M. (2020) 'Europe Needs to Push Back against Trump'. *Foreign Policy* (10 July). https://foreignpolicy.com/2020/07/10/trump-europe-nato-transatlantic-push-back/.

Michel, C. (2020) 'Strategic Autonomy for Europe – the Aim of our Generation'. Speech by President Charles Michel to the Bruegel think tank. https://www.consilium.europa.eu/en/press/press-releases/2020/09/28/l-autonomie-strategique-europeenne-est-l-objectif-de-notre-generation-discours-du-president-charles-michel-au-groupe-de-reflexion-bruegel/.

NATO (2020) 'Statement by the NATO Secretary General on the Open Skies Treaty'. Press Release (2020) 047. https://www.nato.int/cps/en/natohq/news_175945.htm.

Pothier, F. and Vershbow, A. (2017) 'NATO and Trump. The Case for a New Transatlantic Bargain'. Atlantic Council. https://espas.secure.europarl.europa.eu/orbis/sites/default/files/generated/document/en/NATO_and_Trump_web_0623.pdf.

Rankin, J. (2018) 'Merkel Joins Marcon in Calling for a "Real, True European army"'. *The Guardian* (13 November). https://www.theguardian.com/world/2018/nov/13/merkel-joins-macron-in-calling-for-a-real-true-european-army.

Rathbun, B. (2011) 'Before Hegemony: Generalized Trust and the Creation and Design of International Security Organizations'. *International Organization*, Vol. 65, No. 2, pp. 243–73.

Ryan, M. and DeYoung, K. (2021) 'Biden Will Withdraw all U.S. Forces from Afghanistan by Sept. 11, 2021'. *Washington Post* (13 April). https://www.washingtonpost.com/national-security/biden-us-troop-withdrawal-afghanistan/2021/04/13/918c3cae-9beb-11eb-8a83-3bc1fa69c2e8_story.html.

Schmitt, E., Gibbons-Neff, T., Savage, C. and Cooper, H. (2020) 'Trump Is Said To Be Preparing to Withdraw from Afghanistan, Iraq and Somalia'. *New York Times* (16 November). https://www.nytimes.com/2020/11/16/us/politics/trump-troop-withdrawal-afghanistan-somalia-iraq.html.

Smale, A. and Erlanger, S. (2017) 'Merkel, after Discordant G-7 Meeting, Is Looking Past Trump'. *New York Times* (28 May). https://www.nytimes.com/2017/05/28/world/europe/angela-merkel-trump-alliances-g7-leaders.html.

Sperling, J. and Webber, M. (2019) 'Trump's Foreign Policy and NATO: Exit and Voice'. *Review of International Studies*, Vol. 45, No. 3, pp. 511–26.

Staniland, P. (2018) 'Misreading the "Liberal Order": Why We Need New Thinking in American Foreign Policy'. *Lawfare*, 29 July. https://www.lawfareblog.com/misreading-liberal-order-why-we-need-new-thinking-american-foreign-policy.

Taylor, A. and Birnbaum, M. (2020) 'In a Rare Rebuke of Trump, NATO Chief Warns Against Troop Cuts in Afghanistan'. *Washington Post* (17 November). https://www.washingtonpost.com/world/2020/11/17/jens-stoltenberg-afghanistan-trump/.

The Economist (2019) 'Emmanuel Macron Wants Europe: NATO is Becoming Brain-Dead'. (7 November). https://www.economist.com/europe/2019/11/07/emmanuel-macron-warns-europe-nato-is-becoming-brain-dead.

Usherwood, S. (2021) '"Our European Friends and Partners"? Negotiating the Trade and Cooperation Agreement'. *Journal of Common Market Studies*, Vol. 59, No. S1.

Watanabe, C., Kondo, R., Ouchi, N., Wei, H. and Griffy-Brown, C. (2004) 'Institutional Elasticity as a Significant Driver of IT Functionality Development'. *Technological Forecasting and Social Change*, Vol. 71, No. 1, pp. 723–50.

Wheeler, N. (2020) '"A Presumption of Trust" in International Society'. *International Relations*, Vol. 34, No. 4, pp. 634–41.

Williams, M. J. (2020) The United States Needs German Bases More Than Germany Does. *Foreign Policy* (9 June). https://foreignpolicy.com/2020/06/09/germany-troops-withdrawal-nato-trump/.

JCMS 2021 Volume 59. Annual Review. pp. 162–174   DOI: 10.1111/jcms.13226

Controversial Developments of EU–China Relations: Main Drivers and Geopolitical Implications of the Comprehensive Agreement on Investments

MARIO TELÒ
Institut d'Etudes Européennes, Université Libre de Bruxelles, Brussels

I. A New Comprehensive Regime

The size and geopolitical relevance of both the contracting partners makes the new EU–China arrangement (the Comprehensive Agreement on Investments, CAI) not only a new investment regime, but also a relevant international event affecting international relations. Which variables explain the creation of a new international regime? What kind of gains the sides expect from the regime and which responsibilities the two sides delegate to the regime?

The EU and China signed the political authorisation for the CAI after a difficult 35th round of negotiations on 30 December 2020. Before the next French rotating presidency (early 2022) the text agreed in principle upon will be translated, legally finalized and scheduled for eventual Council and EP ratification.[1] For CAI negotiations, the EU Commission took stock of the exclusive competence for large parts of foreign direct investment provided by the Lisbon Treaty (2009), to replace the first-generation bilateral investment treaties (BITs) signed by the Member States with a single EU–China investment agreement of new generation.

This decision looks very relevant for bilateral relations. The idea of a bilateral investment treaty gradually emerged in the context of the global framework provided by the Strategic Partnership signed in 2003.[2] Firstly, Foreign direct investment (FDI) flows between the EU and China are underdeveloped compared to the sizes of the two economies (Dadush et al., 2019). Although trade between the EU and China has very much increased (still unbalanced in favour of China by 300 US billion dollars in 2018), bilateral FDI flows remained less dynamic: from 2008 to 2017, the stock of EU FDI in China grew from EUR 54 billion to EUR 178 billion – an increase of 225%. Meanwhile, the stock of Chinese FDI in the EU rose nearly tenfold, reaching EUR 59 billion in 2017. However, in the most recent years, Chinese FDI has been booming in volume and quality, whereas

[1] European Commission, 'Key Elements of the EU-China Comprehensive Agreement on Investment', 30 December 2020; Factsheet [DE] and [FR].
[2] In fact, the first concrete step was the joint Declaration of February 2012. Point 11 of the final communiqué of the 14th bilateral summit stated: '11. The two sides welcomed companies' readiness to trade and invest in each other's economies. Leaders agreed that a rich in substance EU-China investment agreement would promote and facilitate investment in both directions. Negotiations towards this agreement would include all issues of interest to either side, without prejudice to the final outcome. They agreed to work towards the start of the negotiation as soon as possible.' In 2013, the Commission obtained a unanimous mandate from the Council on the basis of its 'Recommendation for a Council Decision authorising the opening of negotiations on an investment agreement between the European Union and the People's Republic of China' (COM, 2013: 297).

European FDI in China has declined. European investor concerns focused on the obstacles and discriminations affecting market access, investor protection, and obligations to joint venture and transfer of Intellectual Property Rights (IPR).[3] In sum, the pre-CAI situation was seriously unbalanced regarding the welcoming treatment of Chinese investors in Europe compared with that of EU investors in China. In addition, the defensive side of the negotiation for the EU regards the desire to protect its technological edge from Chinese state-owned companies making controversial strategic acquisitions.

The existing bilateral treaties on investments between the individual European member states and China do not include market access nor sustainable development provisions, while the CAI does, although it still excludes trade issues and rules on public procurement, subsidies, and so on. Enhanced reciprocity will eventually characterize mutual concessions regarding improved conditions for access to the EU and Chinese markets for Chinese and EU investors. China's new concessions include protection of EU investments against uneven and unfair treatment, discrimination as well as IPR linked to investments.

Moreover, the EU priority was a 'comprehensive' regime, beyond traditional bilateral investment treaties and according to its strategy for new generation arrangements. Regimes are traditionally single-issue-focusing arrangements. However, the EU was strong enough to establish an original linkage between investment liberalization and sustainable development. This entails several symbolic 'common goods', the subject of already existing multilateral arrangements. Issue linkage is part of the distinctive EU's transformation power (Risse and Börzel, 2015). According to several scholars (Woolcock, 2020) this makes the negotiation process more difficult and time-consuming, notably the last chapter related to the array of issues encompassed by the title 'sustainable development', which includes objectives in the struggle against climate change (effective implementation of the COP 21), as well as core environmental and corporate social responsibility, and one of the most symbolic of EU objectives: China's commitment to 'make continued and sustained efforts' to ratify International Labour Office (ILO) conventions, notably on forced labour and worker's association. The inclusion of this final chapter is relevant when it comes to the inevitable question of asymmetric gains: which actors obtains absolute or relative gains? Each partner had specific symbols to defend: the EU values and beliefs include the expanded application of multilateral conventions supporting climate regimes and defending labour rights. That is why, even if mere instrumental action and calculus are a key, they can hardly be considered as a satisfying explanation (Hall and Taylor, 1996).

In terms of more complex motivations, the consistent implementation of mutual commitments guarantee will be the investment-dispute-settlement-mechanisms available to the states and investors. A new Investment Committee and a working group at the top level (Vice-Presidents on both sides) would be in charge of monitoring the implementation process. Furthermore, the sustainable development commitments will be monitored by a new working group (an independent panel of experts will deal with the dispute settlement mechanism) with involvement of civil society.

---

[3]European Parliament, Directorate-General for External Policies Policy Department: 'EU-China Trade and Investment Relations in Challenging Times', Brussels 2020.

Investment protection will be the object of a commitment by both sides to complete further negotiations within two years of the CAI signature. However, the convergences and the work undertaken in the context of the United Nations Commission on International Trade Law (UNCITRAL) on a Multilateral Investment Court will be a reference, as required by the EU, which aims at replacing the Investor State Dispute Settlement (ISDS) mechanisms in every trade and investment deal.

All in all, explaining such a voluntary agreement between two of the three most relevant actors of global trade is more challenging than expected. It is about deepening the complex institutionalization of the 'Strategic partnership' signed in 2003, by the creation of a new comprehensive regime, providing both sides with reduction of transaction costs, organizational costs and several gains, but also including symbolic achievements supporting multilateral negotiations. How did the drivers of this agreement progress and change, along the seven years of negotiations?

II. Rational Choice or Power Asymmetry?

When it comes to the drivers of such a relevant negotiation, interest-calculation is the first explanation, while the second could be the development of a power asymmetry between rising China and declining EU, and the third one, the changing weight of domestic legitimacy factors.

For both actors, it is a rational choice to better shape their relations regarding reciprocal investments in a period of economic uncertainties. Notably, the imbalance between the EU current recession (according to the best forecasts for 2020 and 2021, from −7 per cent to +4 per cent) and the Chinese growth is pushing the EU to explore options for fruitful cooperation with China. It is relevant for the EU that China (growth rate: +2.3 per cent in 2020, and +7.3 per cent in 2021) has opened up its manufacturing sectors (international maritime transport and air transport, electric cars, digital equipment and health) as well as its service sectors to EU investors: financial, cloud and environmental services, private healthcare, and transport-related services. In the interest of both partners, this may also help by consolidating global supply chains and making them more resilient with positive effects against the multiple de-globalization tendencies.

It was very important for the EU to establish much more than a single-issue regime focusing on mere investment liberalization: a 'level playing field', which firstly means non-discrimination, reciprocity as well as transparency of subsidies as general principles. Accordingly, a high benchmark was set in terms of regulation of Chinese state-owned enterprises, and forced technology transfer via joint-venture authorization to be obtained by EU companies investing in China. As far as the EU is concerned, every observer wonders whether mere interest calculation of benefits is a satisfying explanation, if compared with actors less conditioned by controversial parliamentary ratification. Of course, as in every trade and investment negotiation conducted by the Commission, there is a two-pronged pressure of lobbying: first, that of competing companies, investment funds, and exporting interest groups; and second, the internal inter-state bargaining among the 27. In terms of their protectionism degree (PD), the national governments are classified from France at the top, moving down to Poland, Italy and others, to the traditional free traders: Netherlands, Germany and Sweden. German companies are seen as the CAI winners. However, in the event of a sudden internal asymmetry between national or sectoral interests, how could have the Commission reached the Council unanimous approval, representing 27 national governments? No national government has stopped the CAI negotiation so far. Therefore, it was a convergent and still consensual interest calculation of all the Council members and the Commission.

To understand the extent to which the calculus by the 27 EU MSs fully explains the agreement, we should investigate the evolving preferences of both sides, China and Europe; to what extent and how did the respective priorities change over time, in response to both internal and international factors, as well as to the interpretation of their respective interests? Their respective preferences (notably regarding not only market access and sustainable development but also bilateral/geopolitical implications) are not definitely fixed and the negotiations were often close to failure. Did the power asymmetry between a rising China and a declining EU matter?

Focusing on power and strategic purposes is one alternative to the merely rational choice calculation. In that case, the question is whether this new institutionalization was accelerated and shaped by China's gradual growing superiority as an economic power and agenda-setting power. We know that the global context of the bilateral negotiation dramatically changed during the seven years from 2014 to 2020. The increasingly evident WTO Development Doha Round paralysis, the subsequent proliferation of PTAs (Heydon and Woolcock, 2009; Telò, 2021) and the Donald Trump trade wars encouraged both parties, the EU and China, to look for further convergence, notably in three directions: (a) as strategic actors accustomed to rational calculus, they worked on limiting global fragmentation, uncertainties and unregulated market competition, through greater efficiency and a bilateral arrangement; (b) as actors sharing interests on several common goods, they converged by combining an arrangement based on reciprocity with an upgrading negotiation on sustainable development; (c) they also looked at a combination of bilateral and geopolitical spill-over effect: for example, since the Trump election, on the one hand, the China leadership wanted to show itself as a defender of multilateralism (Davos speeches by Xi Jinping, 2018 and 2021); on the other hand, the EU wished its multiple bilateral and interregional negotiations to go on, also as a way to revive multilateralism: for example, the EU aims to deepen the dialogue with China for the 'Strategic Agenda for Cooperation 2025', while proposing, at the same time, that both sides take stock of the CAI achievements to support multilateral negotiations.

Did China's growing relative economic power make a difference? According to IMF figures, the two giants still are of comparable size. Despite clear evidence that China is a rising power, and expected to become the no. 1 global economy (not just, as now it already is, in PPP terms, see Figure 1), its growth rate is dangerously diminishing and the demography of its ageing society is shifting. Furthermore, the EU is a major trade power, the world's largest trading bloc, and the top trading partner for 80 countries, second only to the US as importer and second only to China as global exporter in 2020. Moreover, according to Lisbon Treaty provisions the EU is acting in trade and investments international negotiations like a state (decisions taken by Community method). As far as the EU is concerned, the CAI was politically relevant. Playing the 'Brussels effect' (Bradford, 2020) by centralizing its multiple international negotiations, notably with the People's Republic of China (PRC), against its dividing policies:

Figure 1: China Already Has the World's Largest Economy at Purchasing Power Parity

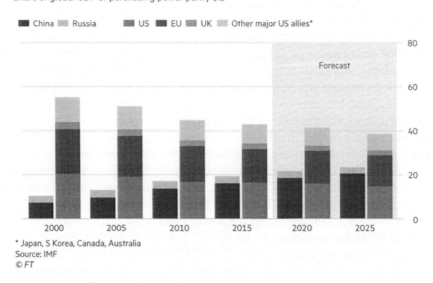

Source: IMF (Commented by Martin Wolf, 2021). [Colour figure can be viewed at wileyonlinelibrary.com]

'17 + 1 regime' with Eastern European and individual agreements with single EU MS, in the context of the Belt and Road Initiative (BRI).

In conclusion, rather than the consequence of a serious power asymmetry in favour of China, CAI is explained by a multidimensional rebalancing in favour of the EU; therefore, the set of drivers for the voluntary creation of such a new regime is, for both the EU and China, inevitably more complex, beyond oversimplification.

III. A Seven-Year Negotiation. Did Actors' Preferences Change According to Geopolitical Variables?

To better explain the CAI multiple causes, we must consider this new regime in the context of the evolving triangular relationship among three trade giants (the US, EU and China). The historically main actor, the US, twice changed its preferences and policies towards both partners during the seven years of CAI negotiations. President Obama tried to implement a grand design, through two pluri-lateral mega-negotiations, both aiming at a soft containment of China's global influence: the Trans-Pacific Partnership (TPP) signed in 2015 with 12 partners of the Asia-Pacific region with the exception of China, and the Transatlantic Trade and Investment Partnership (TTIP) with the EU, negotiated with the purpose of strengthening the weight of the Western bloc in global negotiations

(2013–16). Elected in 2016, Donald Trump decided on immediate withdrawal from the TPP and freezing of the TTIP.

In the first instance, the CAI negotiations (then: BIT) were for China a strategic reaction, aimed at dividing the EU and the US and preventing trade and sustainable development standards, respectively arranged with EU and with 12 Pacific countries (including Japan) to be imposed to China.[4] China reacted with a multiple and vibrant external relations strategy: firstly, deepening the negotiations of the RCEP (Regional Comprehensive Economic Partnership), including the ten ASEAN member states as well as four more democracies, Japan, S. Korea, Australia and New Zealand (Feng and Telò, 2020). This was parallel to various regional and interregional endeavours: founding a new multilateral Asian Infrastructures Investments Bank (AIIB[5]) and launching the ambitious BRI towards Europe, Africa and South America.

Retaliating against the Trump administration's aggressive China policy has been more challenging for China's leadership. The Trump strategy to cope with China growth was aiming at unilaterally changing China's policies (by trade wars). His administration obtained the opposite: domestic complaints, China's trade retaliations and, what matters more, a dynamic acceleration by China of RCEP, taking advantage of the vacuum left by the US, up to its signature on 15 November 2020. China also accepted an improvement of RCEP standards, compared with the very low initial level of mere trade-easing provisions, even at the price of protectionist India's withdrawal in 2020 (Feng and Telò, 2020).

China's interest in the CAI increased with the transition from the Obama to the Trump administration: the assertion of global multilateralism and free trade was consistent with the national interest of opposing isolation. Logically, China had increased interest in achieving the deal with the EU with the double objective of developing bilateral/interregional trade and as a contrast to US unilateral policies.

From its side, during the Obama era, the EU looked at balancing the politically relevant TTIP negotiations with the US administration (defined as an 'economic NATO') by a multiple, poly-gamic, trade strategy, successfully implementing a new generation of interregional and bilateral arrangements with Canada, Korea, Singapore, Japan, MERCOSUR, Mexico and … China (De Block and Lebullenger, 2018). In the Trump's years, and in the context of a weakening WTO and multiple trade wars, the EU was discouraged from reviving a transatlantic unity against China and more interested in a deal with China, according to its new trade and investment strategy.

It is not surprising that the Trump administration condemned the CAI. What dismayed many observers was the Biden administration stance: on the one hand, excluding new trade deals for two years (J. Yellen, US Secretary of the treasury) and on the other (J. Sullivan) criticizing the CAI as a naïve present to the PRC.[6] Is this national security advisor's thesis of EU naivety a serious explanation? CAI as a potential driver for multilateral negotiation upgrading was ignored, while the EU, as a global power comparable with China, wishes to autonomously assert, notably by CAI, not only its own interests, but also its multilateral perspective.

---

[4]However, according to part of the literature, the China's leading group was divided and some could have considered the perspective of joining TPP in a second stage as a stimulus for China's modernization (Zhang, 2018).
[5]The AIIB deserved the definition of 'counter-multilateral' by Keohane (2015), because of its competition with the existing WB and other regional banks
[6]See G. Rachman, 'Europe Has Handed China a Strategic Victory', *Financial Times*, 4.1.2021.

Since the signing of the Strategic Partnership with China (2003), the EU is aware of being under US pressure regarding its partnership with China within a changing triangular game. In October 2003, even the EU's most pro-US leaders, such as the EU Commission President Barroso and the Council President Berlusconi, resisted Vice-President Cheney's opposition to the EU–China Strategic Partnership, criticized for including cooperation on the sensitive Galileo satellite recognition project. Later on, the EU was sidelined by both the Obama's 'pivot to Asia' and subsequent US–China convergence at the climate change summit in Copenhagen (2009). And more recently, it was weakened by the Trump trade wars (2017–19) and *'divide et impera'*, pro-Brexit and anti-EU policies.

All in all, there are many pieces of evidence that, within the context of a troubled and unstable global context, the EU has been ready, for almost twenty years, to assert its interests and multilateral vision at the cost of several trade policy divergences, and not only with the Trump administration which signed a truce with China in January 2020 (the 'Phase-one trade deal' including sectoral openings in several industries, in joint-venture requirements and the financial sector) without consulting the EU – but also with other administrations, in spite of the evident geopolitical implications.

If this analysis is correct, the EU motivations for signing CAI are much more complex than the two opposite explanations mentioned above (mere calculus or naïve subordination to China's power). Other factors played a role in its 30 December 2020 decision. All the recent EU's position papers confirm that the EU is looking, as a long-term process, at enhanced 'Open Strategic Autonomy', not only within a multipolar world order, but also within the NATO alliance.[7] The EU's political action is therefore aiming at diminishing the current global bifurcation and rivalry between the US and China, by multiplying intergovernmental and multilateral regimes, a distinctive EU approach to global governance.

There is a large debate within International Relations Theory about the trade–security nexus. However, even the book which has been considered as a prophecy of the inevitability of a 'Thucydides trap', of military conflict between emerging and declining superpowers (Allison, 2017) indicates regime-building and institution-consolidating as the way to avert the trap.

We emphasize that, despite the criticism by the US administration to the EU - responding to a dramatic change of power relations and becoming the true driver of CAI negotiations – there is no clear evidence of asymmetry between the two negotiating sides. Even if China's relative strength accelerated in the period 2008–16 following the financial crisis and during the pandemic toward the postion of being the first global economy in terms of PPP (see Figure 1), both the EU and China increased their relative weight within an unstable and changing global context. The strategic interaction between the two negotiators, by the creation of a new international investment regime, was still based on the shared expectation of a possible win–win game. The path dependence of the

[7]According to EEAS 'Why Strategic Autonomy Matters?' (3 December 2020): 'The Council already used the concept in November 2013 in relation to defence industry, to strengthen the EU's ability of becoming a better partner through the development of CSDP. In May 2015, the Foreign Affairs Council used the same terminology. It was further elaborated in the 2016 "EU Global Strategy", with a clear reference to "an appropriate level of strategic autonomy". In the November 2016 Council conclusions strategic autonomy was defined as "capacity to act autonomously when and where necessary and with partners wherever possible". And the concept of strategic autonomy has been mentioned again by the Council in 2016, 2017, 2018, 2019, 2020 and lately, even by the European Council in October 2020 in its wider sense. PESCO and the European Defence Fund Regulation have adopted it too.'

pre-existing partnership structured the expectations of what the other will do, shaped the mobilization of bias and, in the end, fostered not only appropriateness to the other, but also concrete progress in the CAI negotiations, in spite of increasing ideational differences, notably about fundamental values (Ding et al., 2018).

While still underpinning a WTO reform, the EU is contributing to the creation of several new bilateral and interregional regimes, including the CAI, framing, and to some extent, binding China's behaviour as far as the crucial issues of investment policy and sustainable development are concerned. This regime does not look so asymmetric, in favour of China: in contrast, the agreement allows a rebalancing in the EU–China relationship, at least on paper. The EU has traditionally been much more open than China to foreign investment: by CAI China commits itself to opening up to the EU in a large number of relevant economic sectors, and with new mechanisms of follow-up monitoring. Last but not least, for the EU the new regime is a consistent component of a complex strategy of favouring multiple cooperation endeavours to counter the risk of global bifurcation, a new Cold War, which it sees as contrary to its interest and values.

IV. EU Preference Changes during Negotiation According to Domestic Legitimacy Imperatives

The gradual maturation of an enhanced EU's autonomy in external relations was accelerated during the seven years of CAI negotiation, started in 2014. Both actors negotiated not only within a changing international environment, but also depending on changing internal variables. When it comes to subjective variables (discourse, ideas, programs; see Schmidt, 2008), China started the negotiations in the context of the Hu Jintao 'peaceful rise' discourse, dependent upon the true critical juncture in post-Maoist China, the Deng Xiaoping opening up policy (1978–79) and the WTO successful membership (2001) (Mavroidis and Sapir, 2021). It signed the CAI in 2020 under the new nationalistic and assertive leadership of Xi Jinping, projecting China role on the world stage since 2013, fully endorsed by the 19th CCP congress in 2018. Successful economic performances providing internal stability by continuous growth, still are the main legitimizing factor for both the Xi Jinping centralism and the CCP authoritarian control on the society.

The European trade and investment policies are framed by the Rome Treaty (Meunier and Nikolaidis, 2005) and the Lisbon treaty: however, starting from 2012, the deepest moment of the Eurozone crisis – the year of ECB President Draghi's famous commitment to 'whatever it takes to save the Euro' – the EU was able to gradually upgrade its internal cohesion and external action, in spite of Brexit, Trump's aggressive policy, and the pandemic. Moreover, after the EU elections of 2019, the new pro-integration leadership showed an enhanced self-confidence and will of innovation, notably by fostering further regional EU integration, by the unprecedented recovery plan ('Next generation EU', 2020), in the context of the COVID crisis and the transition from the declining US Trump administration to the Biden New Deal.

As far as the EU is concerned, two changes took place: first, towards enhanced bilateral prudence, when the Commission proposed to the Council approval of the relevant new China communication of March 2019, 'EU–China. A Strategic Outlook', in which the EU openly recognized China as a 'strategic rival' and 'economic competitor', while reiterating its importance as a 'cooperation partner'.

Secondly, the Commission gradually realized the priority of seriously coping with the internal legitimacy challenges, first of all, with the European Parliament's repeated demands for accountability, notably in the sustainable development chapter of the negotiations and defence of human rights.[8]

These changes in the balance of EU preferences were not enough to stop the negotiations. However, awareness of the need to combine different imperatives in a wiser way than in the past (prudence with partnership; and efficiency with legitimacy) influenced the negotiations. The internal constraint was legally based on the co-decision power provided by the Lisbon treaty to the European Parliament. Accordingly, the EP strengthened its monitoring, between its first 2013 Resolution on the topic, firmly in stressing and obtaining from the Commission, the commitment of ensuring transparency and reciprocity of market access; and its 2017 Resolution, in which it demanded (and obtained) a chapter on 'sustainable development', focused on the international environmental and labour standards as well as on respect for human rights.[9] Usually, the EP is more open to vocal NGO's demands.

These resolutions and transparency confirmed that, within the post-Lisbon treaty context, including the two principles of a value-based trade agenda and of a 'comprehensive approach to external relations' (linking foreign policy and trade to human rights promotion), a mere rational-choice calculation by the Commission would have resulted in an announced adventure, a quasi-boomerang. It is true that the Commission slowly became aware of the internal institutional and societal constraints. But, contrary to her predecessor K. De Gucht's secrecy policy, Cecilia Malmström, in her strategic paper of October 2015 ('Trade for all') already looked as having learned the lesson; the enhanced NGO and civil society role in trade politicization, notably on the occasion of TTIP and CETA negotiations between 2013 and 2016 (Morin and others, 2015), forced the executive body to prioritize transparency, legitimacy and civil society dialogue. As a consequence, a specific programme of dialogue with civil society, in parallel to the CAI negotiations, was implemented.[10] This brings us to a final burning issue.

Explaining the 2020 CAI signing is possible only when taking into account the increasing Commission consciousness – from 2013 to 2020 – of the double risk of non-ratification by the European Parliament and collapsing Council unity. The EU elected assembly is under the influence not only of the general trade politicization, but also, more specifically, of multiple very vocal public opinion campaigns based on the large flows of information against the perceived current authoritarian turn of the Chinese regime under Xi Jinping: repression and security law in Hong Kong, alleged persecution of the Uighur population in Xinjiang, threats to Taiwan and assertiveness in the South China Sea as well as at the Indian border.

Public opinion in many EU countries, including Germany, is divided between CAI supporters and critical streams, combining protectionism and a very assertive notion of

[8]The EU Council decision on the Commission proposal: *The EU Global Human Rights Sanctions Regime* (7 December 2020), makes it possible for the EU to target human rights violations and abuses worldwide.
[9]European Parliament, Resolution of 9 October 2013 on the EU–China negotiations for a bilateral investment agreement, 2013/2674(RSP); European Commission, Impact Assessment Report on the EU–China Investment Relations, SWD (2013)185; European Commission, Sustainability Impact Assessment (SIA) in support of an Investment Agreement between the European Union and the People's Republic of China, Final Report, November 2017.
[10]See for example 'Civil Society Dialogue on the EU–China Comprehensive Agreement on Investment (CAI)'27/01/2021, with participation of 100 NGOs.

normative power Europe, against Beijing. Such new facts and their perception have been provocative enough to push some European parties to require 'targeted sanctions' against China. In 2020–21, the pressures by European society and public opinion arose. In spite of its positive resolution on the successful 'EU–China geographical indications agreement' (2020), the EP strengthened its political demands by the creation of a parliamentary dimension for the CAI's implementation, notably focusing on its sustainable development chapter, including human rights.[11]

It is a matter of fact that, not only populists and protectionists, but also the Greens and part of the Socialists and Liberals oppose the CAI ratification, which is strongly supported only by the European People's Party (EPP). The EU sanctions and the China retaliations of early 2021 have made ratification in 2021 unlikely, in spite of the EU Commission engagement in a civil society dialogue.[12] The evident mistakes of China by retaliating against EU sanctions have united the EP against ratification. Furthermore, member states may also be influenced when deciding their final vote in the Council, by convergence of such internal criticism with the US opposition to CAI. The most likely scenario is a postponement of the EP ratification vote.

Conclusion

We have shown that, even if calculus remains key, multiple factors play a role in the creation and ratification of the new EU–China comprehensive regime. We do not know yet whether they are strong enough to balance the risk of non-ratification. In any case negotiation and ratification represent an extremely relevant laboratory for investment- and trade-regime building and legitimacy in the current era. We investigated the relevance of multiple internal and external driving factors combined with calculus: power relations changing in favour of China, the influence of discourses, notably the EU ideational and institutional setting, including the search of an enhanced 'strategic autonomy' and the increasing weight of domestic legitimacy needs.

We have in particular underlined that, beyond a trivial opposition between realism versus idealism, and interests versus values, ideational differences matter in the oscillations of the negotiation process. The EU worldview is not only different from China's in terms of the basic understanding of values of human rights and democracy, but also for the idea of the necessary interplay between bilateralism/inter-regionalism and multilateralism (Ruggie, 1993; Meyer et al., 2019). The EU is looking for WTO reform, putting an end to the many obscure sides of the China's membership protocol of 2001, whereas China is in favour of status quo and what some American and Chinese scholars (Rodrik, 2017; Qin, 2020) define as the pluralist coexistence of various kind of multilateralisms (plural).

As far as the EU is concerned, the CAI controversy may foster the perspective of a WTO reform by a joint EU–US deal with China. If reviving the traditional EU–US alliance with the aim of containing China is hindered by the multiple transatlantic

---

[11]European Parliament, EPRS, 'EU–China Comprehensive Agreement on Investment, Levelling the Playing Field with China', Briefing, September 2020.
[12]European Commission Position Paper [on the SIA], May 2018. European Commission, Civil Society Dialogue on State of Play of the EU–China Investment Negotiations, 9 July 2020, minutes of 7 August 2020. European Commission Position Paper [on the SIA], May 2018.; European Commission, Civil Society Dialogue on State of Play of the EU-China Investment Negotiations, 9 July 2020, minutes of 7 August 2020.

controversies (digital services tax, carbon border adjustment and so on) and convergence with the US seems to be more difficult, with the US focusing on extreme competition with PRC, the EU may take the opportunity of the new US administration to find common focused proposals, notably for WTO reform.

In particular, the Commission would like to combine its autonomous trade policy with a new transatlantic dynamic of cooperation in 2021: Sabine Weyand, head of the EU trade directorate, and former US trade negotiator Wendy Cutler converged on the idea of establishing a joint 'trade and technology council'. A new, more balanced, transatlantic agenda is about to be negotiated, provided that the US unblocks the dispute settlement system's appellate body (AB). If, according to the EU, a containment policy would not work because of the size, internal performance and the high interdependence of the Chinese economy, including in high tech sectors, WTO reform will be the best test for both allies: against illegal state aids, compulsory technology transfers and subsidies. WTO reform, under EU and US driving pressure would revive the centrality of multilateral cooperation as an avenue, for instance, protecting IPS, regulating state aid, imposing subsidy notification, addressing the status of developing country question, tackling technical barriers to trade (TBTs) and digital regulation. The CAI already entails many steps in this direction.[13]

Thus, the EU Commission is also supporting collective anti-subsidy instruments and sanctions for human rights violations, to be used against Chinese companies and individuals.

In geopolitical terms, for the EU, many factors of uncertainty prevail in the context of the triangular relations. Firstly, very much depends on the other actor's behaviour: is China supporting EU unity or ambiguous divisions such as the 17 + 1 initiative (BRI)? Which balance between continuity and discontinuity will emerge in the policy of the Biden administration towards EU and China? Will the CAI facilitate transatlantic cooperation against China on trade and human rights protection and other issues beyond recent misunderstandings? Are strategic concepts compatible?

Secondly, political factors increasingly matter. For example, Angela Merkel and her likely successor Armin Laschet support the Foreign Affairs Minister Heiko Maas, who jointly with his French colleague elaborated the concept of an 'Alliance for multilateralism'[14] which looks quite different from the 'summit of democracy', suggested by J. Sullivan as a kind of global grand design US leadership aimed at containing China (Ikenberry, 2021).

Thirdly and finally, the geopolitical implications of CAI address the question of the size of the global historical transformation framing the triangular game. In the context of a multipolar global power structure, combined with a strong tendency towards a bifurcation of global economy, politics and supply chains, shifts of economic power made it possible that for the first time the largest global economy will not be a western democracy. How can global and regional institutions and regimes affect the actor's behaviour, notably an authoritarian power?

The WTO paralysis obliged all the actors to look for second-best options, from bilateralism to preferential agreements and to interregional arrangements. On the basis of its

[13]However, the EU MS are still divided as the sensitive issue of allowing Huawei to build 5G systems and national security screening of foreign direct investment.
[14]The idea of an 'Alliance for multilateralism' was launched by Jean-Yves Le Drian and Heiko Maas: 'No, Multilateralism is not Outdated!', *Le Figaro*, 12/11/2019, after the successful meeting of 50 foreign ministers at the UN general assembly.

legal provisions, the EU not only adjusted to the new context as trade and investment arrangements are concerned, but also looked at upgrading their contents and implications, to "new generation" styled agreements, by issue-linkages, with the aim of consolidating and reviving multilateral cooperation (ILO, COP 21, WTO). Such a new set of external policies is interpreted by the EU's discourse and rhetoric's as 'Strategic autonomy', inspired by EU values and interests.

We have shown that CAI represents a major test for the EU's strategic autonomy, much beyond rational choice calculation, and not a naïve attitude. However, the new uncertainties are not only commercial but also political; the paradox to be deepened by further research is that the same internal EU institutional set (Lisbon treaty) allowing this change of external relations, looks not yet fully adapted to deal with the geopolitical consequences of the change the EU itself is fostering by its international trade and investment policies, notably in the Asia-Pacific crucial area. This extremely relevant act of foreign policy has been managed by the Commission so far, and not at all coordinated with the HR for CFSP: the CAI laboratory shows that the EU's institutional set allows for steps towards strategic autonomy, but is not yet adjusted for a correct management of all its geopolitical implications. A revival of the old dilemma is suggested: it is still about the EU's capability-expectations gap?

References

Allison, G. (2017) *Destined for War* (London: Scribe).
Bradford, A. (2020) *The Brussels Effect. How the EU Rules the World* (Oxford: Oxford University Press).
Dadush, U., Domínguez-Jiménez, M. and Gao, T. (2019) 'The State of China–EU Economic Relations', *Bruegel*, Working Paper, 09/2019. www.bruegel.org/wpcontent/uploads/2019/11/WP-2019-09-China-finalincl-edit.pdf
de Block, C. and Lebullenger, J. (eds) (2018) *Génération TAFTA/CETA: Les nouveau partenariats de la mondialisation* (Montréal: Université de Montréal).
Ding, C., Zhang, X. and Telò, M. (2018) *Deepening EU–China Partnership* (Abingdon: Routledge).
Feng, Y. and Telò, M. (eds) (2020) *China and the EU in the Era of Regionalism and Interregionalism* (Berlin: Peter Lang).
Hall, P. and Taylor, R. (1996) 'Political Science and the Three New Institutionalisms'. *Political Studies*, Vol. 44, No. 5, pp. 936–57.
Heydon, K. and Woolcock, S. (2009) *The Rise of Bilateralism* (Tokyo: UN Press).
Ikenberry, J. (2021) *A World Safe for Democracy: Liberal Internationalism and the Crises of Global Order* (Princeton, NJ: Princeton University Press).
Keohane, R. (2015) 'Contested Multilateralism'. In Morin, J. *et al.* (eds) *The Politics of Transatlantic Trade Negotiations* (Abingdon: Routledge), pp. 17–27.
Mavroidis, P. and Sapir, A. (2021) *China and the WTO: Why Multilateralism Still Matters* (Princeton, NJ: Princeton University Press).
Meunier, S. and Nikolaidis, K. (2005) 'The EU as a Trade Power'. In Hill, C. and Smith, M. (eds) *International Relations and the EU* (Oxford: Oxford University Press), pp. 247–68.
Meyer, T., de Sales Marques, J.L. and Telò, M. (eds) (2019) *Regionalism and Multilateralism* (Abingdon: Routledge).

Morin, J.-F. and others (eds) (2015) *The Politics of Transatlantic Trade Negotiations* (Abingdon: Routledge).

Qin, Y. (2020) 'Transnational Governance and Multiple Multilateralism'. In Meyer, T. *et al.* (eds) *Regionalism and Multilateralism* (Abingdon: Routledge), pp. 48–64.

Risse, T. and Börzel, T. (2015) 'The EU and the Diffusion of Regionalism'. In Fawcett, L. (ed.) *Interregionalism and the EU* (Abingdon: Routledge), pp. 51–65.

Rodrick, D. (2017) *Straight Talk on Trade: Ideas for a Sane World Economy* (Princeton, NJ: Princeton University Press).

Ruggie, J. (ed.) (1993) *Multilateralism Matters* (New York: Columbia University Press).

Schmidt, V. (2008) 'Discursive Institutionalism: The Explanatory Power of Ideas and Discourse'. *Annual Review of Political Science*, Vol. 11, No. 1.

Telò, M. (2021) 'The Crisis of International Trade, and its Cultural and Political Implications'. In Meyer, T. (ed.) *Towards a New Multilateralism?* (Abingdon: Routledge).

Wolf, M. (2021) 'Containing China is not a Feasible Option', *Financial Times*, 2 February.

Woolcock, S. (2020) 'Commercial Policy: The E.U. and the World Trade and Investment Order'. In Weyembergh, A. *et al.* (eds) *Supranational Governance at Stake* (Abingdon: Routledge), pp. 211–23.

Zhang, X. (2018) 'Linkage Power: how the Eu and China Managed their Economic and Trade Partnership (1975-2016) in Ding and others Deepening EU-China Partnership'. In *Bridging Institutional and Ideational Differecnes in an Unstable World* (Routledge), pp. 155–64.

JCMS 2021 Volume 59. Annual Review. pp. 175–181   DOI: 10.1111/jcms.13305

Index

Note: Italicised page references indicate information contained in tables.